ISBN: 978129024135

Published by:
HardPress Publishing
8345 NW 66TH ST #2561
MIAMI FL 33166-2626

Email: info@hardpress.net
Web: http://www.hardpress.net

SIGILLVM · UNIVERSITATIS · CALIFORNIENSIS

FIAT LVX

MDCCCLXVIII

EX LIBRIS

M.O. 225 ii.

METEOROLOGICAL OFFICE.

METEOROLOGICAL GLOSSARY

(Fourth Issue)

In continuation of *The Weather Map*, (M.O. 225 i,)

Issued by the Authority of the Meteorological Committee.

LONDON:

PRINTED UNDER THE AUTHORITY OF HIS MAJESTY'S STATIONERY
OFFICE

BY DARLING AND SON, LIMITED, BACON STREET, E.2.

AND TO BE PURCHASED FROM
THE METEOROLOGICAL OFFICE, EXHIBITION ROAD, LONDON, S.W.7.

1918.

Price 1s. *net.*

LIST OF ABBREVIATIONS.

For units or systems of units.

F.P.S. is equivalent to foot-pound-second system of units.

C.G.S   „   „   centimetre-gramme-second system of units.

B.T.U.   „   „   British Thermal units.

The following are also used :—

For the expression of	Abbreviation.	Meaning.
Angle ...	° ′ ″	Degrees, minutes, seconds of arc.
Density ...	g/m^3 g/cc lb/cu. ft.	Grammes per cubic metre. Grammes per cubic centimetre. Pounds per cubic foot.
Length ...	mm cm m k	Millimetre. Centimetre. Metre. Kilometre.
Mass	g kg	Gramme. Kilogramme.
Pressure ...	mb cb	Millibar. Centibar.
Temperature	a C F	Absolute scale of temperature.* Centigrade scale of temperature. Fahrenheit scale of temperature.
Velocity ...	m/s mi/hr	Metres per second. Miles per hour.
Volume ...	cc m^3	Cubic centimetre. Cubic metre.

* The abbreviation "a" is also used to represent a unit or degree of temperature on the absolute scale. For an interval of temperature 1a is the same as 1° C.

METEOROLOGICAL GLOSSARY.

TABLE OF CONTENTS.

The entries marked (I) are also referred to in *The Weather Map*. (M.O. 225 i.)

	Page.		Page.
Absolute Extremes ...	12	Aneroid barometer ...	30
Absolute Humidity ...	290	Aneroidograph ...	30
Absolute Temperature	12	Anthelion	30
Accumulated Temper-	293	Anticyclone (I) ...	30
ature.		Aqueous-vapour ...	31
Actinometer	14	Atmosphere (I) ...	33
Adiabatic	15	Atmospheric Electri-	294
Aërology	16	city.	
Aeroplane Weather ...	16	Audibility	33
Air (I)	19	Aureole	36
Air-Meter	20	Aurora	298
Airship-Weather ...	20	Autumn	36
Altimeter	27	Average	37
Altitude	28	Azimuth	37
Alto-cumulus	28		
Alto-stratus	28	Backing	37
Anabatic	29	Ballon sonde	39
Anemobiagraph ...	29	Balloon Kite	42
Anemogram	29	Bar	43
Anemograph	29	Barogram	43
Anemometer	29	Barograph	43
Anemoscope	29	Barometer	43

(13204r—12.) Wt. 26779—464. 7000. 3/18. D & S. (*S.*) G. 3.

	Page.			Page.
Barometric Tendency	44	Condensation ...	...	70
Beaufort Notation (I)	44	Conduction ...	...	71
Beaufort Scale (I) ...	45	Contingency ...	...	302
Bishop's Ring	46	Convection ...	...	71
Blizzard	46	Corona	...	71
Blue of the Sky ...	46	Correction ...	...	72
Boiling Points ...	300	Correlation ...	...	74
Bora	47	Correlation Ratio	...	302
Breeze	48	Cosecant ...	...	76
Brontometer	49	Cosine	...	76
Buoyancy	49	Cotangent ...	...	76
Buys Ballot's Law (I)	57	Counter Sun ...	...	76
		Cumulo-stratus	...	77
C.G.S.	57	Cumulus ...	...	77
Calm	57	Cyclone (I) ...	...	77
Calorie	301	Cyclostrophic ...	...	77
Celsius	57			
Centibar	58	Damp Air ...	...	77
Centigrade	58	Day Breeze ...	...	77
Centimetre	58	Débacle ...	...	77
Cirro-cumulus ...	58	Dekad	...	78
Cirro-stratus ...	58	Density	...	78
Cirrus	58	Depression ...	...	82
Climate	58	Dew	...	82
Climatic Chart ...	59	Dew-point ...	...	82
Climatology ...	60	Diathermancy ...	...	82
Clouds	60	Diffraction ...	...	83
Cloud Burst	67	Diffusion ...	...	84
Clouds, Weight of ...	67	Diurnal ...	...	85
Col	68	Doldrums ...	...	88
Compass	68	Drought ...	...	88
Component	69	Dry Air ...	...	88

	Page.
Dry Bulb	88
Duration of Rainfall ...	303
Dust	304
Dust-counter	305
Dynamics	89
Dynamic Cooling ...	89
Earth Thermometer ...	89
Eddy	89
Electrification of Water-	337
drops.	
Electrometer	91
Energy	92
Entropy	94
Equation of Time ...	100
Equator	100
Equatorial	101
Equilibrium	102
Equinox	103
Error	104
Evaporation	106
Expansion	109
Exposure	109
Extremes	110
Fahrenheit	110
Fall	111
False Cirrus	306
Fluid	111
Fog	112
Fog Bow	116
Föhn	115

	Page.
Forecast	117
Freezing	118
Frequency	118
Friction	122
Frost	123
Gale	124
Gale Warning	128
Gas	129
Geostrophic	129
Glacier	307
Glazed Frost	129
Glory	130
Gradient	130
Gradient Wind ...	134
Gramme	138
Grass Temperature ...	139
Gravity	308
Great Circle	139
Gulf Stream	139
Gust	140
Gustiness	142
Hail	142
Halo	143
Harmattan	145
Harmonic Analysis ...	311
Haze	145
Heat	145
High (I)	152
Hoar Frost	152
Horizontal	152

	Page.		Page.
Horse Latitudes	... 153	Katabatic ...	... 182
Humidity (I)	... 154	Khamsin ...	... 182
Hurricane ...	... 155	Kilometre ...	... 183
Hydrometer ...	... 158	Lake	... 183
Hydrosphere ...	... 158	Land Breeze ...	... 183
Hyetograph ...	... 158	Lapse	... 183
Hygrograph ...	... 158	Lenticular ...	... 185
Hygrometer ...	... 159	Level	... 185
Hygroscope ...	... 159	Lightning ...	... 186
Hypsometer ...	... 160	„ Protection against	324
		Line Squall ...	... 188
Ice	... 321	Liquid ...	... 189
Iceberg ...	... 161	Low (I) ...	... 189
Incandescence	... 161	Lunar	... 189
Index	... 162		
Index Error ...	... 162	Mackerel Sky ...	... 190
Insolation ...	... 162	Magnetic Needle	... 190
Inversion ...	... 163	Magnetism ...	... 327
Ion	... 164	Mammato-Cumulus ...	... 190
Ionisation ...	... 322	Mares' Tails ...	... 191
Iridescence ...	... 166	Maximum ...	... 191
Irisation ...	... 166	Mean	... 191
Isabnormals ...	... 166	Meniscus ...	... 191
Isanomalies ...	... 166	Mercury ...	... 192
Isentropic ...	... 167	Meteor	... 192
Iso	... 168	Meteorograph ...	... 193
Isobars	... 168	Meteorology ...	... 193
Isohels		Metre	... 193
Isohyets	See Iso.	Microbarograph	... 193
Isopleths		Millibar ...	... 194
Isotherm		Millimetre ...	... 195
Isothermal ...	... 181	Minimum ...	... 195

	Page.		Page.
Mirage	195	Pocky cloud	212
Mist	196	Polar	212
Mistral	197	Pole	212
Mock Sun	197	Potential	213
Mock Sun Ring ...	197	Potential Temperature	213
Monsoon	197	Precipitation	329
Moon	198	Pressure	213
		Prevailing winds ...	213
Nadir	198	Probability	214
Nephoscope	198	Prognostics	215
Nimbus	198	Psychrometer	216
Normal	198	Pumping	216
		Purple Light	217
Observer	203	Pyrheliometer ...	217
Ombrometer	203		
Orientation	203	Radiation	330
Orographic Rain ...	203	Rain	217
Ozone	204	Rainband	218
		Rainbow	218
		Rainday	219
Pampero	204	Raindrops, size of, &c.	334
Paranthelion	204	Rainfall	219
Paraselenae	204	Rainfall, duration of ...	303
Parhelia	204	Raingauge	219
Pentad	205	Rain-spell	219
Periodical	205	Réaumur	219
Persistence	206	Reduction	220
Persistent Rain ...	206	Reduction to Sea Level	220
Phases of the Moon ...	208	Refraction	222
Phenology	210	Registering balloon ...	223
Pilot-balloon	210	Regression-equation ...	339
Pluviograph	211	Relative humidity ...	223
Pluviometer	212	Reversal	224

	Page.		Page.
Ridge	225	Solar Radiation Ther-	238
Rime	225	mometer.	
River	225	Solstice	238
Roaring Forties ...	226	Sounding	238
		Spells of Weather ...	238
		Spring	239
St. Elmo's Fire ...	226	Squall	239
Saturation	226	Stability	239
Scotch Mist	340	Standard Time ...	239
Screen	226	State of the Sky ...	239
Scud	226	Statics	240
Sea-breeze	227	Station	240
Sea-level	227	Statoscope	240
Seasons	227	Storm	241
Secant	231	Storm Cone	241
Secondary	231	Strato-cumulus ...	241
Seismograph	231	Stratosphere	241
Serein	231	Stratus	241
Shamal	231	Summer	241
Shepherd of Banbury	232	Sun	241
Silver Thaw	235	Sun-dial	343
Simoon	235	Sun-dogs	242
Sine	235	Sun Pillar	242
Sine curve	236	Sunset Colours ...	242
Sirocco	237	Sunshine	242
Sleet	237	Sunshine-recorder ...	243
Snow	237	Sunspot Numbers ...	243
Snow crystals ...	237	Surge	244
Soft hail	343	Synoptic	244
Solar Constant ...	237		
Solar Day	238	Tangent	244
Solarisation	238	Temperature (I) ...	244

	Page.		Page.
Temperature Gradient	246	Vapour Tension ...	266
Tension of Vapour ...	247	Vector	266
Terrestrial	247	Veering	267
Terrestrial Magnetism	327	Velocity	267
Thaw	247	Vernier	268
Thermodynamics ...	247	Vertical	268
Thermogram	247	Viscosity	269
Thermograph	247	Visibility	269
Thermometer	248	Vortex	347
Thunder	248		
Thunderstorm ...	249		
Time	252	Water	271
Tornado	252	Water-Atmosphere ...	273
Torricelli	253	Waterspout ...	274
Trade Winds	253	Water-Vapour ...	274
Trajectory	262	Waves	274
Tramontana	263	Waves of Explosion ...	276
Transparency	263	Weather (I)	276
Tropic	263	Weather maxim ...	276
Tropical	263	Wedge	279
Tropopause	263	Weight	279
Troposphere	263	Wet Bulb	279
Trough	263	Whirlwind	280
Twilight	344	Wind	280
Twilight Arch ...	264	Wind Rose	351
Type	264	Winter	288
Typhoon	265	Wireless Telegraphy ...	288
Upbank Thaw	265		
		Zenith	288
V-Shaped depression ...	266	Zodiac	289
Vapour Pressure ...	266	Zodiacal Light ...	289

TABLE OF CONTENTS OF THE WEATHER MAP.

AN INTRODUCTION TO THE GLOSSARY.

(*Now issued as a separate volume.*)

	PAGE.
Meteorology and Military Operations ... ... , ...	3
Weather Records and Climate	5
The Necessity for Forecasts of Weather	7
Modern Meteorology the Work of an Organisation, not of an Individual	8
The Meteorologist at Headquarters `	8
A Map of the Weather	9
The Beaufort Notation	10
A Map of the Winds...	12
The Beaufort Scale	13–14
The Atmosphere	15
Water Vapour : Evaporation and Condensation	17
Temperature and Humidity	19
A Map of Temperature	
Pressure and Its Measurement	21
The Barometer	23
A Map of the Distribution of Pressure	
Isobars	25
A Map of all the Elements together...	26
Lessons from Weather Maps	26
Buys-Ballot's Law and the General Relation of Pressure to Wind	26
Weather and Temperature	30
The Sequence of Weather	31
The Travel of the Centres of Cyclonic Depressions ...	35
Barometric Tendency	41
Veering and Backing of Wind	42
Types of Pressure Distribution	43
The Upper Air. The Dynamics and Physics of the Atmosphere	44
Distribution of Rain and Cloud in Cyclonic Depressions...	50
Climatic Supplement, Charts and Diagrams	55

METEOROLOGICAL GLOSSARY.

CONTAINING INFORMATION IN EXPLANATION OF TECHNICAL METEOROLOGICAL TERMS.

Details as to the use of meteorological instruments are given in the *Observer's Handbook*, and as to the numerical computations in the *Computer's Handbook*, to both of which reference is made in the Glossary when required.

In accordance with the practice of the Oxford Dictionary the initial word of each article is in black type, and words in the body of the text are printed in small capitals when they are the subjects of articles in another part of the glossary.

For the articles in this glossary I am principally indebted to the Staff of the Observatory at Benson, W. H. Dines, F.R.S., and E. V. Newnham, B.Sc.; and of the Branch Office at South Farnborough, Captain C. J. P. Cave, R.E., and R. A. Watson Watt, B.Sc., with Major Taylor, Professor of Meteorology, R.F.C.; and to the staff of the Forecast Division, especially F. J. Brodie, E. L. Hawke, B.A., and Second Lieutenant T. Harris, R.E., who have passed the MS. through the press, and W. Hayes who prepared many of the illustrations.

The revision of the work for the present fourth issue has been carried out by Dr. C. Chree, F.R.S., Superintendent of the Observatory, Richmond. Some new articles have been added at the end of the volume, pp. 290-354.

NAPIER SHAW.

Meteorological Office,
26 October, 1917.

METEOROLOGICAL GLOSSARY.

Absolute Extremes.—The word extreme is often used with reference to temperature to denote the highest and lowest temperatures recorded at an observing station in the course of time. As the observations are generally summarised for a year, extreme temperatures come to mean the highest and lowest temperatures of a year. When the survey is taken over a longer period, 10 years, 20 years, 35 years or 200 years, according to the duration of the observations, the highest and lowest temperatures observed during the whole period are called the absolute extremes. The journalistic expression would be "the record," high or low as the case may be.

The absolute extremes for the British Isles are, highest 310·8a., (100° F.); lowest 245·8a., (−17° F.). Those for Belgium, highest 311·2a., (100·8° F.); lowest 243·2a., (−21·6° F.). The Surface of the Globe, highest 329·7a., (134° F.); lowest 203·2a., (−93·6° F.). In the Upper Air, lowest 182·1a., (−131·6° F.) at a height of 16½ km. over Java.

Absolute Temperature.—The temperature of the centigrade thermometer, increased by 273, more properly called the temperature on the absolute, or thermodynamic scale. The absolute scale is formulated by reasoning about the production of mechanical work at the expense of heat (which is the special province of the science of thermodynamics, see ENTROPY), but for practical purposes the scale may be taken as identical with that based on the change of volume and pressure of one of the permanent gases with heat. For thermometric purposes aiming at the highest degree of refinement the hydrogen scale is used, but for the purposes of meteorological reckoning the differences of behaviour of the permanent gases, Hydrogen, Oxygen, Nitrogen are unimportant. In physical calculations for meteorological purposes the absolute is the natural scale ; the densities of air at any two temperatures on the absolute scale are inversely proportional to the temperatures. Thus the common formula for a gas,

$$\frac{p}{\rho\,(273 + t)} = \frac{p_0}{\rho_0\,(273 + t_0)}$$

where p is the pressure, ρ the density and t the temperature Centigrade of the gas at one time, p_0, ρ_0, t_0 the corresponding values at another, becomes

$$\frac{p}{\rho T} = \frac{p_0}{\rho_0 T_0},$$

where T and T_0 are the temperatures on the absolute centigrade scale. Its most important feature for practical meteorology is that from its definition there can be no negative temperatures. The zero of the absolute scale is the temperature at which all that we call heat would have been spent. In the centigrade scale all temperatures below the freezing point of water have to be prefixed by the negative sign —. This is very inconvenient, especially for recording observations in the upper air, which never gives temperatures above the freezing point in our latitudes at much above 4 kilometres (13,000 feet), and often gives temperatures below the freezing point nearer the surface.

The absolute temperature comes into meteorology in other ways ; for example, the rate at which heat goes out into space from the earth depends, according to Stefan's Law, upon the fourth power of the absolute temperature of the radiant substance. See RADIATION.

Temperatures can also be expressed in an absolute scale of Fahrenheit degrees of which the zero is approximately 459° below the Fahrenheit zero.

Some common temperatures on the absolute scales and their equivalents in Centigrade and Fahrenheit are :—

	Centigrade.		Fahrenheit.	
—	a.	° C.	° F.	af.
The boiling point of helium.	4	−269	−452·2	7·2
The boiling point of nitrogen.	77	−196	−320·8	138·6
The freezing point of mercury.	234·2	−38·8	−37·8	421·6
The freezing point of water.	273	0	32	491·4
The mean temperature of London.	282·7	9·7	49·5	508·9
"Temperate" as shown on an ordinary thermometer.	285·8	12·8	55	514·4
The best temperature for a living room.	290	17	62·6	522·0
A hot summer day ...	300	27	80·6	540·0
The temperature of the human body.	310	37	98·6	558·0
The temperature of the Sun.	6,000	—	—	10,000

Actinometer.—An instrument for measuring the intensity of RADIATION received from the sun. In Michelson's Actinometer, for example, the essential element consists of two strips of different metals fixed together. These are heated by the solar radiation which they absorb, and the amount of bending which results from their unequal expansion is a measure of the rate at which they are receiving radiant energy.

Adiabatic.—The word which is applied in the science of thermodynamics to the corresponding changes which may take place in the pressure and density of a substance when no heat can be communicated to it or withdrawn from it.

In ordinary life we are accustomed to consider that when the temperature of a body rises it is because it takes in *heat* from a fire, from the sun or from some other source, but in the science of thermodynamics it is found to be best to consider the changes which occur when a substance is compressed or expanded without any possibility of heat getting to it or away from it. In the atmosphere such a state of things is practically realised in the interior of a mass of air which is rising to a position of lower pressure, or sinking to one of higher pressure. There is, in consequence, a change of temperature which is called mechanical or dynamical, and which must be regarded as one of the most vital of meteorological phenomena because it accounts largely for the formation and disappearance of cloud, and probably for the whole of our rainfall.

Tyndall illustrated the change of temperature due to sudden compression by pushing in the piston of a closed glass syringe and thus igniting a piece of tinder in the syringe. The heating of a bicycle pump is a common experience due to the same cause.* On the other hand the refrigeration of air is often obtained simply by expansion, particularly in the free atmosphere.

---

* Dangerous heating may result on firing a gun from the sudden compression of gas within the bursting charge of the shell if there are cavities in the explosive therein.

To plan out the changes of temperature of a substance under compression and rarefaction alone, we have to suppose the substance enclosed in a case impermeable to heat—the word adiabatic has been coined to denote impermeable to heat in that sense. The changes of temperature thereby produced are very great, for example :

For adiabatic change of pressure decreasing from 1000 mb. by		The fall of temperature from 290a, 62·6° F., is	
mb.	in.	° C.	° F.
10 or	0·30	0·9 or	1·6
100 ,,	2·95	8·7 ,,	15·7
200 ,,	5·91	18·2 ,,	32·8
300 ,,	8·86	28·4 ,,	51·1
400 ,,	11·81	39·9 ,,	71·8
500 ,,	14·77	52·8 ,,	95·0
600 ,,	17·72	67·6 ,,	121·7
700 ,,	20·67	85·5 ,,	153·9
800 ,,	23·62	108·1 ,,	194·6
900 ,,	26·58	141·3 ,,	254·3

Aërology.—The study of the free air; a word that has come into use recently to indicate that part of meteorology which is concerned with the study of the upper air. Some of the results are given under BALLON-SONDE and PILOT-BALLOON.

Aeroplane weather.—The weather most suitable for aeroplanes is calm clear weather with little or no wind. The only conditions which make it impossible for a good pilot to fly a modern aeroplane are a strong

Diagram showing the pressure in the upper air corresponding with the standard pressure (1013·2 mb.) at the surface and adiabatic lines for saturated air referred to height and temperature. (From Neuhoff Smithsonian Miscellaneous Collections, Vol. 51, No. 4, 1910.)

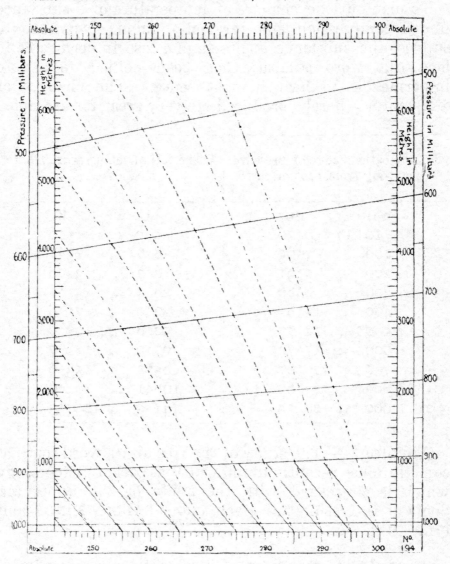

The pressure is shown by full lines crossing the diagram, and the adiabatic lines for saturated air by dotted lines. Temperatures are given in the absolute scale.

The short full lines between the ground and the level of 1,000 metres show the direction of the adiabatic lines for dry air.

GALE or a FOG.· On the other hand many weather conditions may prevent useful work from being done by an aeroplane when it is in the air. The weather affects civilian and military flying in quite different ways. When testing aeroplanes, with a view to finding their rate of climb, top speed when flying level, landing speed, or other aerodynamical quantities it is usually necessary to choose a calm day, when eddies, or large ascending or descending currents, or other conditions prejudicial to accurate testing, are unlikely to occur.

In flying across country the chief danger is that the engine will stop when the aeroplane is over ground on which it is impossible to land. When the engine has stopped the aeroplane must come down somewhere inside a circle whose radius is about equal to five times the height of the aeroplane above the ground. An aeroplane flying at a height of one mile will have an area of about 75 square miles in which it may choose its landing ground, while at a height of 2,000 feet on a calm day the machine has less than 12 square miles to choose from.

In England it is almost always possible to pick out a possible landing ground in a circle containing 75 square miles; but it is frequently impossible to do so in an area of 12 square miles. For this reason clouds below 6,000 feet are one of the chief dangers of cross-country flying, and the lower they are the more dangerous they become.

In flying under war conditions eddies and vertical currents are almost immaterial provided they are not so violent as to impede observations. On the other hand low clouds make observations over an enemy's lines almost impossible, owing to the accuracy of modern anti-aircraft guns. Detached clouds impede, but do not put a stop to, reconnaissance. On days when the clouds are too low to the upper regions, collections of water globules which are called clouds ; in meteorology the dust is regarded as an impurity, and the clouds as an addition to the air, not part of it. The dust, though an impurity, is important, as it makes the formation of cloud and rain possible whenever the temperature of a mass of air gets below the DEW-POINT.

Air-meter.—The name given to an apparatus designed to measure the flow of air. It consists of a light wheel with inclined vanes carried by the spokes, and a set of counting dials to show the number of revolutions of the wheel. Its accuracy can be tested on a whirling table. As generally sold it is the most portable form of ANEMO-METER, its box not being more than four inches each way. But it cannot be used with success by a careless observer.

Airship-weather.—*Favourable weather.*—The most favourable conditions for airships are calms or light airs, with good seeing from above, extending over the whole area to be traversed, and persistent for the whole period, say 24 hours. Detached low clouds may be an advantage, but precipitation, whether in the form of rain, snow or hail, would spoil the occasion. The favourable conditions thus defined are characteristic of the central part of an area of high barometric pressure which, in technical language, is called an ANTICYCLONE. Thus, for operating across the North Sea, the primary meteorological conditions will be favourable when the barometer readings at Helder, Yarmouth and Grisnez are higher than those at surrounding places, because the three places named will then be in the central region of an anticyclone, *cf.* Fig. 3, p. 25.
During an anticyclone the pressure is, as a rule, above the normal for the place ; thus, pressures above 1,020

Plate IX.

AIRSHIP WEATHER. Fig. 1.

DISTRIBUTION OF TEMPERATURE, WEATHER, WIND, AND PRESSURE, 6 P.M. 6th SEPTEMBER, 1915.

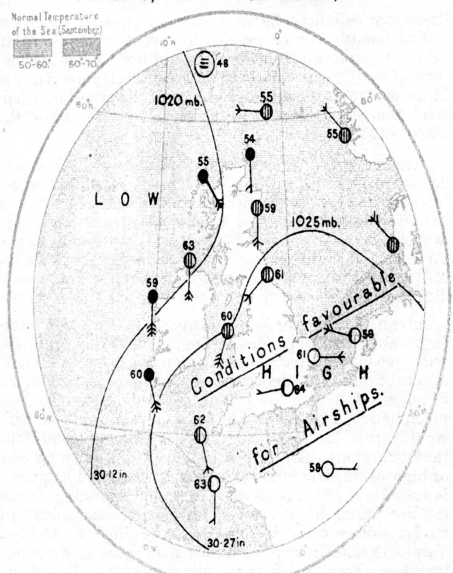

Normal Temperature of the Sea (September)

50°-60°   60°-70°

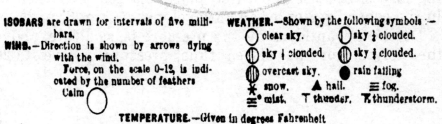

ISOBARS are drawn for intervals of five millibars,

WIND.—Direction is shown by arrows flying with the wind.

Force, on the scale 0-12, is indicated by the number of feathers

Calm

WEATHER.—Shown by the following symbols :—

◯ clear sky.   ◐ sky ½ clouded.

◓ sky ¼ clouded.   ◑ sky ¾ clouded.

◍ overcast sky.   ● rain falling

✳ snow.   ▲ hail.   ≡ fog.

≡° mist.   T thunder.   ⚡ thunderstorm.

TEMPERATURE.—Given in degrees Fahrenheit

millibars (30·1 inches) are generally to be found in anti-cyclones, and this has given rise to the statement that a high barometer in itself indicates favourable conditions for airships and *vice versa*. This is often, but not always, the case. If one plots the pressure on a map the favourable area extends outward from the central region where the highest pressures are found until the pressure begins to fall away rapidly, and then one finds strong winds and, possibly, also rain or snow.

An anticyclone is indicated on a map by drawing lines of equal pressure, ISOBÁRS, which naturally enclose the area of highest pressure. The lines of an anticyclone, generally speaking, run in roughly parallel curves and are easily recognisable on a map, such as the one reproduced here, Fig. 1. The shape is sometimes that of a regular curve, more or less like a circle or an oval, as in this instance, but often it is quite irregular and straggles over a large region. Anywhere near what may be called the top of it, *i.e.*, the region of highest pressure, there are calms or light airs. Further away the winds begin to range themselves in circulation round the central region—easterly winds on the south side, westerly on the north. Further out, as one gets towards the regions of low pressure, the winds become brisker, and on the margins of an anticyclone they may be very strong, but on the eastern side they are generally steady, not changeable or squally.

It is characteristic of an anticyclone that when it is once set up and well marked it generally lasts two or three days; sometimes it is persistent for a week or 10 days, occasionally even more. An anticyclone is, in fact, typical of settled weather, and consequently the setting in of a large anticyclone over the area of operations may be regarded as providing an ample period of favourable weather.

An anticyclone in our neighbourhood generally drifts eastward or north-eastward. It has northerly winds on its eastern or front side, so that the setting in of a northerly wind, veering to N.E., generally means that an anticyclone is coming over, and as it will take two or three days at least to pass, the navigator is practically sure of a few days of fair conditions, and while the central region is going over and the wind is slacking down from north-east to calm, and then changing to south or south-west, there is practically certain to be a perfect day, possibly two or three, for operating an airship.

All that an airship navigator has to do, therefore, to hit upon a favourable time for a raid is to choose the occasion when there is an anticyclone with its central area over southern England or the Channel, advancing slowly eastward, as most of them do. He may then reckon on two or three days' favourable weather, and if he watches the map may extend his forecast day by day as he notes the behaviour of the anticyclone. An anticyclone is such a well-recognised creature in meteorological maps that observations from one half of it are sufficient to go upon in forming a judgment as to its existence. Its end comes with the southerly wind that marks its western side, so that a southerly wind, even a light one, is a warning which no hostile navigator is likely to disregard.

In winter it is often foggy in anticyclonic weather, particularly when the anticyclone is going away, and sometimes it is cloudy and gloomy, but there is never heavy rain in the central region, and seldom any rain at all.

Unfavourable weather. — The most unfavourable weather for hostile operations with airships is cyclonic

Plate X.

AIRSHIP WEATHER. FIG. 2.

DISTRIBUTION OF TEMPERATURE, WEATHER, WIND, AND PRESSURE, 7 A.M. 1st NOVEMBER, 1915.

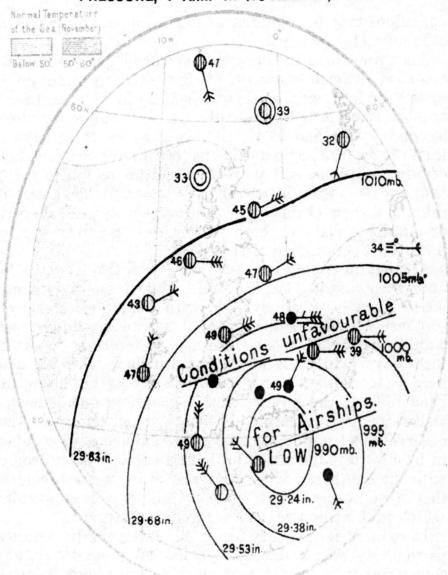

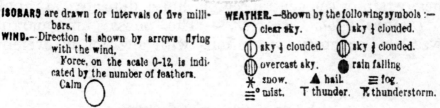

ISOBARS are drawn for intervals of five milli-bars.

WIND.—Direction is shown by arrows flying with the wind,

Force, on the scale 0-12, is indi-cated by the number of feathers.

Calm ◯

WEATHER.—Shown by the following symbols:—

◯ clear sky.   ◗ sky ¼ clouded.

◐ sky ½ clouded.   ◕ sky ¾ clouded.

◍ overcast sky.   ● rain falling

✳ snow.   ▲ hail.   ☰ fog.

☰° mist.   T thunder.   Ҡ thunderstorm.

TEMPERATURE.—Given in degrees Fahrenheit.

weather represented on the map by a region of relatively low barometer round which strong winds circulate. (See figure 2.) It is the opposite of anticyclonic weather. The cyclonic depression passes rapidly across the map and the weather goes through a well-known cycle of phases in the course of twelve to twenty-four hours. A well-developed cyclonic depression makes successful air raiding impossible, partly because of the strength of the wind, which may reach 50, 60 or 70 miles an hour in the upper regions, and still more because of its variability (the wind is gusty and squally and is also liable to regular changes), which may give the ship as much lee-way as traverse. This, in darkness, means losing the course and probably losing the bearings. Besides, there is often heavy rain or snow with cyclonic weather.

In the South of England cyclonic weather generally begins with a southerly or south-westerly wind, and as there is frequently a succession of depressions passing along the same track there are successive fallings and risings of the barometer and successive phases of southerly wind, veering to N.W. with the rising barometer, and backing again to S.W. with a falling barometer.

Between two successive depressions there is often a day of perfect weather, light, transparent airs and clear skies. An airship commander who started at the right time might use this brilliant interval to make a raid, but without extremely expert forecasting, which would require ample telegraphic information, it is too dangerous. He is more likely to wait until the setting in of a northerly or north-easterly wind marks the beginning of an anticyclone.

Risky weather.—Between these two extremes of easily identifiable weather, favourable or unfavourable, there are a number of conditions which may be called risky, periods of slow transition between anticyclonic and cyclonic, or periods of vague type without marked features. These require an expert knowledge of meteorology if they are to be dealt with successfully. So far as we know, hostile aircraft have used special meteorological observations (with pilot balloons) to identify a case in which a strong north-easterly wind, too strong for easy navigation, fell off and became much lighter in the upper air. That is characteristic of easterly and north-easterly winds, but there are exceptions. To make use of the proper occasion in this particular is certainly clever, but it is risky; because we can only take advantage of such cases when we happen to find them, and we do not know any law of their distribution. In this connexion it may be remarked that airships are not likely to take the air at night in a strong wind. Not knowing precisely the distribution of air currents, it is impossible to lay a course for an objective across wind, so the objective must be approached ultimately up wind. That means the slowest speed at the most critical point.

The most risky weather for an airship is when a cyclonic depression with southerly wind in its front advances rapidly eastward and replaces the light airs in front of it. Light airs, it has been remarked, are characteristic of the central region of an anticyclone, but they are also characteristic of the region in front of an advancing depression. Depressions sometimes advance at a rapid rate, say 25 miles an hour—600 miles a day—always in that case from the west or south-west. In winter the risk which an airship runs depends a good deal upon the position of the centre of the depression. On the northern side of it, or in its rear, there is often snow, in the latter case with strong northerly winds.

FIGURE 3.

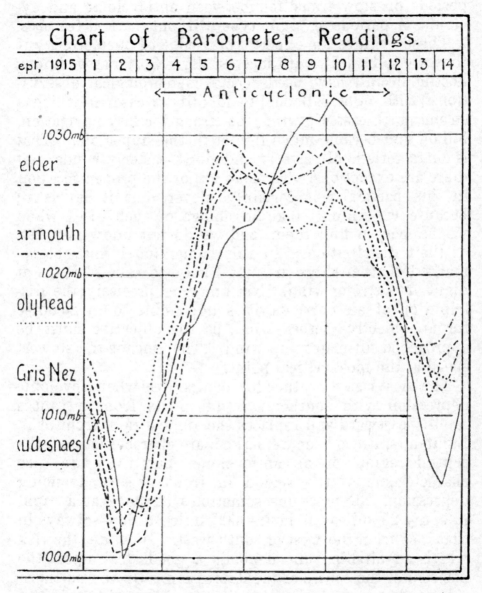

Variations of the Barometric pressure at five stations during the
passage of an anticyclone in September, 1915.

FIGURE 4.

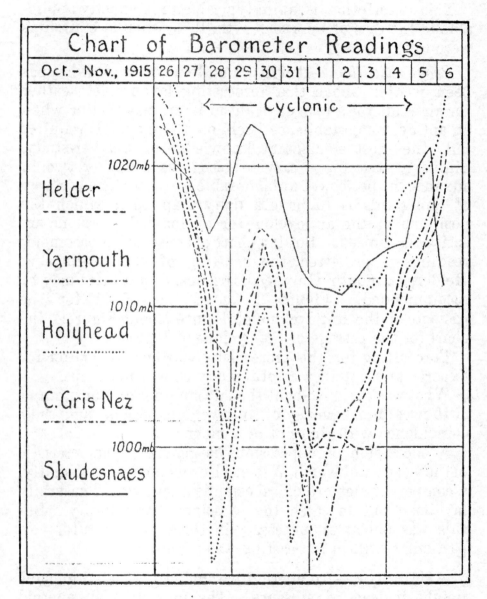

Variations of Barometric pressure during the passage of two consecutive cyclonic depressions in October–November, 1915.

This description is quite typical, and is exactly applicable to the case of February 17th, 1915, when two airships were lost.

Prognostication.—It will be understood from what has been written above that forecasting favourable weather for air raids for a few days ahead is an easy matter when an anticyclone establishes itself on the map. It requires only the most elementary knowledge of weather-study. Similarly it is quite easy to recognise a day or two in advance the periods of unfavourable weather. The best way of doing this is to have a daily map upon which the positions of the anticyclone or cyclonic depressions are easily recognised. But if a chart of consecutive barometer readings is preferred, the charting of the readings at Helder, Yarmouth, Holyhead, Grisnez, Skudesnaes may be recommended. Figure 3 shows the chart for the passage of the anticyclone of Figure 1, and Figure 4 the chart for the passage of the cyclone of Figure 2.

Forecasting for the more risky weather is a matter for experts, and entails a careful study of weather maps.

What was curious about the late summer and autumn of 1915 was the frequency of anticyclonic periods, and their coincidence with times of new moon.

A succession of depressions is generally characteristic of the weather of North-Western Europe, and, consequently, a competent meteorological establishment would naturally lay itself out to catch the occasional opportunity. But this was not at all necessary in the season of 1915. No particular skill in forecasting was required.

Altimeter.—An aneroid barometer graduated to show height instead of pressure. The most that an aneroid barometer can do is to give a satisfactory measure of the pressure of the air. The pressure is very largely affected by the height, and, therefore, whatever indicates the pressure gives a rough indication also of the height.

The accurate determination of the height of a position requires a knowledge of the temperature of the air at successive steps, so that a mean temperature may be obtained for the column between the position and the earth. There are various short ways of making estimates of the temperature of the column, but in any case the temperature at the top and bottom should be noted.*

Altitude.—The angle in a vertical plane subtended at the eye of the observer by the line drawn from the top of an object to the horizon. The word is also used commonly as synonymous with height.

Alto-cumulus.—A form of cloud of middle height (10,000 feet to 25,000 feet). It consists of fleecy groups of cloudlets called by the French " gros-moutons." The separate cloudlets are thick enough to show a darkening of the white ; the similar groups of smaller and higher clouds, cirro-cumulus, show no shadow. See CLOUDS.

Alto-stratus.—A sheet of continuous cloud of middle height, of considerable size and moderate thickness, sometimes covering the whole sky. It must be distinguished from cirro-stratus which is higher and thinner, and stratus without any prefix, which is the lowest form of cloud-sheet.

---

* The pressure at the foot of the column must also be known, and the lack of this knowledge is a source of error with a machine travelling over great distances. A special note on the subject prepared for the *Handbook of Meteorology* can be obtained from the Meteorological Office.

Anabatic.—Referring to the upward motion of air due to convection. A local wind is called anabatic if it is caused by the convection of heated air ; as, for example, the breeze that blows up valleys when the sun warms the ground. See BREEZE.

Anemobiagraph. See ANEMOGRAPH.

Anemogram.—The record of an anemograph.

Anemograph.—An instrument for recording the velocity or force, and sometimes also the direction of the wind. The best known forms of anemograph are the Robinson Cup anemograph similar to that designed by Beckley for Kew Observatory, the Tube anemograph with direction recorder similar to that designed by Dines for Benson Observatory (which might be called the Harpagraph or gust-recorder), the anemobiagraph designed by Halliwell for Negretti and Zambra, the Dines Tube recorder, with direction recorder designed by Rooker for R. W. Munro.

The Royal Observatory at Greenwich and the Observatory of the Mersey Docks and Harbour Board, near Liverpool, have pressure-plate anemographs by Osler.

Anemometer.—An instrument for measuring the velocity or force of the wind. Anemometers register in various ways ; by counting the number of revolutions of cups in a measured time, by the difference of water level in a tube, and in other ways. Information as to the construction and use of various anemometers is given in the *Observer's Handbook.*

Anemoscope.—An instrument for indicating the existence of wind and snowing its direction. The one best known to the Meteorological Office is that designed by Mr. J. Baxendell which is provided with recording mechanism. It is an observatory-instrument, not a portable one.

Aneroid Barometer.—An instrument for determining the pressure of the atmosphere. It consists of a shallow air-tight metal box, usually nearly exhausted of air. The distance between opposite faces of the box alters with change in the surrounding atmospheric pressure, the alteration being shown on a dial by a hand actuated by a suitable train of levers. An aneroid is light, portable and convenient, but should be compared occasionally with a mercury barometer, as an appreciable change of zero sometimes occurs. It is also subject to " creep," *e.g.*, after a recent large fall of pressure—such as may occur when it is used as an ALTIMETER—it will, though under a really constant pressure, show a small spurious further fall, which in the course of an hour may amount to 1 or 2 per cent. of the previous fall. " Creep " in the same direction may be perceptible for several hours, but its rate continually diminishes.

Aneroidograph.—A self-recording aneroid. An aneroid-barometer provided with mechanism for recording the variations of pressure of the atmosphere. See BAROGRAPH.

Anthelion.—A colourless MOCK SUN (see HALO) appearing at the point of the sky opposite to and at the same ALTITUDE as the sun.

Anticyclone.—An anticyclone is a region in which the barometric pressure is high, relatively to its surroundings, and is generally shown on the weather charts by a series of closed isobars, the region of highest pressure being the central region of the anticyclone. In a well-marked anticyclone the isobars are roughly circular or oval curves, the wind blows spirally outwards in accordance with Buys Ballot's Law, and the pressure in the central parts is very seldom under 1,015 millibars or 30·00 inches. See Plate XIII.

Certain parts of the earth, notably large parts of the latitude belts of about 30° N. and 30° S., also continental areas in the winter in temperate latitudes, are anticyclonic regions. In the Azores-anticyclone in summer the pressure is usually about 1,025 millibars, or 30·25 inches, and in winter about 1,020 millibars, or 30·10 inches, and in the Siberian anticyclone of winter the pressure is often as high as 1,050 millibars, or 31·00 inches.

Anticyclones are characterised by calms and light winds and an absence of rain; the desert regions of the earth are anticyclonic regions.' But in the temperate zones, short of gales and strong winds, almost any weather may occasionally occur in an anticyclone. In England they are generally accompanied in winter by dull, cheerless weather and fogs, and in summer by bright, hot weather.

The causes of anticyclones are still unknown. We have learnt in recent years that the temperature of the air in them between the heights of 2 and 10 kilometres (1-6 miles) is higher, but at still greater heights lower than its environment.

For the anticyclone in relation to weather refer to the *Weather Map*, and see also AIRSHIP-WEATHER and ISOBARS.

Aqueous Vapour.*—Aqueous vapour is always present in the atmosphere, and, although it never represents more

---

.* See also HUMIDITY, p. 154, and ABSOLUTE HUMIDITY, p. 290.

than a small fraction of the whole, it has physical properties that give it great importance in meteorology. In a closed space wherever there is a free surface of ice or water, evaporation takes place until the water-vapour exerts a definite pressure of saturation, depending only upon the temperature, and not upon the pressure of the surrounding air. This pressure of saturation is very much greater at high than at low temperatures as is shown in the following table :—

Temperature.		Pressure of Saturation in millibars.	Temperature.		Pressure of Saturation in millibars.
°F	a.		°F	a.	
10	260·8	2·4	60	288·6	17·6
20	266·3	3·7	70	294·1	24·7
30	271·9	5·8	80	299·7	34·6
40	277·5	8·5	90	305·2	47·8
50	283·0	12·2	100	310·8	65·0

A cubic metre of dry air at 1,000 mb. and 289a. weighs 1,206g.

The mass of water contained in saturated air at different temperatures is given in the following table :—

Temperature.		Mass in grammes of water vapour per cubic metre of saturated air.	Temperature.		Mass in grammes of water vapour per cubic metre of saturated air.
°F.	a.		°F.	a.	
32	273·0	5	70	294·1	18
40	277·5	7	80	299·7	25
50	283·0	9	90	305·2	34
60	288·6	13	100	310·8	45

It is easily seen from these figures that saturated air must at once yield rain or snow if cooled, and even air that does not contain all the aqueous-vapour possible will ultimately deposit moisture if sufficiently cooled.

In the passage from the liquid to the gaseous state great quantities of heat are absorbed, 536 calories for every gramme .evaporated at the boiling point, and even more if the water is initially cold. Conversely much heat is yielded up when condensation occurs. See p. 70.

Tyndall has shown that the heat radiated from a black body at the boiling point of water is readily absorbed by aqueous vapour, which must, therefore, have a corresponding power of radiation. Spectrum analysis shows also that some of the visible radiation of the sun is strongly absorbed by the earth's atmosphere.

Atmosphere.—See *Weather Map.* M.O. 225 i., p. 15.

Atmospheric Electricity.—See p. 294.

Audibility.—The audibility of a sound in the atmosphere is measured by the distance from its source at which it becomes inaudible. On a perfectly clear, calm day the sound of a man's voice may be heard for several miles, provided there are no obstructions between the source of sound and the listener; but quite a small amount of wind will cut down the range of audibility enormously.

The sound is not cut down equally in all directions; to leeward, for instance, a sound can usually be heard at a greater distance than it can to windward of the source. This is accounted for by the bending which the sound-rays undergo, owing to the increase in wind-velocity with height above the ground, the rays to leeward of the source being bent downwards while those to windward are bent upwards so that they pass over the head of an observer stationed on the ground. The decrease in all directions in the range of audibility of a sound when there is a wind appears to be due chiefly to the dissipation in the energy of sound as it passes through eddying air. A plane wave-front becomes bent in an irregular manner when it passes through air in irregular or eddying movement. It, therefore, ceases to travel uniformly forward. Part of its energy is carried forward, while the rest is dissipated laterally.

If there were no dissipation of energy in a sound-wave the intensity of the sound would decrease inversely as the square of the distance from the source. Experiments show that, under normal conditions when there is a light wind blowing, the rate of decrease in intensity of sound at a distance of half a mile or more is considerably greater owing to the dissipation of energy than would be expected from the inverse square law. If, for instance, a whistle can be heard at a distance of half a mile, four whistles blown simultaneously should be audible at a distance of a mile ; but the range is actually only increased to about $\frac{3}{4}$ of a mile.

Sounds are usually heard at greater distances during the night than during the day. On calm nights the range of audibility of a sound may be as much as 10 or 20 times as great as it is during the day. This effect is due partly to the increased sensitiveness of the ear at night owing to the decrease in the amount of accidental disturbing waves, partly to the inversion of temperature which commonly occurs on calm, clear nights, and has the effect of bending the sound-waves downwards, but chiefly to the diminution of the amount of disturbance in the atmosphere at night.

Between the source of sound and the extreme range of

audibility areas of silence sometimes appear, in which the sound cannot be heard. This effect has in some cases been attributed to a reversal in the direction of the wind -in the upper layers of the atmosphere. The lower wind would bend the sound rays upwards to windward of the source. On entering the reversed upper wind current these rays would be bent down to the earth again, and would reach it at a point separated from the source of sound by an area of silence. This explanation is quite adequate in many cases in which the places, where the sound is heard again, are to the windward of the source. There are, however, many cases in which areas of silence appear to leeward of the source, and many others in which an area of silence occurs in the form of a ring enclosing the source and surrounded by an area of distinct audibility. In most of the cases where a ring-shaped area of silence has been observed the outer region of distinct audibility begins at a distance of about 100 miles from the source, and may extend to 150 miles or more. The well-known Silvertown explosion is a good example of a case in which a detached area of audibility was separated from the source of sound by an area of silence. In the accompanying map, which is reproduced by permission from the *Quarterly Review*, the two areas of audibility are shown. It will be seen that the outer area, which includes Lincoln, Nottingham and Norwich, lies about 100 miles from the source of sound. The inner area surrounding the source is not symmetrical, being spread out towards the north-west and south-east. Definite evidence was obtained that no sound was heard at various towns within the area of silence.

No very satisfactory explanation of these cases has so far been offered. The wind-distribution necessary to explain them on the wind-refraction theory would be very complicated and would, moreover, in some cases, be of a type which no meteorologist has yet observed.

The effect of FOG on the audibility of sound has been the subject of a considerable amount of discussion. The idea that sound is muffled by a fog seems to be commonly accepted ; but on the other hand the experiments of Henry and Tyndall have failed to give any indication of such an effect. They seem rather to show an increase in audibility in a fog. The effect of the waterdrops themselves has been shown to be too small to affect the propagation of sound waves to an appreciable extent, while the weather conditions usually associated with the production of fog, the homogeneous state of the atmosphere and the INVERSION of temperature, are such as to give rise to increased audibility.

In calm weather the direction of a hidden source of sound may be estimated to a few degrees by turning the head till the sound appears to come from the point towards which the observer is facing. The observer, however, is seldom confident that he has attained such accuracy. In windy weather it is more difficult to estimate the direction of sound.

Aureole.—The luminous area surrounding a light seen through a misty atmosphere.

Aurora.—See p. 298.

Autumn.—Autumn, in meteorology, comprises the three months of September, October and November, the first three months of the farmer's year. In astronomical text-books it is defined as the period commencing with the autumnal equinox and ending with the winter solstice, *i.e.*, from September 23rd to December 22nd, but

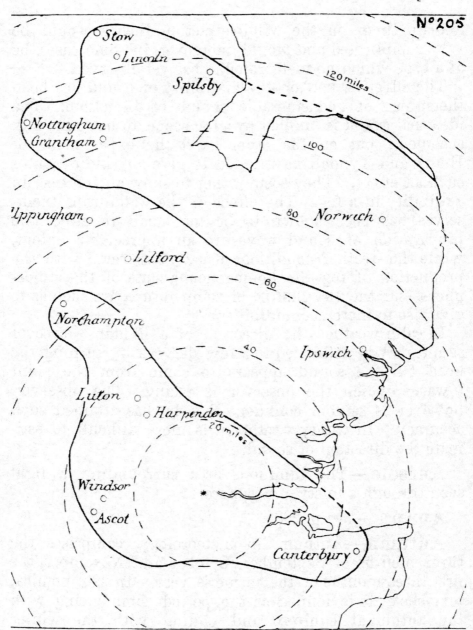

(Reproduced by permission from the Quarterly Review, July, 1917.)

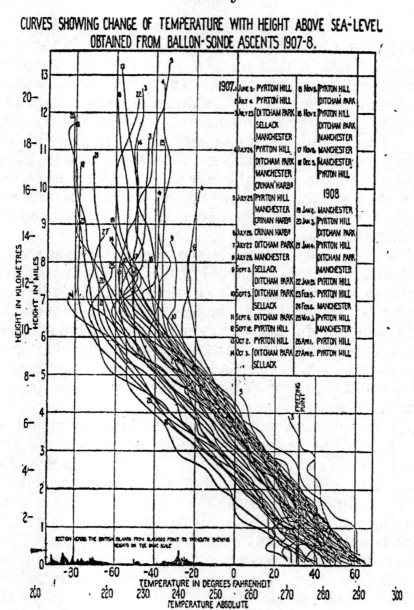

CURVES SHOWING CHANGE OF TEMPERATURE WITH HEIGHT ABOVE SEA-LEVEL OBTAINED FROM BALLON-SONDE ASCENTS 1907-8.

The separate curves represent the relation between temperature and height in miles or kilometres in the atmosphere. The numbers marking the separate curves indicate the date of ascent at the various stations as shown in the tabular columns. The difference of height at which the isothermal layer is reached, and the difference of its temperature for different days or for different localities, is also shown on the diagram by the courses of the lines.

Ballon sonde.—A small balloon usually made of india-rubber, inflated with hydrogen, and used for carrying self-registering instruments into the free atmosphere and thus obtaining records of the pressure, temperature and humidity aloft. The balloons used in England usually have a diameter of about one metre at starting (40 inches nearly), those on the continent nearly two metres. The balloons generally rise until they burst, on account of the diminished external pressure of the air, which may not happen until they have reached a height of 20 kilometres (12½ miles) or more.

After the balloon has burst, the material acts as a kind of parachute and breaks the fall of the instruments, so that they reach the ground without injury. A label is attached, offering a reward to the finder for the return of the instrument, and in that way valuable records are secured.

Sometimes the balloon fails to burst, but develops pin-holes through which the gas leaks. A long TRAJECTORY is the result. One of our records was returned from a Bavarian forest.

In other countries, where much heavier recording instruments are used, two balloons in tandem are employed, one of which bursts, and the other regulates the fall. This mode of arranging the apparatus, with a simple modification, is available for use at sea and many soundings of the air over the sea have been obtained. We have not taken part in that side of the inquiry.

Very remarkable facts about the temperature of the free air have been disclosed by soundings with ballons-sondes. Their general characteristics are shown in the diagram on page 38 which exhibits graphs of temperature and height for ·45 soundings obtained for the Meteorological Office in 1907–8. The reader should notice that, with one or two exceptions, the balloons reached a

NORMAL PRESSURE FOR THE SEVERAL MONTHS AT VARIOUS HEIGHTS OVER S.E. ENGLAND.

(Computed from Sea-level Pressures at Kew, and the Temperatures in Table IV. 2, Computer's Handbook, II. § 2. 53).

Height.	Jan.	Feb.	Mar.	Apr.	May.	June.	July.	Aug.	Sept.	Oct.	Nov.	Dec.	Range.
					Pressure in millibars.								
k													
15	116	116	116	118	121	123	125	125	124	122	119	117	9
14	136	135	136	138	142	144	146	146	145	142	139	137	11
13	159	159	159	162	165	168	170	170	169	166	163	160	11
12	187	186	186	189	193	196	199	198	198	194	191	188	13
11	218	217	217	221	226	229	232	232	231	227	223	220	15
10	255	254	254	259	264	267	270	270	269	265	260	256	16
9	297	297	297	302	307	311	314	313	312	308	303	299	17
8	346	346	346	350	356	360	363	362	361	356	351	347	17
7	401	401	400	405	410	415	417	416	416	411	406	402	17
6	463	462	462	467	472	476	478	478	477	472	468	464	16
5	532	532	531	535	540	544	546	546	545	540	536	533	15
4	610	609	608	612	616	620	621	621	620	616	612	610	13
3	696	695	693	697	701	704	705	705	704	700	697	695	12
2	792	790	789	791	795	797	798	797	798	794	792	790	9
1	899	897	895	897	900	901	902	900	902	898	897	896	7
Gd.	1018	1016	1014	1014	1016	1016	1016	1015	1017	1014	1014	1014	4

Ballon sonde.

TABLE OF RESULTS OBTAINED WITH BALLONS-SONDES IN THE UNITED KINGDOM.

*Normal Temperature at different levels in the atmosphere up to twelve kilometres for the several months of the year.

Height in k.	Jan.	Feb.	Mar.	Apr.	May.	June.	July.	Aug.	Sept.	Oct.	Nov.	Dec.	Year.
	a.	a.	a.	a.	a.	a,	a.	a.	a.	a.	a.	a.	
12	217	218	219	220	221	222	222	221	221	219	218	217	220
11	17	17	17	19	20	21	22	22	21	20	19	18	19
10	20	20	20	22	24	25	26	26	26	24	23	21	23
9	24	23	24	26	29	31	34	33	33	31	28	25	28
8	30	29	30	32	36	38	41	41	41	38	35	32	35
7	37	36	37	39	42	45	47	48	47	45	41	38	42
6	43	43	44	46	49	52	55	55	54	51	49	45	49
5	50	49	50	52	56	59	61	62	61	58	55	52	55
4	57	56	57	59	62	65	67	68	67	64	61	58	62
3	63	62	63	65	68	71	73	74	73	70	67	64	68
2	67	66	67	70	73	76	78	79	78	75	72	69	73
1	71	71	73	76	79	82	83	83	81	79	75	72	77
Ground	76	76	77	82	85	88	89	89	86	83	80	77	82

position (somewhere near ten kilometres), after which the temperature ceased to fall, yet the range of temperature at that level for the whole series is larger than the range at the surface.

Additional soundings have enabled us to put forward a table of the average pressure and temperature of the free air at different levels in the several months of the year, which is given on pp. 40 and 41.

Particulars as to the variation of the meteorological elements, temperature, wind and humidity derived from observations with ballons-sondes, kites and pilot balloons are given in Geophysical Memoirs, No. 5, by Major E. Gold, D.S.O. (published by the Meteorological Office).

Balloon Kite.—For dealing with the general features of the relation of temperature to pressure or height in the upper air of all parts of the globe the ballon-sonde is most effective. In this general inquiry the details due to the smaller irregularities of diurnal or seasonal variation may be disregarded. Such irregularities are specially noteworthy in the lowest kilometre of the atmosphere and are of importance in aviation and gunnery, because changes in the distribution of temperature are necessarily accompanied by changes in the distribution of pressure, and consequently of wind. The first kilometre or 3,000 feet, therefore, requires special attention. Observations of temperature, humidity and wind can be got by means of kites, when there is wind enough ; by captive balloons, when there is little or no wind ; and by the observation balloon or balloon kite in all weathers, except a gale. Special instruments are required for these observations. A special form of meteorograph has been designed by Mr. W. H. Dines for use with kites, but suitable provision has still to be made for kite-balloons and captive balloons.

Bar.—The unit of atmospheric pressure, being equal to the pressure of one million dynes (one megadyne) per square centimetre. The BAR is equal to the pressure of 29·5306 inches, or 750·076 mm. of mercury at 273a (32°F) and in latitude 45°. The name was introduced into practical meteorology by V. Bjerknes, and objection has been raised by McAdie of Harvard College on the ground that the name had been previously appropriated by chemists to the C. G. S. unit of pressure, the dyne per square centimetre. The meteorological bar is thus one million chemical bars, and what chemists call a *bar* we should call a *microbar*. One bar is 100 CENTIBARS or 1,000 MILLIBARS. See p. 194.

Barogram.—The continuous record of atmospheric pressure yielded by a self-recording barometer. See p. 156.

Barograph.—A self-recording barometer, an instrument which records automatically the changes of atmospheric pressure. In one form of mercury barograph the movements of the mercury in a barometer are communicated by a float to a pen in contact with a moving sheet of paper carried by a revolving drum which is driven by clockwork.

The portable barographs which are in common use are arranged to record the variations of pressure shown by an aneroid barometer, and on that account they are sometimes referred to as ANEROIDOGRAPHS. Particulars as to the method of using these instruments are given in the Observer's Handbook. (M.O. Publication 191.)

Barometer.—An instrument for measuring the pressure of the atmosphere. The mercury barometer has been found to be the most satisfactory form for general use. The principle underlying this type of instrument is quite simple. If a glass tube 3 feet long, closed at one end, is filled with mercury, and the open end is temporarily stopped up and immersed in an open vessel of the same liquid, then if the tube is held in a vertical position and the immersed end is re-opened, the mercury will fall until the level inside the tube stands at a height of about 30 inches above the mercury in the trough. The pressure of the atmosphere on the lower mercury-surface balances the tendency of the enclosed column to fall, and the height supported in this way represents the atmospheric pressure at the time. In order to compute the pressure, the length or height of the column of mercury has to be measured. Different mercury barometers vary as regards the method of reading this height, and in all the temperature of the mercury and the latitude of the place must be taken into account.

In the aneroid barometer the pressure of the atmosphere causes deformations in a spring inside a closed metallic box, which has been exhausted of air, and these are communicated to a pointer moving over a suitably engraved scale.

For the purposes of meteorology the pressure of the atmosphere has to be determined to the ten-thousandth part, which is a much higher degree of accuracy than is required in other meteorological measurements. Special contrivances and precautions are therefore required, which are duly set out in the Observer's Handbook.

Barometric tendency.—The change in the barometric pressure within the three hours preceding an observation. See *Weather-Map*, p. 35.

Beaufort notation.—A table of letters for weather. See *Weather-Map*, p. 10.

Beaufort Scale.

Beaufort Scale.—The scale of wind force devised by Admiral Beaufort in 1805. An explanation has been given in the *Weather-Map*, p. 13.

Table of Equivalents in Force and Velocity.

Pressure of Wind on a Plate		Equivalent velocity in miles per hour.	Beaufort Number.	Limits of Velocities.			
in lbs. per square ft.	in Millibars (10³ dynes per cm.²).			Statute Miles per Hour.	Nautical Miles per Hour.	Metres per Second.	Feet per Second.
0	0	0	0	Less than 1	Less than 1	Less than 0·3	Less than 2
·01	·01	2	1	1–3	1–3	0·3–1·5	2–5
·08	·04	5	2	4–7	4–6	1·6–3·3	6–11
·28	·13	10	3	8–12	7–10	3·4–5·4	12–18
·67	·32	15	4	13–18	11–16	5·5–8·0	19–27
1·31	·62	21	5	19–24	17–21	8·1–10·7	28–36
2·3	1·1	27	6	25–31	22–27	10·8–13·8	37–46
3·6	1·7	35	7	32–38	28–33	13·9–17·1	47–56
5·4	2·6	42	8	39–46	34–40	17·2–20·7	57–68
7·7	3·7	50	9	47–54	41–47	20·8–24·4	69–80
10·5	5·0	59	10	55–63	48–55	24·5–28·4	81–93
14·0	6·7	68	11	64–75	56–65	28·5–33·5	94–110
Above 17·0	Above 8·1	Above 75	12	Above 75	Above 65	33·6 or above.	Above 110

Bishop's ring, so named after its first observer, is a dull reddish-brown ring of about 20° outer radius seen round the sun in a clear sky even at mid-day. That it is a CORONA, and not a HALO, is proved by the fact that at times it has been seen to have a red outer margin (see CORONA). It appeared after the great eruption of Krakatoa in 1883, and remained visible till the spring of 1886, and was no doubt due to minute particles shot out by the eruption ; these remained suspended in the atmosphere for a considerable time. The great radius of this corona is explained by the smallness of the particles, and its intensity by their great number. The non-appearance of the other colours of the corona is explained by the presence of particles of many different sizes. Bishop's Ring was seen again after the eruptions of the Souffrière in St. Vincent and Mont Pelée in Martinique in 1902.

Blizzard.—A gale of wind with the temperature below freezing, the air being filled with fine dry snow. The snow may not be actually descending from the clouds but be merely raised from the snow-covered ground. The fine powdery snow peculiar to these storms is formed only at very low temperatures, so that the phenomenon is practically confined to the polar regions and the large land areas of the temperate zone. During a blizzard the temperature often rises, possibly because the violent wind causes a mixing of the lowest layers of the atmosphere and brings down air that is often warmer than the excessively cold air lying near the ground.

Blue of the sky.—Light rays striking particles which are smaller than the wave length of the light are scattered, that is turned aside in all directions. But the short waves composing the blue and violet end of the spectrum are more completely scattered than the long red and yellow waves. Hence light passing through a medium containing a great number of such particles is left with an excess of red, while light emerging laterally has an excess of blue. It is for this reason that soapy water looks yellowish when one looks through it at a source of white light, and bluish when one looks across the direction of illumination. The greater part of the sky appears blue because the light from it consists mainly of light scattered laterally from minute particles in the atmosphere. The smaller the particles the less intense is the light but the greater the proportion of it that is blue. When the particles are larger the proportion of blue is less, as in the whiter sky of a haze. Near the horizon the sky is whiter than at the zenith because the rays of light from that region have passed through a greater thickness of the lower air where large particles are relatively more numerous. Sunset colours are reddish because the rays reaching us directly have lost much of their blue light by lateral scattering. The sky as seen from high mountains and from aeroplanes at a great height is of a deeper but purer blue because there are fewer large particles than at lower altitudes.

Boiling Points.—See p. 300.

Bora.—A cold wind occurring in the northern Adriatic, very violent, which blows from the high plateaus which lie to the northward. These plateaus may become extremely cold in clear winter weather, and passing cyclonic systems allow the air to flow down to lower levels. The actual violence of the wind in a bora is largely due to the weight of the cold air of the plateau causing it to run down the slope like a torrent or cataract

of water. The wind experienced may therefore be independent of Buys Ballot's Law. The adiabatic warming
due to the increased pressure below is not sufficient to
prevent the resulting wind from being cold. In the
Meteorological Office it is proposed to call local winds of
this character "katabatic" in order to distinguish them
from the winds which show the normal relation to the
distribution of atmospheric pressure and are called
" geostrophic " winds.

Breeze.—A wind of moderate strength.

Glacial-breeze.—A cold breeze blowing down the course
of a GLACIER, and owing its origin to the cooling of the air
in contact with the ice. The movement of the air is due
to the gravitation of the air made denser by the cold
surfaces on a slope, and a glacial breeze may be classed
as a typical example of a katabatic wind.

Lake-breeze.—A breeze blowing on to the coast of a lake
in sunny weather during the middle of the day, part
of the convectional circulation induced by the greater
heating of the land than of the water.

Land-breeze.—An off-shore wind occurring at the
margin of a sea or lake during a clear night, due to the
more rapid cooling of the air over the land than over
the water. During the day the conditions are reversed
and the wind blows from the sea to the land, constituting
a SEA-BREEZE. These phenomena are most marked in the
tropics, where the wind arising from other causes is
usually not strong enough to mask the convectional
effect. See also p. 183.

Mountain-breeze.—A night breeze blowing down the

valleys, due to the flowing downward of the air chilled by the cold ground.

These also, as being due to convection in which the colder air takes the leading part, would be classed as katabatic winds, whereas the one next following in which warmed air plays the leading part would be classed as an "anabatic" wind.

Valley-breeze.—A day-breeze that blows up valleys when the sun warms the ground.

Brontometer, from *bronte*, a thunderstorm, a combination of apparatus for following and noting all the details of the phenomena of weather during a thunderstorm.

Buoyancy.—Used generally with regard to ships or balloons to indicate the load which a ship could carry without being completely submerged, or the weight which a balloon or airship can carry without sinking.

In the case of the balloon or airship the buoyancy is due to the displacement of air by hydrogen which is lighter than air. A cubic metre of perfectly dry air at 1000 mb. and 273 a. weighs 1·28 kilogramme, whereas a cubic metre of hydrogen under the same conditions weighs only ·09 kg. It follows that a cubic metre of hydrogen in air at 1000 mb. and 273a. will have a buoyancy represented by the difference, *i.e.*, 1·19 kg. Part of the buoyancy will have to be devoted to supporting the envelope which contains the hydrogen and which adds so little to the volume of air displaced by the hydrogen that, for purposes of calculation, we may regard the displacement of the air by hydrogen as the source of the buoyancy, and count the envelope and other accessories of the same kind as "dead weight."

The gas that is used under the name of hydrogen for filling balloons always contains some impurity that reduces its buoyancy. Water-vapour in the hydrogen and the surrounding air will reduce the buoyancy by an amount varying from 0·2 per cent. to 2 per cent. in the common range of circumstances and the impurities incidental to the manufacture of the gas, or to leakage, may easily reduce the buoyancy by 5 or 10 per cent. Instead, therefore, of taking the buoyancy of a cubic metre of working hydrogen at 1·19 kg. the theoretical figure for pure dry hydrogen in dry air, we may take it at 1·10 kg. per cubic metre at 1000 mb. and 273 a.

The volume of a large airship may be 25,000 m³, the dimensions being 140 m. in length and 15 m. in diameter. The gross buoyancy at 1000 mb. and 273 a. is, in that case, 25,000 × 1·10 kg., or 27,500 kg. In those conditions the relation of pressure to temperature is 3·66:1, see p. 53. In other conditions of pressure and temperature the relation, and therefore the buoyancy, will be different.

The relation between the displacement and the weight supported is given by the equation

$$Q\rho(1-\sigma) = W + L + B$$

where Q is the volume of air displaced, ρ the density of the air, σ the specific gravity of the "hydrogen" referred to air at the same temperature and pressure, W the dead weight, L the portable load, and B the ballast.

Buoyancy in different Atmospheric Conditions and the Limit of Height that an Airship can reach.

The density of air ρ becomes less and less as one ascends in the atmosphere because the pressure diminishes. The temperature diminishes also, and, on that account, there is some compensation for the fall of pressure, but not enough to preserve the buoyancy.

We may suppose that σ, the specific gravity of the hydrogen, remains the same throughout, because, in an airship, the pressure of the hydrogen changes with that of the air in which it floats. Its temperature changes likewise, and, if we leave out of account the heat received or lost in the form of radiation, the fall of temperature of the hydrogen of an ascending balloon is generally more rapid than that of the surrounding air. It would take time for the temperature to become equalised, whereas the adjustment of pressure is practically immediate. Therefore, the hydrogen in a rising airship is rather denser than the result of calculation would give. Thus, to suppose σ to remain constant, is a little more favourable to the navigator than actuality, unless he takes advantage of sunshine.

The buoyancy at any level is determined by the density ρ.

With the assumption that σ remains constant the buoyancy can be computed from the density of the air at the level of standard pressure and temperature by the ordinary gas-equation

$$\frac{p}{p_0} = \frac{\rho}{\rho_0} \times \frac{T}{T_0}$$

Where p, ρ, T are the pressure, density and absolute temperature of the air at the selected level p_0, ρ_0, T_0 are the standard pressure, density and temperature.

The equation of buoyancy becomes

$$Q \times \frac{p}{p_0} \times \frac{T_0}{T} \rho_0 (1-\sigma) = W + L + B.$$

For the figures which we have quoted,

$$p_0 = 1000 \text{ mb}, \text{ T}_0 = 273\text{a}, \rho_0 (1 - \sigma) = 1{\cdot}1 \text{ kg/m}^3$$

and the equation becomes

$$\frac{273 \times 1{\cdot}1}{1000} \frac{p}{T} = \frac{W + L + B}{Q}$$

W and L, the dead weight and the portable load, cannot be altered during a voyage without sacrificing something, but the ballast B is carried for the purpose of adjusting the level. The maximum height will be reached when the ballast is exhausted, that is when B is zero.

In this equation the value of the ratio p/T which determines the density depends upon the pressure and temperature of the air at the time of the flight, but for aeronauts the most important cause of the variation in these elements, and therefore in their ratio, is the change of pressure and temperature of the atmosphere with height. These are so considerable that they overshadow altogether the changes at any chosen level from day to day or from month to month. We can therefore use a table of average monthly values with advantage. The following tables give the average values of p/T for different heights computed from observations of ballons-sondes. From the values p/T the density in grammes per cubic metre can be found by multiplication by 348. (The first table is computed from the pressures in the accompanying table and the temperatures in Table IV. 2, Computer's Handbook, Part II., §2, p. 56, : the second has been prepared by Mr. W. H. Dines, F.R.S., for the *Handbook of Meteorology*).

NORMAL MONTHLY FACTORS p/T FOR THE DENSITY OF AIR AT VARIOUS HEIGHTS OVER S.E. ENGLAND.

k	Jan.	Feb.	Mar.	Ap.	May.	June.	July.	Aug.	Sept.	Oct.	Nov.	Dec.	Year	k
						p/T in millibars/degrees								
15	·53	·54	·53	·54	·55	·56	·57	·57	·56	·56	·55	·54	·55	15
14	·63	·63	·62	·63	·65	·65	·66	·66	·60	·65	·64	·63	·64	14
13	·73	·73	·73	·74	·75	·75	·77	·77	·77	·76	·75	·74	·75	13
12	·86	·86	·85	·87	·88	·89	·90	·89	·90	·89	·88	·86	·88	12
11	1·00	1·00	1·00	1·01	1·03	1·04	1·04	1·04	1·04	1·03	1·01	1·01	1·02	11
10	1·16	1·17	1·17	1·18	1·19	1·19	1·20	1·19	1·19	1·18	1·17	1·16	1·18	10
9	1·32	1·34	1·34	1·34	1·35	1·35	1·35	1·35	1·34	1·34	1·33	1·33	1·34	9
8	1·52	1·52	1·51	1·51	1·52	1·52	1·52	1·52	1·52	1·51	1·52	1·52	1·52	8
7	1·71	1·71	1·69	1·69	1·69	1·69	1·69	1·69	1·70	1·70	1·70	1·70	1·70	7
6	1·93	1·92	1·91	1·91	1·91	1·90	1·88	1·88	1·88	1·88	1·89	1·91	1·90	6
5	2·15	2·15	2·13	2·12	2·11	2·10	2·09	2·09	2·10	2·10	2·12	2·13	2·12	5
4	2·39	2·38	2·38	2·36	2·34	2·33	2·32	2·32	2·33	2·34	2·35	2·36	2·35	4
3	2·66	2·64	2·65	2·61	2·62	2·60	2·58	2·58	2·59	2·60	2·62	2·63	2·62	3
2	2·97	2·95	2·95	2·92	2·91	2·87	2·87	2·87	2·88	2·88	2·91	2·94	2·91	2
1	3·31	3·30	3·29	3·25	3·23	3·19	3·18	3·17	3·20	3·20	3·24	3·27	3·24	1
Gd.	3·66	3·68	3·65	3·62	3·58	3·56	3·53	3·52	3·55	3·57	3·62	3·65	3·60	Gd.

Note: Density is constant throughout the year at 8 k, where $p/T = 1·52$ mb/a and $\rho = 530$ g/m³ $= 231$ gr/ft³.

At greater heights the air is heavier in summer, owing to its higher pressure; at lesser heights the air is lighter in summer, owing to the higher temperature.

NORMAL VALUES OF PRESSURE, TEMPERATURE AND DENSITY IN DIFFERENT REGIONS AT VARIOUS HEIGHTS UP TO 20 K.

Height in Kilo-metres.	England, S.E.			Europe.			Canada.			Equator.		
	T a.	p mb	D p/T	T a.	p mb.	D p/T	T a.	p mb.	D p/T	T a.	p mb.	D p/T
20	219	55	.25	219	55	.25	214	54	.25	193	53	.27
19	219	64	.29	219	64	.29	215	63	.29	193	63	.33
18	219	75	.34	219	75	.34	214	74	.35	193	75	.39
17	219	88	.40	219	88	.40	211	87	.41	193	90	.47
16	219	102	.46	219	102	.46	211	102	.48	195	107	.55
15	219	120	.55	219	120	.55	211	120	.57	198	128	.65
14	219	140	.64	219	140	.64	212	142	.67	203	152	.75
13	219	164	.75	219	164	.75	214	167	.78	211	178	.84
12	219	192	.88	218	192	.88	216	195	.90	219	209	.95
11	220	224	1.02	219	225	1.03	219	228	1.04	227	244	1.18
10	222	261	1.18	222	262	1.18	223	266	1.19	235	283	1.20
9	228	303	1.33	227	305	1.34	229	309	1.35	243	327	1.35
8	234	352	1.50	233	353	1.52	236	358	1.52	251	376	1.50
7	241	407	1.69	241	408	1.69	243	413	1.70	258	430	1.67
6	248	469	1.89	248	470	1.90	251	475	1.90	265	491	1.85
5	255	538	2.11	255	538	2.11	258	543	2.11	272	558	2.05
4	262	615	2.35	261	614	2.35	264	618	2.34	279	632	2.27
3	268	699	2.61	267	699	2.62	270	703	2.60	285	713	2.50
2	273	795	2.91	272	794	2.92	275	798	2.90	290	803	2.77
1	278	900	3.24	277	899	3.25	278	903	3.25	295	903	3.06
0	282	1014	3.60	281	1014	3.62	282	1017	3.60	300	1012	3.38

The figures for Canada above 15 k. are somewhat doubtful, and for the Equator very doubtful, owing to paucity of observations.

With these tables the limiting height of flotation can be approximately determined when the dimensions and particulars of the dead weight, portable load and ballast are known.

For example, in the case of an airship which displaces $25,000m^3$ of air with a dead weight 11,500kg. 9,000kg. ballast, including 2,000kg. of fuel which can be spared, 7,000kg. portable load, including crew, clothing and food, fuel for the return journey, oil armament and working tackle, the right hand side of the equation is reduced to its minimum when the ballast is disposed of, that is when $B = o$, in that case p/T works out to be 2·46. This will be found in the table between 3k and 4k, rather nearer 3k in summer than in winter.

THE EFFECT OF WEATHER UPON BUOYANCY.

The changes of weather affect the buoyancy because they alter the value of p/T at the starting point and at every stage of the course. The value at the starting point determines the amount of ballast that can be carried to begin with, and the value at other stages of the journey determines the height to which the airship can rise with all its ballast expended.

Assuming that the limit of ascent is determined by the value 2·4 for the ratio p/T, we find that the variation in the course of the year 1913 was from 3·5k to 4·1k. The effect of low pressure or high temperature can easily be seen but it is not very pronounced. The difference between the worst occasion and the best from January to May 1913 was about 1,600 ft. It is now recognised that above one kilometre, when pressure is low, temperature is also low, and, consequently, at any level the value of p/T is steadier than the variations at the surface would lead one to expect. In these calculations no allowance has been made for leakage, nor, on the other hand, for compressed hydrogen carried to replace losses.

DEPRESSION PRODUCED BY THE WEIGHT OF A DEPOSIT OF RAIN OR SNOW.

The catchment area may be about 1000 m², and the figures quoted from Josselin by Mödebeck for the weight on that area are—

	Weight.		Maximum depression.
	kg.	kg.	k.
Dew (light)	15	to 50	·03
Dew (heavy)	80	to 240	·15
Rain	200	to 290	·18
Heavy rain	250	to 360	·21
Storm rain	400	to 480	·30
Snow	800	to 1000	·60

According to this table the worst effect, even of snow, would be a depression of 2,000 feet.

DEPRESSION PRODUCED BY DESCENDING WIND.

The calculation is very hazardous; supposing the vertical component of the wind in ordinary circumstances to be from 0·5 to 1·5 m/s, and assuming the ordinary law of resistance, which is true for small areas, the downward force would be ·01 mb. = 10 dynes per cm², say $500 \times 10^4 \times 10$ dynes on the envelope (taking the area to be 500 m²), or 5×10^7 dynes. This is equivalent to a weight of about 50 kg. and is, therefore, unimportant, but it would become important if the downward velocity reached 5 m/s, which it probably may do in a disturbed atmosphere, and in the downrush of a line squall this value might be largely exceeded.

Buys Ballot's Law (see *The Weather Map*).—The law is that if you stand with your back to the wind the atmospheric pressure in the northern hemisphere decreases towards your left and increases towards your right. In the southern hemisphere the reverse is true. The law is a necessary consequence of the earth's rotation.

C.G.S.—Abbreviation for Centimetre Gramme Second, used to denote the organised system of units for the measurement of physical quantities by units which are based upon the centimetre, the gramme, and the second as fundamental units.

Calm.—Absence of appreciable wind ; on the Beaufort Scale 0, *i.e.*, less than 1 mile an hour, or three-tenths of a metre per second.

Calorie.—See p. 301.

Celsius, Anders : an astronomer and physicist, the inventor of the Centigrade thermometer, born at Upsala in 1701. The name Centigrade arises from the division of the interval between the freezing point and boiling point of water into one hundred parts. In continental countries the scale is generally named after the inventor Celsius. It is also not infrequently referred to as the centesimal scale.

Note.—Celsius divided the thermometric interval between freezing and boiling points of water into 100 parts, but he made the former 100° and the latter 0°.

The Centigrade scale now in use was introduced by Christin of Lyons in 1743 (possibly earlier). It has also been claimed for Linné, but the priority is extremely doubtful.

Centibar.—A hundredth part of a "bar" or C.G.S. "atmosphere." See BAR, also see Table of equivalents at the end of this volume.

Centigrade.—A thermometric scale introduced by ANDERS CELSIUS (*q.v.*), which has zero at the melting point of ice, while 100° represents the boiling point of water at a pressure of 760 mm. of mercury. A centigrade degree is 9/5 Fahrenheit degrees. On the centigrade "absolute" scale the freezing point is at 273a, the unit being the same as a centigrade degree.

Centimetre—the hundredth part of a metre. The unit of length on the Centimetre-Gramme-Second system which is universally employed for electrical and magnetic measurements. A metre was originally defined as one ten-millionth part of the earth's quadrant, that is, the distance from the equator to the pole. 1 centimetre is equal to ·394 inch, and 2·54 centimetres to 1 inch, to a high degree of accuracy.

Cirro-cumulus.—A group of fleecy cloudlets or small "flocks" of cloud formed at great heights and showing no shadows. They are called "moutons" in French. See CLOUD.

Cirro-stratus.—A layer of thin, transparent cloud at a high level. See CLOUD.

Cirrus.—Clouds at great height, generally formed into "wisps" of thread-like structure. See CLOUD.

Climate.—A general summary of the weather for any particular locality. When the weather has been observed for a sufficiently long time in any locality we are able to make a useful statement as to the weather which *may* be

Cirrus clouds, Thread or Feather clouds at a height of from five to six miles, and generally of a white colour. They are composed of ice-crystals.

The picture gives an idea of rather more massive structure than is usual with cirrus clouds, but the sweeps and wisps are very characteristic.

experienced at any particular time of the year in that locality. Technically, the climate of a place is represented by the average values of the different meteorological elements, which should include means for each month, as well as means for the whole year. Average extreme values for different periods and ABSOLUTE EXTREMES are of interest, and also the number of rain-days, days of snowfall, frost, hail, thunderstorm, gale, &c., and the frequency of occurrence of winds from different directions. Included also under this heading would be the earliest and latest dates of frost and snow, the average depth of snow lying at different times, and particulars of the temperature of the soil at various depths. In places where the type of weather at a given time of year varies greatly, a long series of observations is needed in order to obtain a fair idea of the different climatic elements. Various kinds of climate are characterised, chiefly with regard to moisture and temperature, as *continental* which is dry, with great extremes of temperature ; *insular* or *oceanic* which is moist and very equable in temperature ; *tropical* in which the seasons depend chiefly upon the time of occurrence of rainfall ; *temperate* in which the seasons are chiefly dependent upon the variation of the daily course of the sun in the sky ; *arctic* in which the year is mainly two long periods of sun and no sun. Local climates, such as those of the Mediterranean in general and of the Riviera in particular, are dependent upon the geographical conditions of land and water. Every climate is to some extent affected by the geographical nature of the surroundings of the locality.

Climatic Chart (see *Weather Map,* p. 88).—A map showing the geographical distribution of some element of climate ; temperature, rainfall and sunshine are the most frequently charted. Charts of normal values of these elements for the British Isles for long periods of years ended 1910 are issued by the Meteorological Office. The word also covers any diagram representing the periodic or secular variation of a climatic factor.

Climatology.—The study of CLIMATE (*q.v.*).

Clouds.—Clouds have been classified into certain typical forms, but there are so many intermediate types that it is sometimes difficult to decide to what class any cloud belongs.

Certain types of cloud and the direction from which they are moving indicate certain states of weather ; certain types of cloud being usually within certain heights, a knowledge of cloud forms enables the observer to make a rough estimate of the height of clouds.

For practical purposes clouds may be divided into cloud sheets and cloud heaps.

CLOUD SHEETS.

Many forms of cloud are obviously in more or less extended sheets, sometimes covering the whole sky, sometimes only covering a small patch. They vary much in thickness, sometimes no blue sky is visible through the sheet, sometimes small patches of blue are visible, sometimes half the sky is blue, at other times the sheet of cloud is represented by a few detached clouds in the blue.

The formation of a sheet of clouds is not well understood. But the following may be on some occasions the method of formation ; it is known that the atmosphere is to a certain extent stratified, and that there may be damp and dry layers; if the pressure over any area is diminished the air in the region will be cooled by expansion; if sufficiently cooled the dew point will be reached, and any damp layer will become a cloudy layer.

Cloud sheets are often seen to be broken up into waves; the waves may not be formed in the cloud itself; if waves are set up in the atmosphere they will be propagated upwards and downwards; in a thin cloud layer the air that rises on the wave crest is cooled by expansion, more condensation occurs and the cloud is thicker; the air that descends in the hollow is warmed by compression and some of the cloud is evaporated, leaving a clear or nearly clear space.

Cloud sheets may sometimes be seen forming at several levels at the same time; over a cyclonic depression there are probably sheets of cloud at several levels.

Cloud sheets may be divided up into three classes which differ in appearance and height. The upper layer, the cirrus clouds, are at heights of from 25,000 to 30,000 feet; the middle layer, the alto clouds, are from 10,000 to 25,000 feet; the lower layer clouds are below 10,000 feet.

THE UPPER LAYER.

The clouds of the upper layer, the CIRRUS CLOUDS, are composed of ice particles, not of water drops as all other clouds. They are of a pure white colour with no shadows except when seen when the sun is low down. They are usually streaky and have a brushed out appearance (mares' tails); they are frequently spoken of as windy looking clouds, but in spite of this appearance they do not necessarily indicate wind. They are often seen in long streaks stretching across the sky, sometimes in parallel bands, seeming by

the effect of perspective to converge. on the horizon
to a V-point. These clouds often move away from the
centres of depressions ; when coming from North-West,
West or South-West they indicate a depression in a
westerly direction, which will probably spread over the
observer ; when seen coming from the North they indicate a depression to the Northward which will probably
move away to the North-East and so not influence the
weather. To observe the motion of clouds, especially of
the high clouds, get a patch of cloud "on" with the
point of a branch or some point of a building ; if one
moves so as to keep the cloud on the point, one's direction
of motion will be towards the direction from which the
cloud is coming. It is often difficult to determine the
motion of the high clouds without a careful observation
of this kind.

Bands of cloud do not necessarily move in the direction
of their length, nor do parallel bands of clouds necessarily
move from their V-point.

HALOS and MOCK SUNS (sun dogs) are seen at times
in cirrus clouds but in no other forms ; a halo is a ring,
sometimes coloured, seen at some distance (22° or more
rarely 46°) from the sun or moon.

Besides the wisps and streaks of cloud of common
cirrus there are other forms :—

CIRRO-CUMULUS : lines or groups of cloud, sometimes detached globules, sometimes waves ; mackerel
sky (French : moutons) ; these clouds are pure white, with
no shadows.

CIRRO-STRATUS : a bank of tangled web sometimes
overspreading the whole sky ; no shadows ; sun pale and
"watery."

CIRRO-NEBULA : similar to last but no visible structure ; a veil of pale white cloud. Precedes depressions.

THE MIDDLE LAYER, ALTO CLOUDS.

The alto clouds are composed of water droplets, not ice particles, therefore halos are never seen ; CORONÆ may be seen ; these are coloured bands quite close round the sun or moon. The alto clouds are not such a pure white as the cirrus clouds, and shadows are visible on them. They may move away from centres of low pressure, like the cirrus clouds. They are, on the average, only half the height of the cirrus clouds, being from 10,000 to 25,000 feet high. The following are the most important varieties :—

ALTO-CUMULUS.—Very like cirro-cumulus, but the cloud masses are larger, and shadows are visible ; sometimes arranged in globular masses (French : Gros moutons), sometimes in waves.

ALTO-CUMULUS CASTELLÁTUS, TURRET CLOUD.—The globular masses of Alto-cumulus are developed upwards into hard-edged clouds like miniature cumulus ; sometimes a large number of clouds almost of exactly the same shape are seen. When coming from a southerly or westerly point, after fine weather, Turret cloud is a sign of approaching thundery conditions.

ALTO-STRATUS.—Very like cirro-stratus, but a thicker and greyer cloud ; halos never seen ; precedes depressions, and does not usually extend so far from the centre as cirro-stratus.

THE LOWER LAYER.

The clouds of the lower layer are below 10,000 feet ; thicker clouds with not such a fine structure as the higher clouds.

STRATO-CUMULUS.—Masses of cloud with some vertical structure appearing in rolls or waves, sometimes covering the whole sky ; sometimes the whole sky is covered with cloud, but the hollows of the waves are lighter and obviously thinner ; blue sky is occasionally seen more or less plainly through the thinner parts. This cloud is common in quiet weather in winter, and sometimes persists for many days together. In summer it is more broken up, and tends to turn into cumulus clouds.

STRATUS.—A uniform layer of cloud which resembles a fog, but does not rest on the ground. Small masses of stratus, more or less in the shape of a lens (lenticular cloud), are often seen near thunder clouds ; they appear dark when seen against the white sides of the thunder clouds.

NIMBUS.—A dark shapeless cloud without structure, from which continuous rain or snow falls ; through openings in this cloud, should such occur, layers of cirro-stratus or alto-stratus may almost always be seen.

SCUD.—Small shapeless clouds with ragged edges ; sometimes seen without other cloud, but usually associated with nimbus and cumulus.

. HEAP CLOUDS.

Clouds with considerable vertical structure, not forming horizontal sheets of cloud. Their formation is due to rising currents of air ; as the air rises it is cooled by expansion till it reaches the dew point when cloud begins to form ; as soon as condensation takes place heat is liberated, and though the air cools as it rises still further, it does not cool so rapidly as it would were no heat liberated by the condensing water vapour. The rising current is due to air heated above its surroundings, and the condensation enables the current to rise considerably

Between pp. 64 *and* 65.

CLOUDS SEEN FROM BELOW: FIGURE 1.

Strato-Cumulus from below.

Cumulo-Nimbus (Thunder-cloud) with "Anvil" extension
of false cirrus, 30th October, 1915.

Strato-cumulus from an aeroplane (4,000 feet).

filled with fog, 300 feet deep, in early morning after
still night.

higher than it would have done had no extra heat been available.

SIMPLE CUMULUS.—This may consist of small clouds with flat base and rounded top or large cauliflower shaped clouds (Woolpack cloud). These clouds commonly form on a summer day, beginning as small clouds, and growing larger by the early afternoon, when the rising currents due to the sun's heat are at a maximum; they usually disappear before sunset.

CUMULO-NIMBUS; SHOWER CLOUD; THUNDER CLOUD.—Sometimes when cumulus grows to large proportions the upper edge is seen to become soft and brushed out into forms somewhat like cirrus (false cirrus); at the same time from the under edge of the cloud, which has been growing very dark, rain begins to fall. Sometimes only a slight shower may result; but if the cloud is large there may be heavy rains and violent thunderstorms. Sometimes the false cirrus is brushed out round the top of the cloud giving it the shape of an anvil; the anvil cloud is usually associated with very violent thunderstorms and falls of hail. Thunder clouds due to the rising currents of a hot day usually disappear about the time of sunset, but often leave the false cirrus.

Cumulus often forms in long lines of cloud presenting the appearance of a succession of clouds or of a wall of cloud extending along the horizon. Any cause that brings masses of air of different temperatures near together brings about the formation of cumulus cloud.

It should be noted that rain, hail, and snow only fall from nimbus or cumulo-nimbus clouds, except the slightest and most transient showers, which may sometimes fall from alto-cumulus or strato-cumulus. Nimbus causes persistent rain or snow, cumulo-nimbus more or less severe showers of rain, hail or snow.

TABULAR STATEMENT OF THE SEVERAL TYPES OF CLOUDS.

I.—CLOUD SHEETS.

Upper cloud layer about 30,000 feet. Clouds composed of ice crystals. With these are sometimes seen halos, or rings, at some distance from the sun and moon.

CIRRUS. Mares' tails; wisps or lines of pure white clouds with no shadows.

CIRRO-CUMULUS. Small speckles and flocks of white clouds; fine ripple clouds; mackerel sky.

CIRRO-STRATUS. A thin sheet of tangled web structure, sometimes covering the whole sky; watery sun or moon.

CIRRO-NEBULA. Similar to last, but a veil of cloud with no visible structure.

Middle cloud layer; 10,000 feet to 25,000 feet. Clouds composed of minute drops of water. Coloured rings sometimes seen quite close to sun and moon, but never halos.

ALTO-CUMULUS. Somewhat similar to cirro-cumulus, but the cloud masses are larger, and show some shadow.

ALTO-CUMULUS CASTELLATUS. Turret cloud; alto-cumulus with upper margins of the cloud masses developed upwards into miniature cumulus, with hard upper edges. (Sign of thunder.)

ALTO-STRATUS. Very like cirro-stratus and cirro-nebula, but a thicker and darker cloud.

Lower cloud layer. Below 7,000 feet.*

STRATO-CUMULUS. Cloud masses with some vertical structure; rolls or waves sometimes covering the whole sky.

STRATUS. A uniform layer of cloud resembling a fog but not resting on the ground.

NIMBUS. Shapeless cloud without structure, from which falls continuous rain or snow.

SCUD. Small shapeless clouds with ragged edges; sometimes seen without other cloud, especially in hilly country; but more commonly seen below other clouds, such as cumulus and nimbus.

---

*. The heights given are only approximate. Thus lower clouds of the strato-cumulus type may rise above 7,000 feet and attain at times the height of the middle cloud layer.

II.—HEAP CLOUDS.

CUMULUS. (Woolpack clouds); clouds with flat base and considerable vertical height. Cauliflower-shaped top.

FRACTO-CUMULUS. Small cumulus with ragged tops.

CUMULO-NIMBUS. (Anvil-, thunder- or shower-cloud). Towering cumulus with the top brushed out in soft wisps or larger masses (false cirrus) and rain cloud at base.

The height of the heap clouds is very variable. Mean height of base, about 4,500 feet; the height of the top varies from about 6,000 to 25,000 feet.

Reproductions of photographs of Strato-cumulus seen from below and from above, also of Cumulo-Nimbus and of a Valley filled with fog are inserted between pages 64 and 65. A photograph representing Cirrus faces page 58, and one representing Mammato-cumulus, page 190.

Cloud-burst.—A term commonly used for very heavy thunder-rain. Extremely heavy downpours are sometimes recorded, which in the course of a very short time tear up the ground and fill up gulleys and watercourses; this happens in hilly and mountainous districts, and is probably due to the sudden cessation of convectional movement, caused possibly by the supply of warm air from the lower part of the atmosphere being cut off as the storm moves over a mountain range. With the cessation of the upward current, the raindrops and hailstones which it had been supporting must fall in a much shorter time than they would have done had the ascensional movement continued.

Clouds, Weight of.—Measurements on the Austrian Alps of the quantity of water suspended in clouds have given $0·35$ g/m³ to $4·8$ g/m³. The water suspended as mist, fog, or cloud may be taken as ranging from $0·1$ to 5 g/m³. (See *Wegener's* Thermodynamics of the Atmosphere, p. 262.)

Col.—The neck of relatively low pressure separating two anticyclones ,(see ISOBARS). One of the most treacherous types of barometric distribution, as it sometimes marks a locality of brilliantly fine weather and sometimes is broken up by thunderstorms. See Plate XIV.

Compass.—A circumference, or dial, graduated into thirty-two equal parts by the points N., N. by E., N.N.E., N.E. by E., N.E. and so on. The cardinal points of the compass are North, South, East and West. The points of the compass are often called ORIENTATION points. A MAGNETIC COMPASS, or MARINER'S COMPASS, is a compass or orientation-card having attached to it one or a series of parallel magnets and supported so that it may turn freely in a horizontal plane. Any magnet sets itself parallel to what is termed the magnetic meridian, but it is only some few countries that have a magnetic meridian the same as the geographical meridian ; they include narrow strips in Arabia, European Russia, Finland, and North Lapland. Even at places within temperate latitudes the angle between the two may amount to 50° or more, and in the Arctic or Antarctic regions the direction of the compass needle may be the opposite of the geographical north and south line. In the neighbourhood of London the needle points about 15° to the west of north, and the amount is slowly decreasing.

In the west of Ireland the declination, or variation, as it is called, is more than 20° W.

Public wind-vanes are often incorrectly set according to magnetic north instead of true north ; caution must be exercised accordingly.

All maps are set out according to true north ; often an orientation mark is given to show the variation of the compass or magnetic declination.

A compass-needle is influenced by magnetic material in its neighbourhood, and therefore in practice should not be used near to articles made of iron or steel.

The variation of the compass and correction of its errors are matters of primary importance for aircraft pilots and are provided for by a special manual.

Component.—A word used to indicate the *steps*, in their various directions, which must be *compounded* or combined geometrically in order to produce a given *displacement*. For example a man going ten steps upstairs arrives in the same position as if he took ten treads forward on the level and then ten rises straight upwards, or equally if he first went up ten rises and then took ten treads forward. The actual distance travelled is the combination of the horizontal distance and the vertical rise. We call the horizontal distance and the vertical rise the *components* and the actual distance the *geometrical sum* or the *resultant* of the components.

It is evident that it is not necessary that the components should be at right angles to each other as the horizontal and vertical are. Any displacement AC is the geometrical sum of the two components AB and BC,. wherever B may be.

This analysis of displacement into components, or combination of component displacements to form a resultant displacement, finds an effective illustration in the effect of leeway on the performance of aircraft. The aircraft must necessarily be carried along by the air in which it travels. If we suppose AB to be the travel of the aircraft through the air in an hour, and BC to represent the travel of the wind in the hour, AC, the resultant, will represent the travel of the aircraft with reference to the fixed earth, or its performance. BC is the leeway, AB is the headway made through the air.

Hence the *performance* is the *geometrical sum* of the *headway* and the *leeway.* See VECTOR.

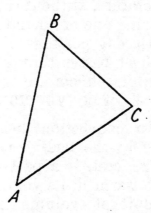

The law of composition of displacements which is thus set out is equally applicable to the composition of velocities, accelerations, and forces. The resultant is always the geometrical sum of the components, and to obtain the geometrical sum, set out a step or line representing the first component, then another step representing the second component : the resultant is the step from the beginning of the first component to the end of the second.

The simplest way of dealing with the magnitudes and angles which come into questions involving geometrical composition is to make a scale-drawing and measure them with a rule and protractor. That is generally accurate enough for most purposes, but the methods of the solution of triangles can be employed if high numerical accuracy is wanted.

Condensation.—The process of formation of a liquid from its vapour. See AQUEOUS VAPOUR.

Conduction.—The process by which heat is transferred by and through matter, from places of high to places of low temperature, without transfer of the matter itself, the process being one of " handing on " of the heat-energy between adjacent portions of matter. It is the process by which heat passes through solids ; in fluids, although it occurs, its effects are usually negligible in comparison with those of CONVECTION. See also p. 146.

Convection.—In convection heat is carried from one place to another by the bodily transfer of the matter containing it. In general, if a part of a fluid, whether liquid or gaseous, is warmed, its volume is increased, and the weight per unit of volume is less than before. The warmed part therefore rises and its place is taken by fresh fluid which is warmed in turn. Conversely, if it is cooled it sinks. Consequently, if heat is supplied to the lower part of a mass of fluid, the heat is disseminated throughout the whole mass by convection, or if the upper part is cooled the temperature of the whole mass is lowered by a similar process.

There are two apparent and important exceptions in meteorology. Fresh water, when below the temperature of 39·1° F., 277a., expands instead of contracting on being further cooled. Hence a pond or lake is cooled bodily down to 39·1° but no further, as winter chills the surface before it freezes. Secondly, heat applied to the bottom of the atmosphere may stay there without being disseminated upwards when the atmosphere is exceptionally stable in the circumstances explained under ENTROPY.

Corona.—A coloured ring, or a series of coloured rings, usually of about 5° radius, surrounding the sun or moon. The space immediately adjacent to the luminary is bluish-white, while this region is bounded on the outside by a brownish red ring, these two together forming the "aureole." In some cases the aureole alone appears, but a complete corona has a set of coloured rings surrounding the aureole, violet inside followed by blue, green, yellow to red on the outside. This series may be repeated several times outwards. The corona is produced by diffraction, that is by the bending of rays of light round the edge of small particles, in this case minute water drops, but sometimes dust (see BISHOP'S RING). If the diffracting particles are of uniform size the colours are pure ; a mixture of many sizes may give the aureole only. The more numerous the particles involved, the greater is the intensity of the colours, while the radius of the corona is inversely proportional to the size of the particles. Thus a corona whose size is increasing indicates that the water particles are diminishing in size, and vice versa. The corona is distinguished from the halo, which is due to REFRACTION, by the fact that the colour sequence is opposite in the two, the red of the halo being inside, that of the corona outside.

Correction.—The alteration of the reading of an instrument in order to allow for unavoidable errors in measurement. The measurement of nearly all quantities is an indirect process, and generally takes the form of reading the position of a pointer or index on a scale. When we wish to know the *pressure* of the atmosphere we read an index on the scale of a barometer ; when we wish to know the *temperature* of the air we read the position of the end of a thread of mercury in a thermometer ; to determine a *height* we use the pressure, though the scale may be graduated in feet or metres.

Almost all measurements are, in fact, ultimately reduced to reading a position or length on a graduated scale and, generally speaking, the reading depends mainly, it is true, on the quantity which the instrument is intended to measure, but also partly upon other quantities. Thus the readings of barometers are generally affected by temperature as well as pressure, those of thermometers by alterations in the glass containing the mercury or spirit. It is the object of the designer and maker of instruments to get rid of these disturbances of the reading as far as possible, either by the selection of special materials or by introducing some device whereby the disturbing effect is automatically corrected. In that case the error, and often the instrument, is said to be *compensated*.

But in most cases the amount of the error has to be determined and allowed for by a suitable *correction*. An ANEROID BAROMETER is often compensated for temperature, and for a mercury barometer the effect of temperature is made out and tabulated and a correction introduced, which is derived from a table, when the temperature of the "attached thermometer" has been noted. In a similar manner the correction of a barometer reading for the variation of GRAVITY at different parts of the earth's surface is worked by means of tables, the variation of gravity with latitude having been previously reduced to a formula, by means of observations from which the figure of the earth has been determined and the change of gravity has been ascertained.

In some measurements, such as the determination of height by the use of an aneroid barometer, corrections are numerous and complicated : the uncorrected reading may even be only a rough approximation not sufficiently accurate for practical purposes.

Correlation.—Two varying quantities are said to be correlated when their variations from their respective mean values are in some way or other mutually connected with each other.

A kind of measure of this connection is given by the " correlation coefficient." This is a decimal lying between + 1 and − 1, which is easily calculated. Values of + 1 and of − 1 show that the two quantities are directly or inversely proportional; that is to say, for any departure from the normal of the one quantity there is a corresponding departure from the normal of the other, always in the same sense or always in the opposite sense. On the other hand values that are nearly nothing show that there is little if any connexion.

It may be of interest to state that the coefficient of correlation between the phases of the moon and the barometric pressure at Greenwich is insignificant.

Modern statistical methods have been frequently applied to meteorological problems. Mr. W. H. Dines, F.R.S., has used the method of correlation with great success in his work on the upper air. His results are published by the Meteorological Office in Geophysical Memoirs No. 2. As examples of correlation coefficients we may give those found by Mr. Dines between the pressure at a height of 9 kilometres and the mean temperature of the air column from 1 to 9 kilometres. For different sets of observations the values found were ·88, ·96, ·90, ·90, 94. The inference to be drawn from such correlation coefficients is that the variations of temperature of the air column from 1 to 9 kilometres are directly dependent upon the pressure at the top of the air column.

Mr. Dines gives correlation coefficients from work on the upper air in various other papers.

Dr.

~~Sir~~ Gilbert Walker, of the Indian Meteorological Service, has used the method of correlation to predict the amount of the Indian Monsoon Rainfall. He has also investigated the connection between sunspots and temperature, sunspots and rainfall, sunspots and pressure by statistical methods.

From various papers the following examples of correlation coefficients have been selected :—

Correlation Coefficient.	Number of Observations.	Variables Correlated.	Reference.
·49	42 (1867–1908).	Height of Nile flood and South American mean pressure in March, April, May.	G. T. Walker, Correlation in Seasonal Variations of Weather. (Memoirs of the Indian Met. Dept., Vol. XXI., Part II.)
− ·47	30 (1880–1909).	Rainfall at Java, October to March, with rainfall at Trinidad the following six months.	R. C. Mossman, Southern Hemisphere Seasonal Correlations. (Symons Met. Mag., Vol. 48, 1913.)
− ·43	34 (1877–1910).	Annual mean temperature at Cairo and annual mean temperature in England, S.W., and South Wales.	J. I. Craig, a See-Saw of Temperature. (Quar. Journal, Roy. Met. Soc., April 1915.)
− ·62	36 (1875–1910).	Mean pressure for March at Azores and in Iceland.	J. P. Van der Stok.

Correlation Coefficient.	Number of Observations.	Variables Correlated.	Reference.
·78	20 (1891–1910).	March barometric gradient at Zikawei (China) and July–August air temperature at Miyako in N.E. Japan.	T. Okada (Monthly Weather Review, U.S.A., Jan., 1916).
— ·81	47 (1869–1915).	Mean pressure for March at Kew and rainfall total for same month at Kew.	E. H. Chapman, The Relation between Atmospheric Pressure and Rainfall. (Quar. Journal, Roy. Met. Soc., 1916.)
·80	20 (1896–1915).	Sunspot numbers and level of Lake Victoria.	M.O. MS.

Cosecant.—In a right angled triangle the ratio of the hypotenuse to one side is the cosecant of the angle opposite to that side ; the ratio is the reciprocal of the sine. See SINE.

Cosine.—In a right angled triangle the ratio of one side to the hypotenuse is the cosine of the angle between them. See SINE.

Cotangent.—In a right angled triangle the ratio of the two sides that form the right-angle is the cotangent of the angle opposite the side taken as the divisor. See SINE.

Counter sun.—See ANTHELION.

Cumulo-stratus.—The name given to a certain combination of cloud forms which is no longer used in the international classification. See CLOUDS.

Cumulus.—The technical name of the woolpack cloud. See CLOUDS.

Cyclone.—A name given to a region of low barometric pressure ; now usually spoken of as a DEPRESSION or a LOW. See ISOBARS.

Cyclostrophic.—See GRADIENT WIND.

Damp Air.—As distinguished from dry air in meteorology, damp air implies a high degree of RELATIVE HUMIDITY (*q.v.*). When its relative humidity equals or exceeds 85 per cent. of saturation air may fairly be called damp. It will deposit some of its moisture in dry woollen fabrics, cordage or other fibrous material, though its water will not condense upon an exposed surface until 100 per cent. is reached. Even the driest air of the atmosphere contains some water vapour, and its relative dampness or dryness can be changed by altering the temperature. Thus the same air may be very dry at 2 o'clock in the afternoon, and very damp, even cloudy, at 8 o'clock in the evening, simply because its temperature has been lowered. At any time of the year, but especially in summer, the dampness of the air is subject to great changes.

Day Breeze.—See SEA BREEZE or BREEZE.

Débacle.—Breaking up of the ice in the spring in rivers and seas ; it lasts from two to six weeks, and takes place between the end of January and the beginning of

May, varying according to locality. The waters are usually free from ice by the end of April-May. At "débacle" the water in rivers rises to the extent of inundating the country for miles around, sometimes stopping all carriage traffic—ferry-boats taking their place. This condition may last for as long as three weeks.

In Russia there are some 110 stations at which observations of the "débacle" are taken. The event takes place earliest in the Caspian, Black and Azov Seas : it commences at the end of February, and the sea along the coast is free of ice by the end of March—the open sea being clear by the end of February. In the Pacific the phenomenon takes place in April, and the sea is clear by May ; in the Baltic usually in March or the beginning of April, the sea being cleared by the beginning of May, but at Reval and Libau this may occur even by the end of March. At Uleaborg the "débacle" is later, there being ice in the sea till the end of May ; and in the Arctic Sea still later, about the end of April, and the sea is not clear till the beginning of June.

In Canada, in Ontario, the occurrence takes place in March, freeing the waters by April, and the same is true in the case of the Maritime provinces. In the St. Lawrence it is a little later, the river being free of ice in May.

Dekad, in Meteorology, a period of ten days, but *decade* is often used for ten years.

Density.—The density of air is one of the things you have to know when you want to calculate the lifting power of a balloon of given size. As applied to air, density is a difficult word to explain because the numerical value depends partly upon the composition of the air, partly upon its pressure, and again partly upon its temperature. Thus it is often said that moist air or damp air is lighter than dry air, warm air is lighter than cold air, and rarefied air is lighter than compressed air, and all these statements are true provided that in each case we remember to introduce the condition "other things being equal."

By the density of a sample of air is to be understood the weight, or better, the mass of a measured volume, a cubic foot, or a cubic metre ; and moist air is lighter than dry air in this sense that a cubic metre of perfectly dry air weighs 1,206 grammes when its barometric pressure is 1,000 millibars, 29·53 inches, and its temperature is 289a. (60·8° F.), whereas if it were saturated air instead of dry air the cubic metre would weigh 1,197 grammes. But if the barometric pressure rose while the change from dry air to saturation was being effected the density would rise in like proportion ; and if the temperature changed the density would change in reversed proportion to the absolute temperature. The formula for the density of air is, therefore, a complicated one

$$\Delta = \Delta_o \frac{p - 3/8\ e}{p_o} \times \frac{T_o}{T'}$$

where

Δ is the density to be computed,

Δ_o is the density of perfectly dry air at pressure p_o and temperature T_o.

If $p_o = 1,000$ mb., 29·53 in., and $T_o = 290$a. then $\Delta_o = 1,201$ g/m³.

p is the barometric pressure in *mb.* of the sample.

e is the pressure of aqueous vapour in the sample.

The following is a complete example of the determination of the density of a sample of air from a reading of the barometer and wet and dry bulb thermometers.

Barometer corrected for temperature 1,010·1 mb. (29·83 in.).
Dry bulb   285·8a. (55·1° F.).
Wet bulb   281·3a. (47·0° F.).

Vapour pressure from humidity tables = 8·2 mb. (0·239 in.).

$$\Delta_o = 1{,}201 \text{ g/m}^3,$$

$$\Delta = 1{,}201 \times \frac{1{,}010{\cdot}1 - 8{\cdot}2 \times 3/8}{1{,}000} \times \frac{290}{285{\cdot}8} \text{ g/m}^3,$$

$$= 1{,}227 \text{ g/m}^3,$$

or 0·0766 lbs. per cubic foot.

Note.—One grain per cubic foot is equivalent to 2·29 g/m³.

Since the reading of a barometer gives the pressure at the level of the mercury in the barometer cistern it must be understood that the density refers to the sample of air at that level. For the value at any other level a correction for level must be made.

The variation of the density of air with pressure and temperature is of great importance in meteorology. Pressure is of course higher in an anticyclone than in a cyclonic depression, and it has recently been made certain that above one kilometre (3,281 feet) the air in the high pressure is warmer than in the low pressure, so the effect of difference of pressure may nearly counterbalance the effect of temperature, and in consequence the density of a column of air in a cyclone may be very little different from that in an anticyclone.

The influence of moisture upon the density of air is not regarded as having the importance in meteorology which used to be attributed to it when it was held to explain the difference between high and low pressure with the accompanying weather.

The following are the average pressures, temperatures and densities of air at different levels above high pressure and low pressure respectively in the British Isles according to the results obtained with registering balloons by Mr. W. H. Dines, F.R.S.

TABLE OF AVERAGE VALUES OF THE PRESSURE, TEMPERATURE AND DENSITY OF AIR IN A REGION OF HIGH AND OF LOW PRESSURE.

Height.		High Pressure.			Low Pressure.		
		Pressure.	Temp.	Density.	Pressure.	Temp.	Density.
1000-ft.	k.	mb.	a.	g/m³	mb.	a.	g/m³
32·809	10	273	226	421	247	225	382
29·528	9	317	233	474	288	226	444
26·247	8	366	240	531	335	227	514
22·966	7	422	247	595	388	232	583
19·685	6	483	254	662	449	240	652
16·406	5	552	261	736	516	248	724
13·124	4	628	267	818	591	255	807
9·843	3	713	272	911	675	263	893
6·562	2	807	277	1012	767	269	992
3·281	1	913	279	1137	870	275	1100
0	0	1031	282	1270	984	279	1226

The densities quoted above are calculated on the assumption that the relative humidity is 75 per cent.

The following are the densities of a few other substances.

*Hydrogen (dry) ... ... 88·74 g/m³
*Carbonic acid gas (dry)... 1,953 g/m²
Water ... ... 1·000 g/cc (at 277a.)
Sea water... ... ... 1·01 to 1·05 g/cc.
Mercury ... ... 13·596 g/cc (at 273a.)
Petrol ... ... 0·68 to 0·72 g/cc.

See also under BUOYANCY.

Depression.—A region of low barometric pressure surrounded on all sides by higher pressures. See ISOBARS, and Plate XI.

Dew.—The name given to the deposit of drops of water which forms upon grass, leaves, &c., when they become cooled, by radiating heat to the sky on a clear night, to such an extent that their temperature is below the saturation or DEW POINT of the air which surrounds them.

The last part of the process of the formation of dew is in no way different from that which operates when a glass of ice-cooled water covers itself with water drops indoors, or when a deposit of moisture is formed by breathing on a window-pane.

Dew-point.—The temperature of saturation of air, that is to say, the temperature which marks the limit to which air can be cooled without causing condensation, either in the form of cloud if the cooling is taking place in the free air, or on the sides of the vessel if it is enclosed. See AQUEOUS VAPOUR.

Diathermancy.—Diathermanous.—The power of allowing heat in the form of radiation to pass in the same way that light passes through glass. Rock salt is

---

* At a pressure of 1,000 mb. and temperature of 273a.

peculiarly diathermanous, water, on the contrary, and glass are not.

All forms of energy which are "radiated" and in connection with which the word "ray" is used, such as rays of light, heat rays, X-rays, radio-telegraphic rays, travel by wave motion and have some properties in common. One of the most characteristic is that described as transparency and opacity with regard to light. But the same substances are not similarly transparent for all kinds of rays. · X-rays and electric rays make no difficulty about going through walls which stop light; and sound-waves often find a way where light cannot follow. The question of transparency and opacity for different kinds of rays is one of bewildering complexity. The study of DIATHERMANCY deals with that part of the subject which is concerned with the transmission of heat in the form of wave motion.

Diffraction.—The process by which rays of different colour are separated one from another when a beam of light passes an obstacle of any shape. In reality the shape of the obstacle must be carefully chosen in relation to the shape of the beam to make the phenomenon easily apparent. Perhaps the simplest experiment is to draw a greasy finger across a plate of glass and to look through the glass at the bright line of an incandescent electric lamp, taking care that the plate is turned so that the lines left by the finger on the glass are parallel to the bright line. Those who are unfamiliar with the experiment will be surprised at the brilliancy of the colours which are produced by the simple process. In more scientific form when the lines are ruled regularly on the glass by a suitable dividing engine we get a diffraction-grating, one of the most delicate of all optical instruments.

For scientific experiments in diffraction either a bright line of light formed by a slit in front of a lamp with a linear obstacle, or a bright point of light with a circular obstacle may be used, and many remarkable results can be shown with these simple means. For example, when the distances are properly adjusted a bright spot will be found at the central point of the shadow of a circular disc, thrown by a bright point of light, and again on looking past a needle at a line of light parallel to the needle a great play of colours will be seen.

The phenomena of diffraction are explained by the hypothesis that the actual transmission of light is not a direct projection of the light along straight lines from any luminous point, but the spreading out of waves with a spherical wave-front central at the luminous point. They are exhibited in the atmosphere principally by the formation of CORONAE round the sun and moon, and sometimes also by the IRIDESCENCE of CLOUDS.

Diffusion.—The slow molecular process by which supernatant fluids mix in spite of the differences in their density. The molecular forces or motions which come into play in diffusion are perhaps most effectively illustrated by the tenacity with which the mixture maintains its composition when once the mixing has taken place. For example, whisky is lighter than water and a separate layer of the spirit can be floated on the top of water by judicious manipulation. The spirit and water will then slowly mix by diffusion, even if there be no stirring, due to thermal convection or mechanical operation. But when the spirit and water have become mixed no amount of allowing to stand will cause the water to settle to the bottom and leave the whisky in a separate layer at the top. Once mixed they are mixed for ever, owing to the power of diffusion.

The process of diffusion follows certain definite rules, which are similar in type to those for the diffusion of heat by thermal conduction, and the diffusion of velocity through a viscous mass, but it takes so long a time for any appreciable effect to be produced, that in practice diffusion only completes the process of mixing which has been begun by stirring or convection. Major G. I. Taylor has recently shown that in the atmosphere mixing by turbulent motion (see EDDY) follows a similar law, but with a different characteristic constant that brings diffusion by turbulent motion among the operative forces in Meteorology.

Diurnal.—The word, which means " recurring day by day," is used to indicate the changes in the meteorological elements which take place within the twenty-four hours of the day. Thus, by the diurnal change of pressure is meant a slight rise of the barometric pressure between about 4 a.m. and 10 a.m., and between 16 h. (4 p.m.) and 22 h. (10 p.m.) with corresponding falls between. In this change it is the "semidiurnal" variation which is the most striking because it occurs (with different intensity) all round a whole meridian simultaneously, and sweeps round the globe from meridian to meridian about three and a half hours in front of the sun.

Other elements also show noteworthy diurnal variations. We give here diagrams showing the diurnal variation of pressure, temperature, humidity and wind velocity at Kew for January and July as representing winter and summer respectively.

DIURNAL VARIATION IN SUMMER.

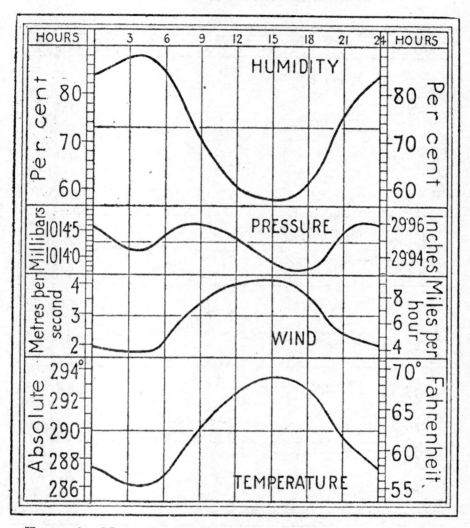

From the Normals for July.

Averages of not less than twenty-five years of Hourly Readings at Kew Observatory. For the Diurnal Variation of wind-speed through the different months at the summit of the Eiffel Tower, Paris, see p. 287.

DIURNAL VARIATION IN WINTER.

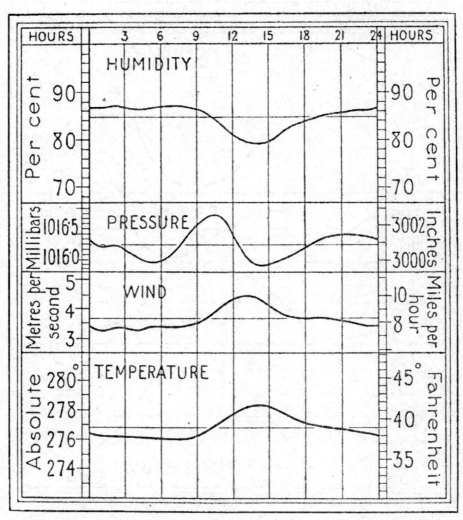

From the Normals for January.

Averages of not less than twenty-five years of Hourly Readings at Kew Observatory.

Doldrums.—The equatorial belt of calms and light variable airs, accompanied by heavy rains, thunderstorms and squalls. The belt follows the sun in his movement North and South, but its movement is not so great as that of the sun, and lags behind it by one to two months.

Drought.—Dryness due to lack of rain. According to the classification of the British Rainfall Organization an *absolute drought* is a period of more than 14 consecutive days without one-hundredth of an inch of rain on any one day, and a *partial drought* is a period of more than 28 consecutive days the mean rainfall of which does not exceed ·01 inch per day, or the total fall for the 28 days at most barely exceeds a quarter of an inch.

Dry Air.—The words are used in two senses. In a book on physics or chemistry dry air means air that carries no water-vapour at all, but in ordinary practice it is used for the atmosphere when it contains a smaller proportion of water-vapour than usual. Water evaporates from wet surfaces exposed to the air unless the atmosphere is completely saturated. If we call air containing 85 per cent. or more of the possible amount of water-vapour damp, we may call air with less than 60 per cent. dry, and understand thereby that EVAPORATION is rapid and roads, grass, &c., dry quickly.

The letter " y " has recently been added to the Beaufort Notation (see *Weather Map*, p. 10) to signify air with less than 60 per cent. of the possible amount of water-vapour. The following table shows for different dry-bulb temperatures the smallest depression of the wet-bulb which would justify the use of the letter " y " in reporting the " present weather."

Dry Bulb.	*Depression of Wet-bulb.*
a	a
271 or below	1
273 (F.P.) or 1a above or below	2
275—281	3
282—292	4
293—305	5
above 305	$5\frac{1}{2}$

It is found from the hourly readings of the Meteorological Office Observatories that out of a thousand hours Aberdeen has 37 hours of " dry air " thus defined, Valencia 6, Falmouth 19 and Kew 90. Had the limit been set at 50 per cent. instead of 60, the figures would have been only 4, 1, 1 and 19 respectively (see p. 224).

Dry bulb.—A curious name given to an ordinary thermometer used to determine the temperature of the air, in order to distinguish it from the wet bulb. No special precautions are taken to keep a " dry bulb " dry beyond protecting it from falling rain in a screen. But it is true enough that if the dry bulb gets a film of water upon it by condensation it will not be in a proper condition to record the temperature of the air until it has got quite dry again.

Dynamics.—The study of the motion of bodies in relation to the forces which control the motion. The fundamental principle of dynamics is that if a moving body is *let alone* it will go on moving. It is a vulgar error to suppose that it will stop.

Dynamic Cooling.—The fall of temperature which occurs automatically throughout a mass of air when it expands on the release of pressure. (See ADIABATIC.) Examples of the expansion under reduced pressure and consequent cooling are to be found in the flow of air up a mountain slope with the formation of cloud at the top.

Earth - Thermometer.—A mercury - thermometer suspended in a tube sunk into the earth, or an electrical resistance thermometer buried in a trench—usually at depths of one foot and four feet—for measuring the temperature of the ground. See *Observer's Handbook.*

Eddy.—"The water that by some interruption in its course runs contrary to the direction of the tide or current. (Adm. Smyth); a circular motion in water, a small whirlpool,"—according to the New English Dictionary.

Eddies are formed in water whenever the water flows rapidly past an obstacle. Numbers of them can be seen as little whirling dimples or depressions on the surface close to the side of a ship which is moving through the water. In the atmosphere similar eddies on a larger scale are shown by the little whirls of dust and leaves sometimes formed at street corners and other places which present suitable obstacles. The peculiarity of these wind eddies is that they seem to last for a little while with an independent existence of their own. They sometimes attain considerable dimensions and, in fact, they seem to pass by insensible degrees from the corner eddy to the whirlwind, the dust-storm, the waterspout, the tornado, the hurricane, and finally the cyclonic.depression. It is not easy to draw the line and say where the mechanical effect of an obstacle has been lost, and the creation of a set of parallel circular isobars has begun, but it serves no useful purpose to class as identical phenomena the street corner eddy twenty feet high and six feet wide and the cyclonic depression a thousand miles across and three or four miles high.

The special characteristic of every eddy is that it must have an axis to which the circular motion can be referred. The axis need not be straight nor need it be fixed in shape or position. The best example of an eddy is the vortex-ring or smoke ring which can be produced by suddenly projecting a puff of air, laden with smoke to make the motion visible, through a circular opening. In that case the axis of the eddy is ring shaped; the circular motion is through the ring in the direction in which it is travelling and back again round the outside. The ring-eddy is very durable, but the condition of its durability is that the axis should form a ring. If the continuity of the ring is broken by some obstacle the eddy rapidly disappears in irregular motion.

It is on that account that the eddy motion of the atmosphere is so difficult to deal with. When air flows past an obstacle a succession of incomplete eddies are periodically formed, detached, disintegrated and reformed. There is a pulsating formation of ill-defined eddies. The same kind of thing must occur when the wind blows on the face of a cliff, forming a cliff-eddy with an axis, roughly speaking, along the line of the cliff and the circular motion in a vertical plane.

Whenever wind passes over the ground, even smooth ground, the air near the ground is full of partially formed, rapidly disintegrating eddies, and the motion is known as turbulent, to distinguish it from what is known as stream-line motion, in which there is no circular motion. The existence of these eddies is doubtless shown on an anemogram as gusts, but the axes of these eddies are so irregular that they have hitherto evaded classification. Irregular eddy motion is of great importance in meteorology, because it represents the process by which the slow mixing of layers of air takes place, which is an essential part in the production of thick layers of fog. Moreover, all movements due to convection must give rise to current and return current which at least simulates eddy motion.

Electrometer.—An instrument for measuring electromotive force, or potential difference. An ordinary battery has an electromotive force of at least a volt and shows a corresponding potential-difference on an electrometer when the poles of the battery are connected to the electrodes (connecting clamps) of the electrometer. A fully charged secondary battery shows a potential-difference of about two volts. In the atmosphere near the ground there is, on the average at most stations, a potential-difference exceeding 100 volts for a difference of level of one metre, due to the electrification of the air. It can be measured by an electrometer using a burning match or a water-dropper or a radio active substance as "collector." The potential-difference in the atmosphere measured in this way is very variable, especially during rain.

The potential-difference necessary to cause a spark between two metal balls through one centimetre of air at ordinary pressure is about 30,000 volts, which suggests that the potential-differences necessary to produce a discharge of lightning are enormous.

Energy.—Used frequently in meteorology in the general sense of vigour or activity. Thus, a cyclone is said to develop greater energy when its character, as exhibited by a low barometer, steep gradients and strong winds, becomes more pronounced. But there is a technical dynamical sense of the word, the use of which is sometimes required in meteorology, and which must become more general when the physical explanation of the phenomena of weather is studied, because all the phenomena of weather are examples of the " transformations of energy " in the physical sense.

The most important conception with regard to energy is its division into two kinds, kinetic energy and potential energy, which are mutually convertible. A clock-weight gives a good idea of potential energy. When the clock is wound up the weight has potential energy in virtue of its position; it will utilise that energy in driving the clock until it is "run down" and can go no further. Potential energy must be restored to it by winding up before it can do any more driving. The potential energy in this case is measured by the amount of the weight and the vertical distance through which it is wound up. In dynamical measure the potential energy of the raised weight is *mgh*, where *m* is the mass of the clock-weight, *h* the vertical distance through which it is wound up, *g* the acceleration of gravity. It is to the mysterious action of gravity that the energy is due :—hence the necessity for taking gravity into account in measuring the energy.

Using the simple product *mgh* as a measure of the potential energy of gravitation, by a simple formula for bodies falling freely under the action of gravity, we have

$$mgh = \tfrac{1}{2}mv^2$$

where *v* is the velocity acquired by a body falling through a height *h*, or, speaking in terms of energy, by losing the potential energy of the height *h*. It thus obtains a certain amount of motion which represents kinetic energy, in exchange for its potential energy. The kinetic energy is expressed by the apparently artificial formula $\tfrac{1}{2}mv^2$. In virtue of its motion it has the power of doing "work": if it were not for unavoidable friction the mass could get itself up-hill again through the height *h* by the use of its motion, and thus sacrifice its kinetic energy in favour of an equivalent amount of potential energy.

The exchange of potential and kinetic energy can be seen going on in a high degree of perfection in a swinging pendulum. At the top of the swing the energy is all potential, at the bottom all kinetic. The swings get gradually smaller because in every swing a little of the energy is wasted in bending the cord or in overcoming the resistance of the air.

What we get in return for the loss of energy in friction is a little HEAT, and one of the great conclusions of physical science in the middle of the nineteenth century was to show that heat is also a form of energy but a very special form, that is to say, its transformation is subject to peculiar laws. Heat is often measured by rise of temperature of water (or its equivalent in some other substance). Calling this form of energy thermal energy and measuring it by the product of the " water equivalent," M, and the rise of temperature $A-A_0$ produced therein, we have three forms of energy all convertible under certain laws, viz. :—

Potential energy	...	mgh
Kinetic energy ...	...	$\frac{1}{2}mv^2$
Thermal energy...	...	$M(A-A_0)$

We have mentioned only a lifted clock-weight as an example of potential energy, but there are many others, a coiled spring that will fly back when it is let go, compressed gas in a cylinder that will drive an engine when it is turned on, every combination, in fact, that is dormant until it is set agoing and then becomes active.

From the dynamical point of view, the study of nature is simply the study of transformations of energy.

In meteorology kinetic energy is represented by the winds ; potential energy by the distribution of pressure at any level, by the electrical potential of the air and by the varying distribution of density in the atmosphere, causing convection ; thermal energy by the changes of temperature due to the effect of the sun or other causes. It is the study of the interchange of these forms of energy which constitutes the science of dynamical meteorology.

Entropy.—A term introduced by R. Clausius to be used with temperature to identify the thermal condition of a substance with regard to a transformation of its heat into some other form of energy. It involves one of the most difficult conceptions in the theory of heat, about which some confusion has arisen.

The transformation of heat into other forms of energy, in other words, the use of heat to do work, is necessarily connected with the expansion of the working substance under its own pressure, as in the cylinder of a gas engine, and the condition of a given quantity of the substance at any stage of its operations is completely specified by its volume and its pressure. Generally speaking (for example, in the atmosphere) changes of volume and pressure go on simultaneously, but for simplifying ideas and leading on to calculation it is useful to suppose the stages to be kept separate, so that when the substance is expanding the pressure is maintained constant by supplying, in fact, the necessary quantity of heat to keep it so, and, on the other hand, when the pressure is being varied the volume is kept constant; this again by the addition or subtraction of a suitable quantity of heat. While the change of pressure is in progress, and generally, also, while the change of volume is going on, the temperature is changing, and heat is passing into or out of the substance. The question arises whether the condition of the substance cannot be specified by the amount of heat that it has in store and the temperature that has been acquired just as completely as by the pressure and volume.

To realise that idea it is necessary to regard the processes of supplying or removing heat and changing the temperature as separate and independent, and it is this step that makes the conception useful and at the same time difficult. .

For we are accustomed to associate the warming of a substance, *i.e.*, the raising of its temperature, with supplying it with heat. If we wish to warm anything we put it near a fire and let it get warmer by taking in heat, but in thermodynamics we separate the change of temperature from the supply of heat altogether by supposing the substance is "working." Thus, when heat is supplied the temperature must not rise; the substance must do a suitable amount of work instead; and if heat is to be removed the temperature must be kept up by working upon the substance. The temperature can thus be kept constant while heat is supplied or removed. And, on the other hand, if the temperature is to be changed it must be changed dynamically not thermally, that is to say, by work done or received, not by heat communicated or removed.

So we get two aspects of the process of the transformation of heat into another form of energy by working, first, alterations of pressure and volume, each independently, the adjustments being made by adding or removing heat as may be required, and secondly, alterations of heat and temperature independently, the adjustments being made by work done or received. Both represent the process of using heat to perform mechanical work or *vice versâ*.

In the mechanical aspect of the process, when we are considering an alteration of volume at constant pressure, $p(v-v_{0})$ is the work done, and in the thermal aspect of the process $H-H_{0}$ is the amount of heat disposed of. There is equality between the two.

But if we consider more closely what happens in this

case we shall see that quantities of heat ought also to be regarded as a product, so that $H - H_o$ should be expressed as $T(\phi - \phi_o)$ where T is the absolute temperature and ϕ the entropy.

The reason for this will be clear if we consider what happens if a substance works under adiabatic conditions, as we may suppose an isolated mass of air to do if it rises automatically in the atmosphere into regions of lower pressure, or conversely if it sinks. In that case it neither loses nor gains any heat by simple transference across its boundary ; but as it is working it is drawing upon its store of heat, and its temperature falls. If the process is arrested at any stage, part of the store of heat will have been lost through working, so in spite of the adiabatic isolation part of the heat has gone all the same. From the general thermodynamic properties of all substances, it is shown that it is not H, the store of heat, that remains the same in adiabatic changes, but H/T, the ratio of the store of heat to the temperature at which it entered. We call this ratio the *entropy*, and an adiabatic line which conditions thermal isolation and therefore equality of entropy is called an isentropic. If a new quantity of heat h is added at a temperature T the entropy is increased by h/T. If it is taken away again at a lower temperature T' the entropy is reduced by h/T'.

In the technical language of thermodynamics the mechanical work for an elementary cycle of changes is $\delta p. \delta v$, and the element of heat $\delta T. \delta \phi$. The conversion of heat into some other form of energy by working is expressed by the equation

$$\delta T. \delta \phi = \delta p. \delta v$$

when heat is measured in dynamical units.

D

It is useful in meteorology to consider these aspects of the science of heat although they may seem to be far away from ordinary experience because, from certain aspects, the problem of dynamical meteorology seems to be more closely associated with these strange ideas than those which we regard as common. For example, it may seem natural to suppose that if we could succeed in completely churning the atmosphere up to, say, 10 kilometres (6 miles) we should have got it uniform in temperature or isothermal throughout. That seems reasonable, because if we want to get a bath of liquid uniform in temperature throughout we stir it up; but it is not true. In the case of the atmosphere there is the difference in pressure to deal with, and, in consequence of that, complete mixing up would result, not in equality, but in a difference of temperature of about 100° C. between top and bottom, supposing the whole atmosphere dry. The resulting state would not, in fact, be isothermal; the temperature at any point would depend upon its level and there would be a temperature difference of 1° C. for every hundred metres. But it would be perfectly isentropic. The entropy would be the same everywhere throughout the whole mass. And its state would be very peculiar, for if you increased the entropy of any part of it by warming it slightly the warmed portion would go right to the top of the isentropic mass. It would find itself a little warmer, and therefore a little lighter specifically than its environment, all the way up. In this respect we may contrast the properties of an isentropic and an isothermal atmosphere. In an isentropic atmosphere each unit mass has the same entropy at all levels, but the temperatures are lower in the upper levels. In an isothermal atmosphere the temperature is the samè at all levels, but the entropy is greater at the higher levels.

An isothermal atmosphere represents great stability as regards vertical movements, any portion which is carried upward mechanically becomes colder than its surroundings and must sink again to its own place, but an ISENTROPIC atmosphere is in the curious state of neutral equilibrium which is called " labile." So long as it is not warmed or cooled it is immaterial to a particular specimen where it finds itself, but if it is warmed, ever so little, it must go to the top, or cooled, ever so little, to the bottom.

In the actual atmosphere above the level of ten kilometres (more or less) the state is isothermal ; below that level, in consequence of convection, it tends towards the isentropic state, but stops short of reaching it by a variable amount in different levels. The condition is completely defined at any level by the statement of its entropy and its temperature, together with its composition which depends on the amount of water-vapour contained in it.

Speaking in general terms the entropy increases, but only slightly, as we go upward from the surface through the TROPOSPHERE until the STRATOSPHERE is reached, and from the boundary upwards the entropy increases rapidly.

If the atmosphere were free from the complications arising from the condensation of water-vapour the definition of the state of a sample of air at any time by its temperature and entropy would be comparatively simple. High entropy and high level go together ; stability depends upon the air with the largest stock of entropy having found its level. In so far as the atmosphere approaches the isentropic state, results due to convection may be expected, but in so far as it approaches the isothermal state, and stability supervenes, convection becomes unlikely.

Equation of Time.—The interval between two successive transits of the sun over the meridian is the true solar day, and the time based on this length is called apparent time. The length of the true solar day varies at different times of the year, and to avoid the inconvenience of want of uniformity in the length of the day, an imaginary body called the mean sun may be supposed to revolve uniformly round the Earth and complete each revolution in a time equal to the average length of the true solar day ; the time referred to this standard is called mean time. To convert mean time into apparent time, and vice versa, the correction known as the equation of time must be applied. The equation of time varies at different times of the year ; its value may be obtained from the Nautical, or other Almanac. See also *Observer's Handbook.*

Equator.—" The line " of sailors. An imaginary line on the earth's surface separating the northern hemisphere from the southern hemisphere. The use of the word " hemisphere " suggests that the earth is regarded as a sphere, and on a spherical globe representing the earth the equator is the line formed by the intersection with the surface of a plane drawn at right angles to the polar axis and bisecting it.

The position of the equator is identified by the vertical or plumb line being at right angles to the polar axis, and any complications introduced by the irregularity of the figure of the earth have to work from that datum. Latitude is measured from the equator northward through 90° to the North pole, southward through 90° to the South pole.

By geodesic calculation it has been found that the

diameter of the globe from a point of the equator to its
antipodes is 12,756,776 metres, whereas the polar axis
is 12,713,818 metres.*

Equatorial.—Originally only an adjective derived
from equator; thus, the equatorial regions are the regions
in the neighbourhood of " the line," but a meteorologist
thinks of them as regions of rather low atmospheric
pressure lying between the two belts of high pressure
which are found in either hemisphere just north or south
of the tropics. In this region the rotation of the earth
has little or no influence in adjusting the wind to balance
the distribution of pressure. The adjustment necessary
for persistence can only be reached by the curvature of
the air's path. It is perhaps for that reason that the
regions about ten degrees north and south of the Equator
are the regions in which tropical revolving storms originate.

The adjective has also come to be used with regard
to wind to mean a wind that is composed of air which
has come from lower latitudes, whatever may be its
direction at the time, as distinguished from a polar wind
which is composed of air that has travelled from higher
latitudes. Typical equatorial winds are generally from
South-West or between South and West, and Polar winds
from North-East or between North and East. It is a
question of considerable meteorological interest to consider in special cases whether a South-East wind or a
North-West wind is actually equatorial or polar. Equatorial winds are generally warm, polar winds cold, but
north-easterly winds are sometimes very warm and sometimes very cold ; a north-wester almost always cold.

---

* U.S. Coast and Geodetic Survey.

Equilibrium.—Properly speaking, the balancing of two or more forces in such a way that the combined effect is the same as if there were no forces acting at all, so that the body upon which they act, if at rest, remains at rest and if in motion, it goes on moving without any alteration of its velocity. In the case of a hammock slung by a cord at each end, the forces acting along the cords and the weight balance each other and the hammock with its load is supported at rest. It is, therefore, not unusual to say that the load is in equilibrium, but it is an unfortunate use of the word because the state of rest is only a special case. In meteorology we are very frequently concerned with equilibrium of forces associated not with rest but with the uniform motion of the body upon which they act. For example, raindrops are all impelled downwards by their weight, and their motion is resisted by the air through which they move, and after a very brief interval from the start the resistance of the air balances the weight and the drops fall with a uniform* speed (which depends upon their size) as if there were no longer any gravity or any air. The same is equally true of a falling bomb, but the time required to reach the limiting velocity is much greater. From the moment of its release it acquires velocity from its weight, but if the height is sufficiently great it reaches a limiting velocity when the weight is balanced by the friction of the air and no further increase of velocity occurs.

So, on the other hand, a pilot balloon rises with a uniform velocity as soon as the balloon is moving upwards fast enough for the buoyancy of the balloon, the weight

---

* Mr. W. H. Dines points out that the speed is not strictly uniform but diminishes with the increasing density of the air in the lower layers.

of the balloon and the friction of the air to get into equilibrium.

So, also, in the case of a train running with uniform speed along a level ; the rails push the train forward, the resistance of the air holds it back ; there is equilibrium which we recognise by the fact that the speed is uniform.

There are some other cases in which the word equilibrium is used that are more difficult. It is sometimes said, for example, that there is equilibrium between the wind velocity and the barometric gradient, but it is a peculiar kind of equilibrium : the wind is kept moving without change of speed in a great circle of the earth but not in a straight line through space. The balance of forces in this case is the same as that which obtains when we consider the motion of the moon round the earth, the force of gravitation on the moon is " balanced " by the moon's motion, a convenient form of expression but one which requires some explanation before its meaning is quite clear.

Equinox.—The time of the year when the astronomical day and night are equal, each lasting twelve hours. At the equinox the sun is " on the Equator " or is " crossing the line." It is on the horizon in the morning exactly in the east, and exactly in the west in the evening all over the world. Sunrise occurs at the same time all along a meridian. The sun is visible by refraction for a little longer than the duration of the astronomical day.

There are two equinoxes. The spring or vernal equinox about the 21st March, and the autumnal equinox about the 22nd September. The currently accepted phrase " equinoctial gales " indicates that the equinoxes are regarded in some quarters as the times of the year when gales are specially frequent ; but on our coasts the equinoxes mark the beginning and the end of the season of gales rather than its culmination. Winter is really the season for gales.

Erg.—See under HEAT.

Error.—In all the sciences dependent upon observation of the size of things the word error has a numerical sense which must not be confused with the ordinary trivial sense of a mistake or fault. Errors in the latter sense have to be avoided by skill and care, so they never occur, or hardly ever ; but when everything possible in that respect has been done there are always *errors* in the technical sense, due to imperfections of the instrument, or its adjustment, or to difficulty arising from changes in the element while it is being measured. In this sense *error* is difference between the reading of the assumed measure and the true measure of the element. The size of the residual error is a good indication of the degree of nicety to which the measurement can be carried. Pressure is the only meteorological element which is read to a very high degree of accuracy, such as one hundredth per cent. ; the temperature of the air can be *read* to the tenth of a degree, or within less than one per cent., reckoning on the absolute scale, as one must do for all calculations of density, but the temperature of the air is not " known " to that degree of accuracy, because it is subject to local and temporary fluctuations. An accuracy within one per cent. or even five per cent. is often acceptable.

What is aimed at is to improve the instruments and the methods of reading, so that there is no systematic error. that is to say, no error that is known always to be present and to affect the measurement in the same way.

When that stage has been reached, and we have no good reason for thinking that the figure given by the reading is in any way biassed, we have what is called the residual error which has been made the subject of prolonged study, and has led to the application of the laws of mathematical probability. These have a real practical application in all cases where we deal with very large numbers of observations.

In that case the frequency of occurrence of errors of given magnitude follows a well-known law called the law of error, from which we are able to compute what is called the " probable error " of an observation, a term which frequently occurs. It only means that in any particular case the actual error is no more likely to be greater than the "probable error" than it is to be less, so that the chances of the error being as great as the probable errors are one in two.

The chances of an error being twice the probable error on either side of the true value are 10 in 57, for three times 10 in 238, while for four times the probable error the chances are 1 in 147 and for five times 1 in 1,388. If the chances of an error on one side only are required the second of each pair of figures given above must be doubled.

The study of laws of error is of great practical importance in all actuarial questions, and now forms part of the science of statistics. There are various forms of numerical error that call for notice. In dealing with accurate timing, for example, by means of a clock or chronometer, there is the *index* error, or clock error, and the *rate* error, the amount by which the clock is gaining or losing. Every instrument is liable to index error, on account of the index being inaccurately set, and every instrument is also liable to a scale error, on account of the scale being imperfectly graduated. Before trusting implicitly to the readings of any instrument it is desirable that the user of it should become acquainted with its ways and habits in respect of error. This is particularly the case with instruments used by aviators, namely, altimeters, anemometers, aneroids, compasses, and so on.

Evaporation.—The process of conversion of water from the liquid to the gaseous form at the free surface of water in the presence of air, or from the solid to the gaseous form from the surface of ice. It expresses itself by the gradual disappearance of drops of dew after sunrise, the drying of roofs and roads after rain, the loss of water from cisterns and reservoirs in drought. There is also copious evaporation from the stomata of the leaves of plants.

The atmosphere is very rarely completely saturated, so that evaporation is always going on when water surfaces are freely exposed. The rate of evaporation depends upon a number of conditions. One of the chief is the "drying power" of the air and is represented by the difference between the amount of water-vapour which would saturate it and the amount which it holds at the time : that again depends on the relative humidity and the temperature. The drying power of air below the freezing point is very small but, in spite of that, the disappearance of snow by evaporation is surprisingly rapid.

The other important condition is the nature of the surface of the water from which the evaporation takes place. There are all stages of cleanliness of the surface from the chemically pure water surface which is very seldom realised in practice, to the complete superficial film of oil which arrests evaporation altogether. Besides

Evaporation from the Surface of Water.

	30 years Average, London, Camden Square.		1914. Great Britain, mean of 14 stations.		South Africa, Bulawayo, 20° 2' S., 28° 58' E.		Egypt, Wadi Halfa, 21° 55' N., 31° 20' E.		Australia, Cue, W.A., 27° 27' S., 117° 52' E.		Tasmania, Hobart, 42° 53' S., 147° 20' E.	
	in.	mm.	in.	mm.	in.	mm.	in.	mm.	in.	mm.	in.	mm.
January ...	·11	2·8	·10	2·5	8·94	227	11·10	282	21·46	545	5·87	149
February ...	·26	6·6	·45	11·4	7·40	188	12·64	321	17·13	435	4·21	107
March ...	·66	16·8	·78	19·8	8·74	222	17·96	456	16·78	426	3·03	77
April ...	1·55	39·4	2·13	54·1	8·90	226	21·85	555	11·22	285	1·97	50
May ...	2·38	60·5	2·54	64·5	9·02	229	25·52	648	7·48	190	1·22	31
June ...	2·90	73·7	3·23	82·0	7·99	203	25·28	642	4·84	123	0·67	17
July ...	3·07	78·0	3·07	78·0	8·07	205	23·82	605	5·35	136	0·83	21
August ...	2·36	59·9	2·38	60·5	12·84	326	22·84	580	6·26	159	1·30	33
September ...	1·37	34·8	2·03	51·6	14·73	374	22·92	582	9·13	232	1·77	45
October ...	·62	15·8	·87	22·1	14·96	380	20·08	510	13·39	340	3·07	78
November ...	·24	6·1	·41	10·4	10·79	274	15·12	384	18·00	457	4·02	102
December ...	·10	2·5	·26	6·6	9·84	250	10·75	273	22·37	568	4·88	124
Year ...	15·62	396·9	18·25	463·5	122·22	3104	229·88	5838	153·41	3896	32·84	834

these conditions, temperature and wind have to be considered, so that the measure of evaporation is the end of a very intricate story. Still, in dry countries like Egypt, South Africa and Australia it is a matter of serious economic importance. , It is generally given on the analogy of rainfall as the depth of water evaporated.

Some results are given on page 107.

The differences shown in this table illustrate quite forcibly the influence which evaporation may exercise upon climate, but the figures must not be taken as strictly comparable as the actual amount of evaporation depends upon so many conditions. The measurements given for Egypt are taken from a Wild's gauge which holds only a small body of water and gives a high figure for evaporation.

See Keeling : Evaporation in Egypt and the Sudan (1909).
Craig : Cairo Scientific Journal, May (1912).

Expansion.—The increase in the size of a sample of material, which may be due to heat or to the release of mechanical strain, or the absorption of moisture or some other physical or chemical change.

The size may be taken as the length or volume, sometimes as the area. In the science of heat the fractional increase of length or volume for one degree of temperature is called the coefficient of thermal expansion. Thus, the co-efficient of " linear " expansion with heat of the brass used for barometer scales is 0.0000102 per degree Fahrenheit, which means that for $1°F$. the length of the scale increases by 102 ten-millionth parts of its length at the standard temperature ($62°$ F.). The co-efficient of " cubical " expansion of mercury is $.0001010$, which means that the volume of a quantity of mercury increases by 1.01 ten-thousandth of its bulk at the standard temperature ($32°$ F.) for $1°$ F. The corresponding expansions and coefficients for 1° C. or 1a. are larger in the ratio of 18 to 10.

Expansion of volume alters the density of a substance, and changes of density are therefore numerically related to expansion.

The expansion of a gas may be caused either by reduction of pressure or by increase of temperature. So in order to see the effect of temperature alone we must keep the pressure constant. In these circumstances the coefficient of expansion is ·00366 for 1a. referred to 273a. as standard, or ·002 for 1° F. referred to 41° F. as standard.

Exposure.—In meteorology, the method of presentation of an instrument .to that element which it is destined to measure or record, or the situation of the station with regard to the phenomenon or phenomena there to be observed. If meteorological observations are to be of much value attention must be paid to the manner of the exposure of the instruments.

Details are to be found in the *Observer's Handbook.* Uniformity of exposure is of the greatest importance and for that reason the pattern of the thermometer-screen has been standardized in most countries, while in these Islands, a standard height above ground for the rain-gauge has likewise been fixed. A SUNSHINE RECORDER demands an entirely unobstructed horizon near sunrise and sunset at all times of the year. The question of the exposure of ANEMOMETERS is one of great difficulty. The extent of the GUSTINESS of the wind as exhibited on the trace of the tube-anemometer is a fair index of the excellence of the exposure.

At Aberdeen Observatory, two anemometers are exposed, one at an elevation of 30 feet above the other.

The results are noticeably different; and the same statement applies in an even more marked degree to the two anemometers at Falmouth, one exposed upon the Observatory roof and one upon the tower of Pendennis Castle.

Extremes.—Generally used with reference to temperature or wind; in the first case to mean the highest and lowest temperatures recorded at an observing station in a day, a month or a year. The maximum and minimum temperatures are the extremes for the day; in 1914 the extremes for Greenwich for January were 55° F. and 20° F., and for July 92° F. and 45° F. When the observations for a series of years are available we may find the normal or average extremes and ABSOLUTE EXTREMES.

With regard to wind the highest wind recorded in a gust shown on a tube-anemogram is the extreme wind, and the highest wind-force on the Beaufort Scale noted by an observer in the course of a gale is logged as the extreme for that gale. The strongest gust for the British Isles is given on p. 142, the highest hourly wind velocity is 34·9 m/s (78 mi/hr) recorded at Fleetwood in 1894.

Fahrenheit, Gabriel Daniel.—The improver of the thermometer and barometer, born 1686 at Dantzig. He used mercury instead of spirit of wine for thermometers and avoided negative temperatures by marking the freezing point of water 32°; the boiling point of water was subsequently marked 212°.

The Fahrenheit scale is still in common use in English-speaking countries, and it has advantages because the size of the degree is convenient and temperatures below 0° F. are of rare occurrence at the Earth's surface, except in the polar (Arctic and Antarctic) regions and the continental countries bordering thereupon. In fact, the range

0° F. to 100° F. is a very serviceable range for the climates of the temperate zone. But the investigation of the upper air has necessitated the frequent use of temperatures on the negative side of the Fahrenheit zero, temperatures as much as 100° below zero occur, and to have the zero in the middle of the working scale is very inconvenient. In the physical laboratory too, temperatures approaching 500°F. below the freezing point are realised in experiments on the condensation of hydrogen and helium.

Probably the best scale for all purposes would be in Fahrenheit degrees measured from 459° below the Fahrenheit zero which is computed to be within half a degree of the zero of absolute temperature. In that case 500° would correspond with 41° F. or 5° C. But the growing prevalence of the Centigrade or Celsius scale in countries which do not speak English has led to the use of temperatures measured in the centesimal degrees from the zero of absolute temperature computed as 273° below the freezing point of water.

For a table of conversion of the various scales in use see page 355.

Fall.—"The fall of the leaf" in common use with American writers for Autumn.

Fluid.—A substance which flows, to be distinguished from a solid which will not flow. Some fluids are very viscous, like pitch or treacle, and take a long time to flow, others are mobile, like water or petrol, and take very little time to flow until the surface becomes level. Gases are included in the general term fluid, because they also will flow through a pipe. Their peculiarity is that they can be not only compressed by pressure but also expanded indefinitely on the release of pressure. The density, *i.e.*, the amount that can be got into a limited space, is, in fact, almost exactly proportional to the pressure.

So when we find a large mass of gaseous fluid like the atmosphere lying upon the earth's surface, it is dense in the surface layer which has to carry the weight of all there is above it; and as the pressure gets less and less, upward, the density gets less and less until space is reached. We do not know what happens where the atmosphere merges into space, but we are sure that the earth, with the aid of gravity, carries its atmosphere along without losing any appreciable amount into the void.

Fog.—Obscurity of the atmosphere which impedes navigation or locomotion. It may be due to a cloud of water particles at the surface, as sea-fogs and valley-fogs generally are, but an effective fog can be produced by clouds of dust; that is often the case off the West coast of Africa during the season of the HARMATTAN. In towns true water-fogs are generally rendered more opaque by loading with smoke, and in some cases in towns obscurity of the atmosphere that hardly amounts to fog may be due to the condensation produced by the gaseous products of combustion under the action of sunlight.

Sea-fog is apparently due most frequently to the passage of air over sea water colder than itself; there is first the cooling of the air by the contact with the cold water, and then the mixing up of the air near the surface by the eddy motion resulting in the cooling of a considerable thickness below the dewpoint. (See G. I. Taylor, *Scientific Results of the Voyage of the "Scotia,"* 1913.) Sea-fog is most prevalent in spring and summer when the air is warming rapidly. It does not often occur in the winter. See p. 121.

Land-fog, on the other hand, is an autumn or winter fog; it is generally due to cold air passing over relatively warm, moist ground. The process of cooling may be either by radiation or by a change of wind, but again eddy motion is necessary to mix the warm, moist air close to the ground with the cold flood. Fogs of this kind are not infrequent in the early mornings of summer, but they persist sometimes through the day in autumn and winter. Autumn is their special season.

Anticyclonic weather with light airs is very favourable for land-fog, and the ending of a period of anticyclonic weather is nearly always fog. Fog on our coasts is generally included in the forecasts for the British Isles when the wind changes from a Northerly or Easterly to a Southerly point. For the monthly percentage-frequency of fog and mist in the English Channel see p. 121.

The conditions for fog in London are set out in a Report of the Meteorological Office on fogs. (M.O. publication No. 160.)

The frequency of fog at the observing hours, according to the returns for the past 20 years from British Stations for the *Daily Weather Report*, is shewn in the following table. It should be noted that up to the end of June, 1908, the morning and mid-day hours of observation were 8h. and 14h. instead of 7h. and 13h., and that at Oxford the observing hours have been, and are still, 8h. and 20h., not 7h. and 18h. The following are the yearly frequencies of observations of fog at 1h. (or 3h.) in the past two years:—

Wick	10	Donaghadee	18	Spurn Head	10
Stornoway	0	Holyhead	13	Yarmouth	8
Malin Head	10	Pembroke	18	Eskdalemuir	3
Blacksod Point	9	Portland Bill	5	Benson	2
Valencia	3	Dungeness	15	London	3
Scilly	20	Tynemouth	1		

AVERAGE NUMBER OF OBSERVATIONS OF FOG IN A

Number of Years of Observations at		—	Station.	7h.			13h.		
7h.	13h.			Summer.	Winter.	Year.	Summer.	Winter.	Year.
20	20	North Coast.	Sumburgh Head...	10	2	12	4	1	5
20	20		Stornoway ...	2	1	3	0	0	0
8	8		Castlebay	9	2	11	3	1	4
20	5		Wick	11	1	12	8	1	9
20	20		Nairn	3	2	5	2	2	4
20	20		Aberdeen	4	1	5	1	0	1
20	—		Leith	2	7	9	—	—	—
20	20	East Coast.	N. Shields ...	8	8	16	2	4	6
20	20		Spurn Head ...	7	12	19	3	5	8
20	20		Great Yarmouth...	5	25	30	1	10	11
12	7		Clacton-on-Sea ...	1	6	7	0	2	2
20	20	West Coast.	Malin Head ...	8	3	11	4	1	5
20	20		{ Belmullet { Blacksod Point }	3	2	5	1	1	2
20	20		Valencia	2	2	4	0	0	0
20	20		Roche's Point ...	8	5	13	3	2	5
20	13		Donaghadee ...	7	3	10	2	2	4
20	—		Liverpool (Bidston Observatory).	1	6	7	—	—	—
20	20		Holyhead	16	9	25	9	4	13
20	17		Pembroke... ...	11	7	18	6	3	9
20	20	South Coast.	Scilly (St. Mary's)	14	6	20	7	4	11
20	20		Jersey (St. Aubin's)	5	5	10	1	2	3
20	20		{ Hurst Castle } Portland Bill }	5	5	10	4	2	6
20	20		Dungeness ...	7	10	17	2	3	5
8	—		Dover	3	7	10	—	—	—
20	20	Inland.	London	3	19	22	0	7	7
17	—		Oxford	4	24	28	—	—	—
20	13		{ Loughborough } Nottingham }	5	20	25	0	6	6
12	—		Bath	1	5	6	—	—	—
20	4		Birr Castle ...	4	6	10	0	2	2

NOTE.—Summer (April to September) contains 183 days, and

YEAR AT VARIOUS STATIONS IN THE BRITISH ISLES.

18h.			21h.			Station.		Number of Years of Observations at	
Summer.	Winter.	Year.	Summer.	Winter.	Year.			18h.	21h.
6	1	7	9	1	10	Sumburgh Head...	North Coast.	20	7
1	0	1	0	0	0	Stornoway ...		20	7
7	2	9	3	0	3	Castlebay		8	7
7	1	8	6	2	8	Wick		20	5
2	2	4	—	—	—	Nairn ...		20	—
3	0	3	—	—	—	Aberdeen ...		20	—
0	2	2	—	—	—	Leith ...		20	—
3	4	7	4	6	10	N. Shields ...	East Coast.	20	2
3	7	10	4	6	10	Spurn Head ...		20	7
1	9	10	1	8	9	Great Yarmouth...		20	7
0	2	2	0	1	1	Clacton-on-Sea ...		12	7
6	3	9	1	1	2	Malin Head ...	West Coast.	20	7
2	2	4	4	2	6	{ Belmullet {Blacksod Point }		20	7
1	0	1	0	0	0	Valencia		20	2
4	3	7	—	—	—	Roche's Point ...		20	—
2	2	4	3	4	7	Donaghadee ...		20	7
0	1	1	—	—	—	Liverpool (Bidston Observatory).		20	—
9	7	16	8	4	12	Holyhead		20	—
6	5	11	7	5	12	Pembroke... ...		20	7
9	6	15	10	5	15	Scilly (St. Mary's)	South Coast.	20	8
3	4	7	2	1	3	Jersey (St. Aubin's		20	7
4	2	6	3	2	5	{ Hurst Castle { Portland Bill }		20	7
2	3	5	—	—	—	Dungeness ...		20	—
0	2	2	—	—	—	Dover		8	—
0	6	6	1	8	9	London	Inland.	20	5
0	4	4	—	—	—	Oxford		17	—
0	6	6	0	5	5	{ Loughborough { Nottingham }		20	7
0	2	2	—	—	—	Bath		12	—
0	1	1	—	—	—	Birr Castle ...		20	—

Winter (October to March) 182 days, in leap year 183 days.

Fog Bow.—A white rainbow of about 40° radius seen opposite the sun in fog. Its outer margin has a reddish, and its inner a bluish tinge, but the middle of the band is quite white. The bow is produced in the same way as the ordinary rainbow but owing to the smallness of the drops, under 0·025 mm., the colours are mixed and the bow is nearly white.

Föhn.—The name given to certain dry, warm, relaxing winds of the valleys on the Northern side of the Alps. The general direction of the Föhn winds is from the South. The peculiar character of the air is accounted for by supposing that it comes from over the plains on the Southern side of the ridge. In its elevation it becomes dynamically cooled, and if condensation occurs and rain or snow is formed in it, the fall of temperature is so much restricted on account of the latent heat of the vapour which is condensed and left behind, that the air which forces its way down into the valleys on the north side, being dynamically warmed and dried, appears as a warm, dry wind. Some of the details of the process are still obscure because warm air does not naturally flow downhill, but the main outline of the process is certainly established and the subject has been studied in detail by Austrian meteorologists.

The Chinook wind of the Western prairies of America which comes down from the Rocky Mountains as a warm, dry wind evaporating a good deal of the prairie snow in winter is of similar character, and various other examples of what is known in meteorology as the Föhn effect occur from time to time on many hill sides. In regions like Norway, Greenland and the Antarctic Continent it complicates the temperature measurements very seriously.

Forecast.—The name given by Admiral R. FitzRoy to a statement of the weather to be anticipated in the near future from a study of a synoptic chart or "weather map." In the Meteorological Office the period of anticipation of a forecast does not exceed twenty-four hours, but when conditions shown on the map are favourable a more general statement of the probable weather for two or three days is given in a form which is called "the further outlook."

In practice a forecast includes—

(1) A statement of the direction and force of the surface-wind and the changes therein which are expected within the period of the forecast.

(2) A statement of the state of the sky (as regards clouds), precipitation (rain, hail, snow or sleet) and temperature, whether it will be high or low for the time of year, or higher or lower than at the time of making the forecast.

(3) A note as to the probability of such occurrences as night-frost, fog, or thunder.

For these statements the forecaster depends upon the changes in the distribution of pressure which are indicated on the map, although these changes are not described in the forecast. They are, however, set out in a preliminary statement called the "general inference," and for the information of airmen the anticipated changes in the pressure gradient over the several districts are formulated and are expressed as an addition to the forecast giving the "wind at 1,500 feet." That height is chosen because the wind at that level is generally in close agreement with that computed from the distribution of pressure at the surface,

The direction and velocity quoted for 1,500 feet are sufficiently applicable for heights up to 3,000 or 4,000 feet, as changes in the wind above the level of 1,500 feet are generally gradual. A Southerly, South-westerly, Westerly or North-westerly wind generally gets gradually stronger at higher levels, but an Easterly wind often falls lighter and is replaced in the highest levels by a wind from a Westerly quarter, though that is not always the case. The motion of clouds, or the measurement of air-currents by observations of a pilot balloon, are the only means available at present for guidance as to the changes in the higher level.

Freezing.—With reference to weather this word is used when the temperature of the air is below the freezing point of water 32° F., 273a., 0° C.

American writers use the term "a freeze" where we are accustomed to use "frost" to indicate freezing conditions persistent for a sufficient time to characterise the weather.

Frequency :—The number of times that a particular phenomenon of weather has happened in the course of a given period of time, generally a number of years. Here, for example, is a summary of the spells of wind from the Easterly quarter, according to the direction of the isobars, over S.E. England and Northern France in nine years. Taking January, for instance, the nine years supply a total of 279 days, of which 58 were days of East wind. These consisted of one sequence of eight consecutive days of East wind, one sequence of six days, three sequences of four, two sequences of three and seven sequences of two days, with finally twelve isolated days of East wind.

Frequency Table.—Number of Spells of Wind of Specified Duration from N.E., E. or S.E., during the nine years 1904–1912 inclusive. England, South-East, and Northern France.

Duration of Spell. Days.	January. No.	February. No.	March. No.	April. No.	May. No.	June. No.	July. No.	August. No.	September. No.	October. No.	November. No.	December. No.
1	12	7	13	15	15	19	13	13	11	12	13	11
2	7	3	3	3	10	7	6	5	8	4	4	2
3	2	5	4	3	3	3	4	—	3	7	1	2
4	3	—	3	3	1	1	4	2	6	1	2	—
5	—	1	—	1	4	—	—	—	1	1	1	—
6	1	—	1	2	1	2	—	2	—	—	1	1
7	—	—	—	2	1	—	—	—	—	2	—	1
8	1	1	—	1	—	—	—	—	1	1	1	1
9	—	—	—	1	—	—	—	—	—	—	—	—
10	—	—	—	—	—	—	—	—	—	—	—	—
11	—	—	—	—	—	—	—	1	—	—	—	—
12	—	—	—	—	—	—	—	—	—	—	—	—
13	—	1	1	—	—	—	—	—	—	—	—	—
Total No. of days of East wind.	58	44	63	71	74	65	53	55	76	75	53	42
Total number of days of observations.	279	255	279	270	279	270	279	279	270	279	270	279

In this case the number of years over which the observations extend is given, quite an arbitrary number, and thus the numbers for frequency of occurrence have to be considered with reference to the number of years selected. It is, however, usual to reduce frequency figures to a yearly average.

Here, for example, is the average frequency of GEOSTROPHIC winds from different quarters over the South-East of England and Northern France obtained from observations for the nine years, 1904–1912.

Frequency of winds (geostrophic) from different quarters.
Average Number of Days in the several months of the year in which the Wind is from a specified quarter. South-East of England and Northern France.

—	N.E.	E.	S E.	S.	S.W.	W.	N.W.	N.	Calms.	Total.
January ...	3	2	2	2	9	6	2	1	4	31
February ..	3	1	1	4	7	6	3	2	1	28
March ...	4	2	1	3	7	5	2	2	5	31
April ...	5	2	1	2	6	5	2	4	3	30
May ...	4	2	2	2	5	4	2	2	6	29
June ...	5	1	1	3	6	4	3	4	3	30
July ...	4	1	1	1	6	5	3	4	6	31
August ...	2	1	1	2	10	6	3	2	4	31
September	4	3	2	2	5	4	3	4	3	30
October ...	3	3	2	5	7	3	3	2	4	32
November	3	2	1	3	7	7	2	1	4	30
December..	1	2	2	7	10	4	2	1	2	31

The treatment of fractional parts of a day accounts for the two discordant totals.

In view of the awkwardness of having to bear in mind the possible number of occurrences, while considering the actual or average number, it is convenient to use the percentage frequency instead of the actual frequency. This plan is often adopted for giving the results of observations at sea, which are made six times a day, or every four hours.

For example, the percentage frequency of fog in the English Channel is given by the figures in the following table :—

Percentage Frequency of Fog and Mist in the English Channel.

[Based on four-hourly observations from ships during the 15 years 1891–1905.]

Month.	Number of observations.	Percentage of whole number of observations. Fog.	Percentage of whole number of observations. Mist.
January ...	1,187	2·5	15·8
February ...	1,185	2·8	22·9
March ...	1,241	3·8	24·5
April ...	1,424	4·8	24·4
May ...	1,501	4·4	26·9
June ...	1,363	5·6	30·2
July ...	1,260	3·8	26·3
August ...	1,206	3·2	17·3
September ...	1,264	1·3	17·0
October ...	1,454	1·6	16·5
November ...	1,284	1·1	15·0
December ...	1,294	1·5	18·2

Friction.—A word used somewhat vaguely in meteor-ological writings in dealing with the effect of the surface of the sea or of the land, with its obstacles in the form of irregularity of surface, hills, buildings, or trees upon the flow of air in the lower layers of the atmosphere. The effect of the irregularities of surface is to produce turbu-lent motion in the lowest layer which gradually spreads upwards, if the wind. goes on blowing, and consists of irregular eddies approaching to regularity in the case of a cliff eddy which can 'be noticed when a strong wind blows directly on to a cliff and produces an eddy with a horizontal axis. An account of the eddy caused by the Eastern face of the rock of Gibraltar is given in the Journal of the Aeronautical Society, Vol. 18, 1914, p. 184.

The general effect of this so-called friction is to reduce the flow of air past an anemometer so that the recorded wind velocity is below that which would be experienced if the anemometer were high enough to be out of the reach of the surface effect. Numerical values for this effect are of great practical importance, because they are concerned with the change of velocity in the immediate neighbourhood of the ground. But it is not easy to obtain them, because every exposure near land or sea is more or less affected, and, therefore, no proper standard of reference can be obtained by direct observation. Recourse is, therefore, had to the computation of the wind from the distribution of pressure, the so-called "geostrophic" or GRADIENT WIND.

From the comparison of a long series of geostrophic and observed winds we conclude that over the open sea, or on an exposed spit of flat sand like Spurn Head, the wind loses one-third of its velocity from "friction," and at other well-exposed stations the loss is, on the average, as

much as 60 per cent., but for any particular anemometer
it is different for winds from different quarters because
the exposure seaward or landward is different. Information on this point for a number of Meteorological
Office stations is given in a memoir by Mr. J. Fairgrieve
(*Geophysical Memoirs*, Vol. 1, p. 189), and information
for other stations is in process of compilation at the
Meteorological Office.

The consequence of this effect can sometimes be seen in
weather maps. On one occasion when the whole of the
British Isles was covered with parallel isobars running
nearly West and East, all the stations on the Western
side gave the wind as force 8 (42 mi/hr) while those on
the Eastern side gave force 5 (21 mi/hr), so that the
velocity was reduced by one-half in consequence of the
"friction" of the land. If the velocity at the exposed
Western stations be taken at two-thirds the velocity of
the wind free from friction, we get the following interesting result which is probably correct enough for practical
use :—One-third of the velocity is lost by the sea friction
on the Western side, and one-third more by the land
friction of the country between West and East.

Frost.—According to British meteorological practice
frost occurs when the temperature of the air is below
the freezing point of water (see FREEZING); it may be
either local, as a ground-frost, a spring-frost or a night-
frost often is, or general, such as a frost which gives
bearing ice in the course of three or four days. But the
word would hardly be used unless there were water or
plants or something else to be frozen, so that its use is
generally restricted to the lowest levels of the atmosphere.
We should hardly speak of a frost in relation to the cold
of the upper air, or even of a mountain top.

Meteorologically, the difference between the conditions for a general frost and those for a local frost is so great that different words are needed. The American meteorologists have some reason, therefore, in speaking of a general meteorological frost as "a freeze."

The British Isles are accessible for a freeze or general frost in two ways, first by Northerly winds bringing cold air from the Arctic regions over the North Atlantic, round a high pressure lying over the Greenland-Iceland region, secondly by Easterly or South-Easterly winds coming round a high pressure over Scandinavia and Northern Europe, which in the winter is persistently cold. The Northerly wind has to cross a considerable stretch of the north-eastern extension of the Gulf-stream water, so that it has to travel quickly to avoid being warmed. Consequently, Northerly "freezes" are generally short and sharp. The more prolonged frosts are generally caused by the Easterly winds which have only a short stretch of sea to cross. A long freeze may begin with a Northerly wind, and snow, followed by a persistent Easterly wind.

The short frosts, or night frosts, may occur with very light winds from any quarter except between South and West ; they are characteristic of clear nights, with great loss of heat from the ground by radiation to the clear sky. The conditions are set out in detail in a pamphlet prepared in the Meteorological Office and reprinted in " *Forecasting Weather*," Chapter XII.

Low temperatures are often quoted as *degrees of frost*, meaning thereby the number of degrees below the freezing point of water.

Gale.—Wind with an hourly velocity of more than 17m/s, or 39mi/hr. The figure is selected as the lower limit of force 8 on the Beaufort Scale. A wind estimated as force 8 or more is counted a gale.

The relation of the estimation to the measured hourly velocity is subject to some uncertainty on account of the incessant fluctuations of velocity in a strong wind which are known as GUSTINESS. They are not shown in the records of the cup anemometer which were used for computing the equivalents.

The number of gales recorded for any locality depends largely on the exposure of the anemometer, as the table on the next page shows.

Judging by this table, anyone who is unacquainted with the practical difficulties of anemometry would be tempted to draw the conclusion that the localities represented by Kew, Falmouth, Aberdeen, Valencia and Yarmouth are immune from gales, or nearly so.

For any purpose of aërial navigation such a conclusion would be egregiously untrue. It is true of the anemometers, but not of the free air above them. The records, which in these particular cases go back to 1868, are good enough when we are concerned only with comparing the wind of to-day with that of yesterday, or any other day in the last forty-seven years, and of determining normals for reference, the diurnal and seasonal variation, and so on ; but when we want to compare one locality with another we must face the problem of making allowance for the exposure of the anemometer.

To meet this requirement we propose to give the basic characteristics of the localities under our observation as regards wind in terms of GRADIENT WIND, or more strictly *geostrophic* wind. It is a very voluminous inquiry, but is now nearly completed, and some of the results will be included in this volume.

Gales recorded at British Anemometer Stations.

Number of hours in each month during which the mean Wind Velocity recorded by certain anemometers was equivalent to Gale-force on the average of seven years 1908 to 1914 inclusive.

Station.	July.	August.	September.	October.	November.	December.	January.	February.	March.	April.	May.	June.	Year.
Valencia	0	0	0	0	3	5	2	5	1	0	0	0	16
Kingstown	0	2	1	5	8	19	4	14	7	3	1	1	65
Fleetwood	7	2	8	7	21	13	12	14	7	4	4	1	100
Holyhead	0	1	1	3	17	10	8	10	4	1	1	0	56
Scilly	1	3	4	10	20	46	25	29	37	5	3	0	183
Falmouth (Observatory)	0	0	0	0	0	1	0	0	0	0	0	0	1
Deerness	0	0	2	2	8	19	42	9	9	8	2	0	101
Aberdeen	0	0	0	0	0	0	8	1	1	0	0	0	2
Yarmouth	0	0	0	4	1	2	0	1	3	0	0	0	19
Kew	0	0	0	0	0	0	0	0	0	0	0	0	0

The seasonal variation may be expressed as follows :—

Odds against the occurrence of a Gale on any day in the various months of the year over the several sections of the British and Irish Coasts.

Based upon records extending over the 40 years 1876–1915.

COASTS.	January.	February.	March.	April.	May.	June.	July.	August.	September.	October.	November.	December.	Year.
Scotland, N.E.	5	6	7	15	27	74	102	43	17	8	5	5	10
,, E.	8	10	10	26	43	74	77	61	20	11	8	10	15
,, N.W.	5	6	9	19	30	74	61	43	14	10	6	5	11
,, W.	7	7	11	22	43	74	102	33	17	6	7	6	13
Ireland, N.W.	4	5	6	12	25	37	30	23	10	8	4	4	8
,, S.W.	4	5	7	14	25	59	61	21	15	8	5	4	9
Irish Sea	5	6	6	15	30	42	43	23	14	8	5	5	9
St. George's Channel	6	7	8	20	38	74	77	30	19	8	6	5	11
Bristol Channel	5	5	8	14	33	42	43	17	13	6	5	4	9
England, S.W.	6	6	8	18	27	74	61	23	22	8	5	5	10
,, S.	8	8	12	26	51	99	51	21	24	9	7	6	13
,, S.E.	9	11	14	32	61	149	77	30	29	10	7	7	16
,, E.	12	12	16	29	61	149	154	51	42	12	9	9	19
,, N.E.	7	8	9	24	43	74	77	61	22	10	9	7	14

(The figures represent in each case the "odds against one.")

The "favourite" day is 28th January in Ireland, N.W., the odds about which are just 21 to 19 against, or nearly even.

For special localities tables of local statistics must be consulted. Some guidance may be obtained from the diagrams given under the heading *wind*.

Gale-Warning.—Notice of threatening atmospherical disturbances on or near the coasts of the British Islands are issued by telegraph from the Meteorological Office to a number of ports and fishery-stations. The issue of a warning indicates that an atmospheric disturbance is in existence which will probably cause a GALE (Force 8 by BEAUFORT SCALE) within a distance of (say) 50 miles of the place to which the warning is sent. The place itself may be comparatively sheltered, and the wind may not attain the force of a gale there. The meaning of the warning is simply " Look out. Bad weather of such and such a character is probably approaching you."

The fact that such a notice has been received is made known* by hoisting in a conspicuous position a black canvas cone (gale-cone) 3 feet high and 3 feet wide at the base, which has the appearance of a triangle when hoisted.

The " *South cone* " (point downwards) is hoisted in anticipation of gales and strong winds—

From S.E. veering to S.W., W., or N.W.
    „   S.W.   „   W. or N.W.
    „   W.   „   N.W.

The " *North cone* " (point upwards) is hoisted in anticipation of gales and strong winds—

From S.E., E. or N.E., backing to N.
    „   N.W. veering to N., N.E., or E.
    „   N.   „   N.E. or E.
    „   N.E.   „   E.

---

* The display of cones and issue of notices to the general public has been suspended during the war.

The warning is intended to continue from the time the telegram leaves the Meteorological Office until 8 p.m. the following day.

The gale-warning service of the British Isles was established under the direction of the late Admiral FitzRoy in 1861, and has been maintained in operation ever since, with a slight interruption in 1867.

Gas.—The name used for any kind of fluid which has unlimited capacity for expansion under diminishing pressure. It is to be distinguished from a liquid which has only a limited capacity for expansion under reduced pressure.

A liquid may occupy only the lower part of a vessel like a bottle; it will flow to the bottom of the vessel and leave a "free" surface. But a gas cannot be located in that way; its volume is determined not by the amount of material but by the size of the vessel which contains it and by the pressure upon its boundaries.

There are many different kinds of gas, such as nitrogen, hydrogen, carbonic acid, coal-gas, marsh-gas, and so on; but the word is often used when coal-gas is meant, and recently it has been used for heavy poisonous gas of unspecified composition. In scientific practice gas means any substance which obeys approximately the gaseous laws; these laws are two, viz. :—

1. When the temperature is kept constant the pressure of a given mass of gas is inversely proportional to the volume which it occupies, or the density is directly proportional to the pressure.

2. When the volume is kept constant the pressure is proportional to the absolute temperature, or when the pressure is kept constant the volume is proportional to the absolute temperature.

Geostrophic.—See GRADIENT WIND.

Glazed Frost.—When rain falls with the air-temperature below the freezing point a layer of smooth ice, which may attain considerable thickness, is formed upon all objects exposed to it. This is known as glazed frost. The accumulation of ice is frequently sufficient to bring down telegraph wires. In these islands the phenomenon is one of comparative rarity.

It must be distinguished from SILVER THAW, which occurs when a warm, damp wind supervenes upon severe cold, the moisture condensing on still-freezing surfaces and thus producing a coat of ice, similar in appearance to glazed frost. Super-cooled water-drops are said to be the cause of glazed frost.

Glory.—The system of coloured rings surrounding the shadow of the observer's head on a bank of cloud or fog or even of dew. It is a diffraction-effect due to the bending of rays of light round small obstacles, water-drops in this case. As in all diffraction effects the violet ring is nearest the centre, followed outwards by blue, green, orange, and red on the outside; the blue and violet are seldom seen. A Glory may be seen surrounding the shadow of an aeroplane on a cloud.

Gradient.—A convenient word rather overworked in modern meteorology. We use it in pressure gradient, temperature gradient, potential gradient, to denote different ideas. In pressure gradient for any locality we imagine the distribution of sea-level pressure to be mapped out by isobars; take a line through the locality at right angles to the isobars nearest to it on either side and measure the step of barometric pressure which corresponds with a measured distance along the line from high pressure to low. This use of gradient was introduced by Thomas Stevenson, C.E., of the Board of Northern Lights. It corresponds with an engineer's use of the word gradient in specifying a slope from a map of contours, but to get the pressure-gradient we have first to determine the line along which the slope is steepest, so that pressure-gradient has a definite direction. There is a convention that the distance to be taken is 15 nautical miles and the step of pressure is to be given in hundredths of an inch. The gradient will work out at practically the same figure if the distance is a geographical degree and the step of pressure is given in millimetres. To get the same figure for the gradient with the step of pressure in millibars the distance would have to be taken as 45 nautical miles. But numerical values of the gradient are very seldom quoted.

Temperature gradient may be based on the same idea and give the rate of change of temperature, along the horizontal through a locality, at right angles to the isotherms, as obtained from a chart of isotherms properly corrected for height. But it is much more frequently used to indicate the step of temperature for a kilometre step of vertical height. Used in this sense temperature gradient may be positive or negative, and by international agreement the temperature gradient is positive when the step is towards lower temperature for increasing height, because temperature generally decreases aloft; but it does not always do so. The change from positive to negative temperature gradient is called an INVERSION of temperature gradient or simply an " inversion ", and so an " inversion " comes to mean a region where temperature increases with height.

Potential gradient is used for the change of atmospheric

electrical potential in the vertical, and for that alone. It is generally given in volts per metre. That also may be positive or negative and is taken to be positive when the potential increases with height.

The word LAPSE (*q.v.*) has been adopted as a better name than gradient for these rates of change in the vertical.

The pressure gradient is the one which comes most frequently into practical consideration, as it is closely related to the direction and force of the wind, so that the idea of pressure gradient should always be present in the mind of a student of weather maps, though the gradient may seldom be evaluated in figures. On looking over a map the localities where the gradient is steep will always be noticeable by the closeness of the isobars. The determination of the pressure gradient is comparatively easy when the isobars in the locality are free from local irregularity and nearly parallel. There is then no difficulty in identifying the direction of the gradient, because the line drawn at right angles to successive isobars is approximately straight for a sufficient distance on the map. Experience is required to make a workable estimate of the gradient when the isobars are irregular. In practice the gradient is not taken by setting out a length of 15 or 60 or 45 nautical miles, but by scaling the distance apart of consecutive isobars. It is most convenient to express this distance in nautical miles, because 60 nautical miles make up a degree of latitude, and every map made for meteorological purposes is scaled according to latitude. If, for example, isobars are drawn for steps of millibars, and the shortest line drawn to bridge two

5

isobars across a station scales out at 75 nautical miles ; the gradient is 1 millibar (0·03 m.) for 15 nautical miles, or 3 on the conventional scale of pressure gradients. For calculation in C.G.S. units it is convenient to have the gradient expressed in terms of millibars for 100 kilometres.

It is best to use a large scale map for obtaining pressure gradients so that intermediate isobars can be inserted by estimation when those drawn for the ordinary steps are not regular, but with the best maps the estimation of the gradient is sometimes uncertain on account of local irregularities of pressure which may be indicated on a barogram but cannot be allowed for in a map based on telegraphic reports from stations 100 miles (160 kilometres) apart.

Some of the steepest authentic gradients that have been noted on British weather maps are :—

Date and Place.	Gradient.	
	International measure.	Millibars per 100 kilometre.
1912, August 26, East Anglia (Norwich floods).	11·0	13·2
1907, February 20, between Iceland and Faroe.	10·0	12·0
1912, November 26, West of Scotland.	9·7	11·7

Gradient Wind.—The flow of air which is necessary to balance the pressure-gradient. The direction of the gradient wind is along the isobars, and the velocity is so adjusted that there is equilibrium between the force pressing the air inwards, towards the low pressure, and the centrifugal action to which the moving air is subject in consequence of its motion.

In the case of the atmosphere the centrifugal action may be due to two separate causes; the first is the tendency of moving air to deviate from a GREAT CIRCLE in consequence of the rotation of the earth; the deviation is towards the right of the air as it moves in the Northern hemisphere, and towards the left in the Southern. The second is the centrifugal force of rotation in a circle round a central point according to the well-known formula for any spinning body. In this case we regard the air as spinning round an axis through the centre of its path. This part of the centrifugal action is due to the curvature of the path on the earth's surface. Both components of the centrifugal action are in the line of the pressure gradient: the part due to the rotation of the earth is always tending to the right in the Northern hemisphere, the part due to the curvature of the path goes against the gradient from low to high when the curvature is cyclonic, and with the gradient when it is anticyclonic, so that in the one case we have the gradient balancing the sum of the components due to the earth's rotation and the spin, and in the other case the gradient and the spin-component balance the action due to the earth's rotation.

The formal reasoning which leads up to this result is given at the end of this article. The method used therein for calculating the effect of the rotation of the earth was suggested to the writer in 1904 by Sir John Eliot, F.R.S., Director of the Indian Meteorological Service.

For the sake of brevity in reference to these two components it is very convenient to have separate names for them. . Let us call the one due to the rotation of the earth the *geostrophic* component,* and the one due to the curvature of the path the *cyclostrophic* component.

Consider the relative magnitude of these components under different conditions. It will be noticed that the geostrophic component depends upon latitude, the cyclostrophic component does not, so, other things being equal, their relative importance will depend upon the latitude; so we will take three cases, one near the equator at latitude 10° within the equatorial belt of low pressure, one near the pole latitude 80° of undetermined meteorological character, and one, half-way, between, in latitude 45°, a region of highs and lows travelling Eastward.

Using V to denote the wind-velocity, when the radius of the path is 120 nautical miles the cyclostrophic component is equal to the geostrophic—

in latitude 10° when V is 5·6 metres per second ;

in latitude 45° when V is 22·9 metres per second ;

in latitude 80° when V is 31·9 metres per second.

It will be seen that in the equatorial region the cyclostrophic component is dominant as soon as the wind reaches a very moderate velocity.

---

* A table to find the geostrophic component is given on pp. 172, 173.

EQUATION FOR GEOSTROPHIC WIND.

The Relation between the Earth's Rotation and the Pressure Distribution for Great-Circle-Motion of Air.

The rotation ω of the earth about the polar axis can be resolved into $\omega \sin \phi$ about the vertical at the place where latitude is ϕ and $\omega \cos \phi$ about a line through the earth's centre parallel to the tangent line.

The latter produces no effect in deviating an air current any more than the polar rotation does on a current at the equator.

The former corresponds with the rotation of the earth's surface counterclockwise in the Northern Hemisphere and clockwise in the Southern Hemisphere under the moving air with an angular velocity $\omega \sin \phi$. We therefore regard the surface over which the wind is moving as a flat disc rotating with an angular velocity $\omega \sin \phi$.

By the end of an interval t the air will have travelled Vt, where V is the "wind-velocity," and the earth underneath its new position will be at a distance $Vt \times \omega t \sin \phi$, measured along a small circle,

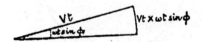

from its position at the beginning of the time t.

Taking it to be at right angles to the path, in the limit when t is small, the distance the air will appear to have become displaced to the right over the earth is $V \omega t^2 \sin \phi$.

This displacement on the "$\frac{1}{2} g t^2$" law (since initially there was no transverse velocity) is what would be produced by a transverse acceleration

$$2 \omega V \sin \phi.$$

$\therefore$ the effect of the earth's rotation is equivalent to an acceleration $2 \omega V \sin \phi$, at right angles to the path directed to the right in the Northern Hemisphere, and to the left in the Southern Hemisphere.

In order to keep the air on the great circle, a force corresponding with an equal but oppositely directed acceleration is necessary. This force is supplied by the pressure distribution.

EQUATION FOR CYCLOSTROPHIC WIND.

Force necessary to balance the acceleration of air moving uniformly in a small circle, assuming the earth is not rotating.

Let A be the pole of circle PRQ. Join PQ, cutting the radius OA in N. Acceleration of particle moving uniformly along the small circle with velocity V is $\dfrac{V^2}{PN}$ along $PN = \dfrac{V^2}{R\sin\rho}$ where $R =$ radius of earth; and ρ is the angular radius of the small circle representing the path.

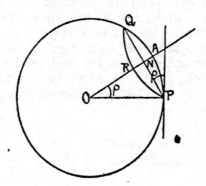

The horizontal component of this acceleration, that is, the component along the tangent at P, is $\dfrac{V^2\cos\rho}{R\sin\rho} = \dfrac{V^2}{R}\cot\rho$.

GENERAL EQUATION CONNECTING PRESSURE—GRADIENT, EARTH'S ROTATION, CURVATURE OF PATH OF AIR AND WIND VELOCITY.

I. *Cyclonic motion.* The force required to keep the air moving on a great circle in spite of the rotation of the earth must be such as to give an acceleration $2\omega V \sin\phi$ directed over the path to the left in the Northern Hemisphere. It must also compensate an acceleration due to the curvature of the path, $V^2 \cot\rho / R$, by a force directed towards the low pressure side of the isobar.

For steady motion these two combined are equivalent to the acceleration due to the gradient of pressure, *i.e.*, $\dfrac{\gamma}{D}$ where D is the density of the air, and γ the pressure gradient, directed towards the low pressure side.

$$\therefore \frac{\gamma}{D} = 2\,\omega\,V \sin \phi + \frac{V^2}{R} \cot \rho.$$

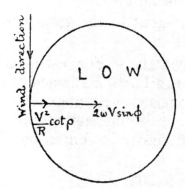

II. *Anticyclonic motion.* In this case $2\,\omega\,V \sin \phi$ and $\frac{\gamma}{D}$ are directed outwards from the region of high pressure, and the equation becomes

$$\frac{\gamma}{D} = 2\,\omega\,V \sin \phi - \frac{V^2}{R} \cot \rho.$$

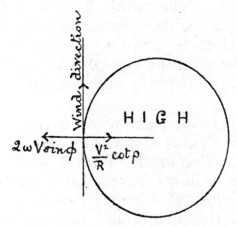

Gramme.—The unit of mass on the C.G.S. system. It is one-thousandth part of the standard kilogramme, which was originally constructed to represent the weight of a litre (cubic decimetre) of water.

A gramme is equivalent to 15·4 grains, or rather more than one-thirtieth of an ounce.

A pound is equivalent to 454 grammes. For GRAMME-CALORIE see p. 301.

Grass-temperature.—For estimating the effect of RADIATION from the Earth's surface at night a minimum thermometer is exposed just above the surface of short grass, so that the bulb does not actually touch the grass. Abroad the thermometer is sometimes laid on the grass itself.

Gravity.—See p. 308.

Great Circle.—A line on the earth's surface which lies in a plane through the centre of the earth's figure. All meridian lines are great circles so is also the equator, but all lines of latitude, with the exception of the equator, are small circles since their planes do not pass through the earth's centre. The visible horizon is a small circle.

The great circle which passes through two points on the earth's surface is made up of the shortest and the longest track between the two points. The shortest track is less than a semicircle, the longest greater than a semicircle.

Gulf Stream.—A warm ocean current that flows out of the Gulf of Mexico along the coast of Florida. It is ascribed to the action of the TRADE WINDS which cause a mass of water to flow into the Gulf from the East. The current near Florida is strengthened by water which branches from the main trade wind current and flows outside the Antilles. The Gulf Stream flows Northward into the region of prevailing Westerly winds, which cause a current to flow slowly Eastward across the Atlantic ; this current, also called the Gulf Stream, carries water from the Gulf Stream proper to the coasts of Europe. The air no doubt has its temperature slightly raised by the warm current, but our temperate climate is due to prevailing Westerly and South Westerly winds, which are also the cause of the Eastward extension of the Gulf Stream.

Gust.—A "coup de vent." The word was used originally for any transient blast of wind, but is now limited to the comparatively rapid fluctuations in the strength of the wind which are specially characteristic of winds near the surface of the earth, and are probably due to the turbulent or eddy motion arising from the FRICTION offered by the ground to the flow of the current of air.

The subject of gusts, as indicated by a tube-anemograph, has been investigated for the Advisory Committee for Aeronautics by the Meteorological Office, and the results are contained in four reports on Wind Structure published in the annual reports of the Committee. The number and extent of the fluctuations are very irregular ; they have been counted as seventeen in the minute, but another count would probably give a different figure. If the wind be regarded as fluctuating between a gust and a lull, the range between gusts and lulls is dependent on the one hand on the mean velocity of the wind, and on the other hand upon the nature of the exposure of the anemometer. Expressing the fluctuations as a percentage of the mean velocity we get the following results for various anemometers. (*Report of the Advisory Committee*, 1910.)

Anemometer.	Range of Fluctuation as a Percentage of the Mean Velocity.
Southport (Marshside)	30 per cent.
Scilly (St. Mary's)	50 ,,
Shoeburyness, E.N.E. wind ...	30 ,,
,, W. wind	80 ,,
Holyhead (Salt Island)	50 ,,
Falmouth (Pendennis), S. wind ...	25 ,,
,, ,, W. wind ...	50 ,,
Aberdeen	100 ,,
Alnwick	80 ,,
Kew	100 ,,

In this table a fluctuation of 100 per cent. means that a wind with a mean velocity of 30 miles per hour fluctuates over a range of 30 miles per hour, between 15 miles an hour and 45 miles an hour, in consequence of the gustiness.

The most gusty exposure within the experience of the Meteorological Office is at Dyce, in Aberdeenshire, where, for the purpose of inquiry, an anemometer was installed by Dr. J. E. Crombie, with its head projecting 15 feet above the tree-tops of a small wood.

Gusts are to be distinguished from squalls. A squall is a blast of wind occurring suddenly, lasting for some minutes at least, and dying away as suddenly. A squall is attributable to meteorological causes, whereas gusts are the result of mechanical interference with the steady flow of air.

The strongest gusts recorded on anemometers of the Meteorological Office in recent years are :—

		m/s.	mi/hr.
1905.	Pendennis,	46·0	103
1906.	Scilly,	38·4	86
1907.	Southport,	36·2	81
1908.	Scilly,	37·6	84
1909.	Scilly,	40·2	90
1910.	Pendennis,	38·9	87
1911.	Eskdalemuir,	40·2	90
1912.	Pendennis,	43·8	98
1913.	Southport,	38·4	86
1914.	Quilty,	41·0	92
1915.	Pendennis,	40·0	89
1916.	Pendennis,	40·8	91

Gustiness.—The name given to the factor which is used to define the range of the gusts shown on the record of an anemometer. The gustiness of an interval is the factor, (maximum velocity − minimum velocity) ÷ mean velocity.

The figures given for the fluctuations of wind in the records of various anemometers given above may be called the "percentage gustiness" of the winds. To obtain an estimate of the relative gustiness of the winds in the upper air, Mr. J. S. Dines used the pull of a kite wire defining the gustiness as

(maximum pull—minimum pull) ÷ mean pull.

Using this method it appears that gustiness falls off rapidly in the first 500 feet of ascent, and thereafter it is irregular. (*Second Report on Wind Structure*, p. 10.)

Hail.—Usually described as frozen raindrops, though hailstones are often very much larger than any raindrop an possibly be. Hail is formed in the columns of rapidly ascending air that are part of the mechanical process of a rain-storm or thunderstorm. They are associated with the cumulo-nimbus type of cloud. The convection currents which begin with instability in the atmosphere result, first in heavy cloud, and then in raindrops still carried upward in air which is automatically becoming colder in consequence of the diminished pressure. So the drops may freeze, and then any further upward journey may result in condensation in the form of ice on the already formed hailstone.

To maintain a mass of water or ice in the air a very vigorous ascending current is required. If a raindrop reaches a certain size it is broken up into smaller drops by the current which is necessary to keep it from falling, but when the hailstone is once formed there is no limitation of that kind upon its growth.

From their structure, which is often very composite, it is clear that hailstones have a long history, and from their size, which may be large enough to give measurements, it is said, of three or four inches in diameter, a pound or more in weight, they must have required ascending currents of great velocity to support them.

There is, however, evidence to show that some of the strongest winds of the earth are katabatic winds, that is, they are due to falling air, so it requires only a special adjustment of the temperature of the environment to give rise to currents of rising air, anabatic winds, of the most violent character. (SOFT HAIL, see p. 343.)

Halo.—The term halo is an inclusive one applied to all the optical phenomena produced by regular REFRACTION, with or without accompanying reflection, of the

rays of the sun or moon in clouds consisting of ice-crystals (see CLOUD, Cirro-Nebula). The most common halo is a luminous ring of ′22° radius surrounding the sun or moon, the space within it appearing less bright than the rest of the sky. The ring, if faint, is white—if more strongly developed its inner edge is a pure red, while yellow and green follow, more faintly. Next in order of frequency of occurrence is a similar but larger ring of 46° radius. MOCK SUNS are simply more brilliant patches occurring at certain definite points in a halo system. There is a great variety of minor and rarer halo phenomena. (For some of these see *Observer's Handbook*, p. 57.) In polar regions, where ice crystals extend much lower in the atmosphere, halo systems attain great brilliance and complexity.

Halos are very varied in form, they are produced by the REFRACTION of the sun's rays, or the moon's rays, through a cloud of ice crystals forming what is called cirro-nebula or cirrus-haze, one of the highest forms of cloud. They are of great interest from the point of view of the physics of the atmosphere, but they have no meteorological significance. In weather lore they are often spoken of as presaging storms and it is possible that the ice cloud is one of the earliest results of the fall of pressure with which the storm is associated ; but the formation of a halo is not by any means a necessary step in the preparation of a storm ; many storms arrive without announcing their coming in that way. Moreover, the appearance of a halo at the end of a spell of dirty weather is said to be a sign of clearing. We may perhaps conclude that cirro-nebula, with no other clouds in the sky to interfere (the condition for seeing a halo), may be found at the beginning or the end of a depression.

Harmattan.—A very dry wind which is prevalent in Western Africa during the dry season (November to March). During these months, (the winter of the Northern Hemisphere) the air over the desert of Sahara cools rapidly, owing to its clearness and lack of moisture, so that it tends to flow outwards to the coast, especially south-westwards to the Gulf of Guinea, and replace the lighter air there. Being here both dry and relatively cool, it forms a welcome relief from the steady damp heat of the tropics, and from its health-giving powers it is known locally as "The Doctor," in spite of the fact that it carries with it from the desert great quantities of impalpable dust, which penetrates into houses by every crack. This dust is often carried in sufficient quantity to form a thick haze, which impedes navigation on the rivers.

Harmonic Analysis.—See p. 311.

Haze.—Obscurity of the atmosphere which may occur in dry weather and may be due to dust or smoke, or merely to irregularities of density and consequent irregular refraction of the light by which distant objects are seen. During HARMATTAN winds off the West Coast of Africa, dust haze is thick enough to be classed as fog. At sea the weather is often classed as hazy when there is no distant horizon, and yet no visible mist or fog. The obscurity may, however, be due to water particles. It would therefore be desirable to limit the use of the word haze to occasions when the air is not very damp, that is when there is a noticeable difference between readings of the wet and the dry bulb thermometers.

Heat.—The name used for the immediate cause of the sensation of warmth, a primary sensation which is easily recognised and needs no explanation. As used in relation to the weather, heat and cold are familiar words for opposite extremes of temperature of the air. What the American writers call a heat-wave is a spell of hot weather in which the maximum temperatures reach 90° or 100° F. (above 305a.), and a cold-wave is a spell of the opposite character during which temperatures in the neighbourhood of the Fahrenheit zero, or 32 degrees of frost, may be experienced. In continental climates, during the passage of severe cyclonic depressions, the transitions from heat to cold are sometimes extremely abrupt and far-reaching; a difference of temperature of 50° F. in a few hours is not unknown. We have visitations of similar character in this country, but they are less intense. A few days in succession with a temperature over 80° F. would suffice for a heat-wave, and a few days with 10° of frost would certainly be called a cold-wave. One of the most noticeable features of our climate is the succession of cold spells which interrupt the genial weather of late spring and early summer. They are not very intense, but a drop in the mean temperature of the day from 55° F. to 45° F., which roughly defines them, produces a very distinct impression.

As used in connexion with the study of the atmosphere heat has another sense which must not be overlooked. It denotes the physical quantity, the reception of which makes things warmer, and its departure makes them colder. If you wish to make water hot, you supply heat to it from a fire or a gas-burner or, in modern days, by an electric heater, a very convenient contrivance for getting heat exactly where you want it. On the other hand, if you want water to become cooler, you leave it where its heat can escape, by CONDUCTION, aided by CONVECTION or by RADIATION. You can also warm water by adding some hot water to it, or cool it by adding cold water to it. Either process suggests the idea of having the same quantity of heat to deal with altogether, but distributing it, or diluting it, by mixing.

The idea of having a definite quantity of heat to deal with, and passing it from one body to another is so easily appreciated and so generally applicable, that the older philosophers used to talk confidently of heat as a substance which they called Caloric, and which might be transferred from one body to another without losing its identity. They measured heat, as we do still, by noting by how much it would raise the temperature of a measured quantity of water. For students of physics the unit of heat is still a *gramme-calorie*, the heat which will raise a gramme of water through one degree centigrade. To raise m grammes from $t_1°$C to $t_2°$C, $m(t_2 - t_1)$ gramme calories are required. The amount can be recovered, if none has been lost meanwhile, by cooling the water. If we wish to be very precise, a small correction is required on account of the variation in what is called the capacity for heat of water at different temperatures, but that need not detain us.

For students of engineering the unit, called the British Thermal Unit, is a pound-Fahrenheit unit instead of the gramme-centigrade unit, and the heat required to raise m pounds of water from $t_1°$F to $t_2°$F is $m(t_2 - t_1)$ B.T.U.

It is in many ways a misfortune that students of Physics and Engineering do not use the same unit. It is no doubt a good mental exercise to learn to use either indiscriminately without confusion, but it takes time.

From measurements of heat we get the idea that with different substances the same change of temperature requires different quantities of heat; the substances have different capacities for heat. We define *capacity for heat* as the heat required to raise a unit of the substance (1 gramme or 1 lb.) through 1 degree.

It is a remarkable fact that of all common substances water has the greatest capacity for heat. It takes one unit to raise the temperature of a unit mass of water one degree, it takes less than a unit, sometimes only a small fraction of a unit, to raise the temperature of the same amount of another substance through one degree. We give the name *specific heat* to the ratio of the capacity for heat of any substance to the capacity for heat of water. Numerically, specific heat is the same as the capacity for heat in thermal units.

The specific heat of water is 1, the specific heat of any other common substance is less than 1. The specific heat of copper is only 1/11. So the heat which will raise the temperature of a pound of copper 1° will only raise the temperature of a pound of water 1/11°, or the heat which will raise the temperature of a mass of water 1° will raise the temperature of the same mass of copper 11°.

This peculiar property of water makes it very useful for storing heat and carrying it about. From that point of view it is the best of all substances for cooling the condenser of an engine, for distributing heat at a moderate temperature in a circulating system, and for many other economic purposes.

In meteorology its influence is very wide. Large masses of water, of which the ocean is a magnificent example, are huge store houses which take up immense quantities of heat from the air when it is warm and give it out again when the air is cold, with very little change in its own temperature, so that a large lake, and still more the ocean, has a great influence in reducing the extremes of temperature of summer and winter, and of day and night, in the countries which border it.

There is another remarkable storage of heat in which water takes a predominant share that is dealt with in physical science under the name of *latent heat.*

Water at 288a. (59° F.) cannot be evaporated into water-vapour unless every gramme of it is supplied with 589 calories of heat, which produce no effect at all upon the temperature. The water is at 288a. to start with, and the water-vapour is at exactly the same temperature and yet 589 calories of heat have gone. They are *latent* in the water-vapour but produce no effect on the thermometer. You can get them back again easily enough if you condense the vapour back again into water, but you must manage somehow to take away the heat while the condensation is taking place. The separation of the " waters that are above the firmament from the waters that are below the firmament," or in modern language, the evaporation of water from the sea or a lake or the wet earth and its condensation in the form of clouds and rain, implies the transference of enormous quantities of heat from the surface to the upper air, the dynamical effect of which belongs to another chapter of the romantic story of heat which deserves more than the few words which we can afford for it. Readers can find an interesting account in Tyndall's *Heat a Mode of Motion.*

The idea of heat as an indestructible substance, caloric, which could be transferred from one body to another without loss, became untenable when it was found that when air was allowed to expand in a cylinder it cooled spontaneously to an extent that corresponded exactly, so far as could be ascertained, with the means then available, with the amount of mechanical work that the cylinder was allowed to do. It was the last step in the process of reasoning by which men had come to the conclusion that, when *mechanical work* was devoted to churning water or some other frictional process, heat was actually produced, not brought from some other substance but created by the frictional process.

It took many years for men to reconcile themselves to so novel an idea, and a good deal of ingenuity was devoted to trying to evade it, but it has now become the foundation stone of physical science. Heat is not an unalterable indestructible substance but a form of *energy*. It can do mechanical work in a steam-engine or a gas engine or an oil-engine, but for every foot-pound[*] of work that is done a corresponding amount of heat must disappear, and in place of it a corresponding amount of some other form of energy is produced. A good deal of heat, besides, may be wasted in the process so far as practical purposes are concerned. In a steam engine, of the whole amount of heat used, only one tenth may be transformed, the rest wasted, as we have said; but it is still there raising the temperature of the water of the condenser or performing some other unproductive but necessary duty.

There is, therefore, a numerical equivalent between heat and other forms of energy.

We give the relation :—

    1 B.T.U. is equivalent to 777 foot-pounds of energy.

    1 gramme-calorie = 42,640 gramme-centimetres.

               = 41,830,000 ergs.

---

[*] A *foot-pound* of work is the work done in lifting one pound through a distance of one foot.

A *gramme-centimetre* is the work done lifting one gramme through one centimetre.

An *erg* is the absolute unit of work on the C.G.S. system; 1 gramme centimetre = 981 ergs.

We have led-up to this statement in order to point out how extraordinarily powerful heat can be in producing mechanical energy.

If, in the operations of nature, one single cubic metre of air gets its temperature reduced by 1° C. in such a way that the heat is converted into work by being made to move air, the equivalent of energy would be a cubic metre of air moving with a velocity of nearly 45 m/s. (101 mi/hr.).

So familiar have we become with heat as a form of energy that we measure the heat of sunlight in joules* and the intensity of sunshine in watts per square centimetre, *i.e.*, the number of joules falling on one square centimetre per second.

THE SPECIFIC HEAT OF AIR.

The foregoing statement is necessary to lead up to a matter of fundamental importance in the physics of the atmosphere, namely the heat that is required or used to alter the temperature of air in the processes of weather ; in technical language this is the capacity for heat of air or the specific heat of air.

We have explained that when air is allowed to do work on its environment, in expanding, heat disappears, or more strictly is transformed. So the amount of heat required to warm air through a certain number of degrees depends upon how much expansion is allowed during the process. The most economical way of warming air from the

---

* A *joule* is a more convenient unit than the small unit, the erg ; one joule = ten million ergs (10^7 ergs) and one calorie = 4·18 joules.

The *watt* is a unit of power, that is, rate of doing work ; a power of one watt does one joule of work per second.

thermal point of view is to prevent its expanding altogether ; it then has " constant volume " and its specific heat is 0˙1715 calories per gramme per degree at 273 a. It is remarkable, but true, that if you have a bottle full of air, it will take more heat to raise the temperature of each gramme of it by a degree if you take the stopper out while the warming is going on, than if you keep it tight. The difference between warming a bottle of air with the stopper in and with it out, simple as it may seem, has got in it the whole principle of heat as a form of energy.

The effect of leaving the stopper out is that the pressure of the air inside the bottle is the atmospheric pressure for the time being and is therefore practically constant throughout the brief operation. So we get the specific heat of air at constant pressure 0˙2417 gramme-calories per gramme per degree, or 1˙010 joules. The specific heat of air at constant volume is 0˙72 joules. The difference of the two represents the heat equivalent of the work used in expanding unit mass of the gas against atmospheric pressure.

High.—Sometimes used as a contraction for high barometric pressure. The technical term anticyclone was coined by Sir F. Galton for the purpose, but, whether for the sake of brevity or for some other reason, a " high " is often spoken of.

Hoar Frost.—A feathery deposit of ice formed upon leaves and twigs in the same way as DEW (*q.v.*) by the cooling of exposed objects through the radiation of their heat to the clear sky.

Horizontal—in the plane of the horizon. The surface of still water is horizontal. In dynamics and physics a

horizontal line is a line at right-angles to the direction
of the force of gravity which is vertical and identified by
the plumb line.

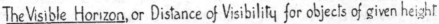

The Visible Horizon, or Distance of Visibility for objects of given height

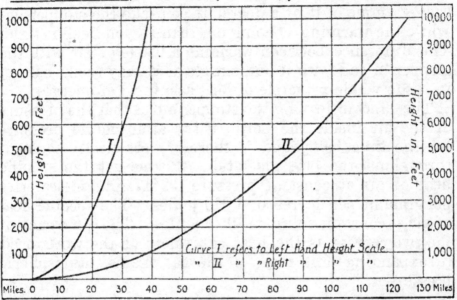

Diagram showing the relation between the height of an observation
point in feet and the distance of the Visible Horizon in miles
(*neglecting refraction*), or the height in feet of a cloud or other
distant object and the distance in miles at which it is visible on the
horizon.

The "sensible or visible horizon" which is visible
from a ship at sea, the line where sea and sky apparently
join, is a circle surrounding the observer a little below
the plane of the horizon in consequence of the level
of the earth's surface being curved and not flat. The
depth of the "sensible horizon" below the "rational
horizon" or horizontal plane is approximately the same
as the elevation of the point from which the "sensible

horizon " is viewed. Apart from any influence of the atmosphere the distance of the visible horizon for an elevation of 100 feet (30 metres) is about 12 miles. The actual distance is about 2 miles greater on account of refraction. It varies as the square root of the height, so that it would require a height of 400 feet to give a horizon 24 miles off. A level canopy of clouds 10,000 feet high is visible from a point on the earth's surface for a distance of about 125 miles, or the visible canopy has a width of 250 miles.

Horse Latitudes.—The belts of calms, light winds and fine, clear weather between the TRADE WIND belts and the prevailing Westerly winds of higher latitudes. The belts move North and South after the Sun in a similar way to the DOLDRUMS *q.v.*

Humidity, in a general sense means dampness, but in meteorology it is used for RELATIVE HUMIDITY and means the ratio of the actual amount of aqueous vapour in a measured volume of air to the amount which the volume would contain if the air were saturated. (See AQUEOUS VAPOUR.) In practice, at climatological stations, the humidity of air is determined from the readings of the dry and wet bulbs with the aid of tables prepared for the purpose and called humidity tables or psychrometric tables. But humidity is the most variable of the ordinary meteorological elements, as it depends not only on the sample of air under observation but also on its temperature. Hence the record of a self-recording hair-hygrometer which can be obtained in a form not much different from an ordinary barograph gives a most instructive record. In the spring and summer it sometimes shows very high humidity in the night and early morning, approaching or actually reaching saturation, and very great dryness, perhaps only from 15 to 20 per cent. humidity, in the sunny part of the day, with very rapid changes soon after sunrise and towards sunset.* These are the changes which correspond with the characteristic changes in the feeling of the air at the beginning and end of the day.

Hurricane—in French, ouragan, in German, Danish and Swedish, orkan. " A name [of Spanish or Portuguese origin] given primarily to the violent wind-storms of the West Indies which are cyclones of diameter of from 50 to 1,000 miles, wherein the air moves with a velocity of from 80 to 130 miles an hour round a central calm space which, with the whole system, advances in a straight or curved track ; hence any storm or tempest in which the wind blows with terrific violence " (New English Dictionary). The hurricanes of the Western Pacific Ocean are called typhoons in China, and .baguios in the Philippine Islands. Those of the Indian Ocean, which are experienced in India, are called by the Indian meteorologists cyclones of the Arabian Sea or of the Bay of Bengal ; while the hurricanes of the South Indian Ocean which visit Mauritius are also called cyclones.

Shakespeare uses the word hurricano for a water-spout.

Overleaf is a reproduction of a barogram showing the variation of pressure during a cyclone which passed over Cocos Island, Sumatra, in 1909, November 27th. It is interesting to notice that in spite of the rapid fall of pressure with the onset of the cyclone the diurnal variation of the barometer is still apparent and it reappears before the normal level is recovered.

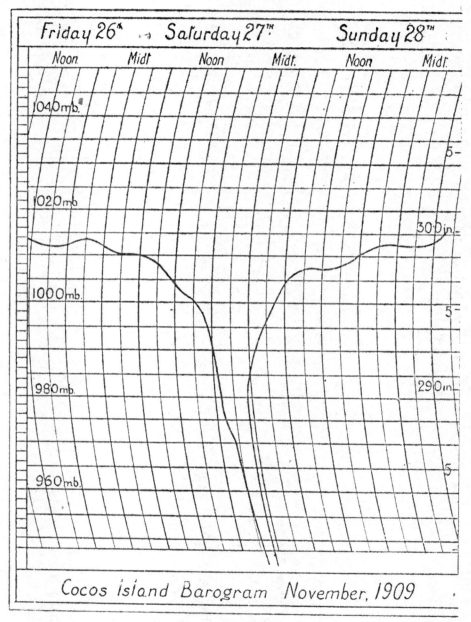

Cocos Island Barogram   November, 1909

The occurrence of hurricanes shows a marked seasonal variation. The following table is taken from the *Barometer Manual for the Use of Seamen.*

Table of recorded Hurricanes, Cyclones, and Typhoons, in various parts of the World.

Region and Period.	January.	February.	March.	April.	May.	June.	July.	August.	September.	October.	November.	December.	Total.
West Indies, 300 years ...	5	7	11	6	5	10	42	96	80	69	17	7	355
South Indian Ocean (38 years, 1848–1885).	71	61	59	50	19	3	2	—	—	5	25	33	328
Bombay, 25 years ...	1	1	1	5	9	2	4	5	8	12	9	5	62
Bay of Bengal, 139 years	2	—	2	9	21	10	3	4	6	31	18	9	115
China Sea, 85 years ...	5	1	5	5	11	10	22	40	58	35	16	6	214
Arabian Sea, 1877–1903...	—	—	—	1	5	6	—	—	—	2	7	—	21
Bay of Bengal, 1877–1903	—	—	—	1	8	4	4	2	6	8	17	6	56
South Pacific, 1789–1891	36	22	35	8	1	—	—	—	2	1	4	16	125

The force of the wind which is experienced in hurricanes is equalled, if not surpassed, in the tornadoes which occur on the American Continent, but the area affected by a tornado is generally a narrow strip a few miles at most in width.

In the Beaufort Scale of wind force the name hurricane is given to a wind of force 12, and its velocity equivalent is set at an hourly velocity exceeding 34 m/s, or 75 mi/hr, but from what has been said under GUST it must be understood that at all ordinary exposures a wind with an hourly velocity of 75 miles an hour will include gusts of considerably higher velocity, reaching a hundred miles an hour or more. The strongest recorded gust in the British Isles marked 103 mi/hr on the anemometer at Pendennis Castle on March 14, 1905.

Hydrometer.—An instrument for measuring the density or specific gravity of sea-water. (See *Marine Observer's Handbook*, M.O. Publication 218.)

Hydrosphere.—The name given to the layer of water of irregular shape and depth lying on the earth's surface, between the geosphere, or the solid earth below, and the atmosphere, the gaseous envelope above.

Hyetograph. — A self-recording RAIN-GAUGE, an instrument for recording automatically and graphically the fall of rain. (See *Observer's Handbook*.)

Hygrograph.—A self-recording HYGROMETER, an instrument for recording automatically the humidity of the atmosphere. Some form of hair-hygrometer is generally employed for the purpose.

Hygrometer.—An instrument for determining the humidity of the atmosphere. Almost all materials exposed to the weather are affected by the humidity of the air, so that it is easy to form a rough estimate of whether the air is damp or dry. Many different materials such as hair catgut, the awm or beard of the wild oat, flannel, have been used in instruments to give an indication of the state of the atmosphere in this respect. But for the purposes of meteorology there are three well-known forms of hygrometer : the hair-hygrometer, the indications of which depend upon the length of a hair or a bundle of hairs exposed to air of different states of moisture ; the dew-point hygrometer, in which a polished surface is artificially cooled until a deposit of dew is produced and the DEW-POINT determined ; and the PSYCHROMETER, or wet and dry bulb hygrometer, in which the temperatures of a bulb covered with moistened muslin and of a dry bulb close to it are read and the humidity determined by tables.

The psychrometer is in almost universal use at meteorological stations, as it is the least dependent upon the skill of the observer ; but a few hair-hygrometers are also employed for eye observations, and for automatic records either at the surface or in soundings with kites or BALLONS-SONDES the hair-hygrometer is generally used.

Hygroscope.—An instrument for showing whether the air is dry or damp. If its indications are sufficiently regular to permit of graduations, it can be made into a HYGROMETER. Any substance which is *hygroscopic*, that is to say, which is affected in shape, size, or appearance by the variations of moisture in the air can be used as a hygroscope. A bundle of seaweed is sometimes used, (the hygroscopic substance in that case is the salt) ; the ordinary " Jacky and Jenny " in a toy house with a catgut support is another example.

Hypsometer.—The word is derived from *hupsos*, and means an instrument for measuring height, but it is employed exclusively for apparatus for determining very precisely the temperature of the boiling point of water. That amounts to the same thing as measuring the pressure at which the water is boiled, because the boiling point depends upon the pressure of the atmosphere, and a table of the relation between the two makes the reading of the temperature equivalent to a reading of the barometer.

Table of the boiling point of water under pressures occurring in the atmosphere up to about 8000 *feet.*

Boiling Point.	Pressure.	
	Millimetres of mercury at 0°C. sea level, lat. 45°.	Millibars.
a.	mm.	mb.
374	787·67	1050·12
373	760·00	1013·23
372	733·16	977·45
371	707·13	942·74
370	681·88	909·08
369	657·40	876·44
368	633·66	844·79
367	610·64	814·10
366	588·33	784·36
365	566·71	755·54
364	545·77	727·62

From the pressure (with a *corresponding reading lower down, which may, should, or must be assumed*) the height can be computed.

The hypsometer has advantages for measuring heights as a substitute for a mercury barometer, which is a troublesome instrument to carry on a journey of exploration. With a pair of thermometers that have all modern improvements, and with careful manipulation, the temperature can be measured to one-thousandth of a degree, corresponding approximately with ·001 inch, or 03 millibar, that is to say, the pressure can be determined to the equivalent of one foot of height. That, however, is not to be attained by the inexpert traveller in a hurry.

Ice.—See p. 321.

Iceberg.—A large mass of ice that breaks away from the tongue of a glacier running into the sea and floats away. An account of the subject is given in the *Seaman's Handbook*. Icebergs drift with favourable winds and currents into latitudes of forty or fifty degrees. The final period of their life history is not very well understood ; there seems to be a sudden ending that is not accounted for. Nobody has apparently " stood by " an iceberg on the track of Atlantic steamers until the end came. Nor do we know through how many seasons, for example, a North Atlantic iceberg floats, or lies aground, between its " calving " and its dissolution. It probably weathers one season but collapses in the second.

Incandescence.—The spontaneous glow of a substance in consequence of its temperature. The word is now quite familiar in consequence of the incandescent or glow-lamp which is luminous on account of the temperature to which the carbon or metallic filament is raised by the electric current. Every substance becomes incandescent when heated to a sufficiently high temperature : thus lightning is presumably incandescent air, the sun incandescent vapour. The temperature at which incandescence begins is different with different substances, so the following figures are only roughly approximate :—Red hot covers a wide range beginning with 800a. Dull red is about 1000a. Cherry red 1200a. Orange 1400a. White hot 1500a. The sun 6000a. Carbon melts at 4300a, platinum at 2000a.

Index, the pointer which moves on the scale of an instrument and by which the reading is taken. Two indexes, the two hands or fingers, are required to tell the time by a watch, but only one index is required in reading the barometer. The index in this case is the top of the mercury column, so also in the ordinary thermometer the end of the mercury is the index. In a maximum thermometer the outer end of the detached thread of mercury is the index. In a minimum thermometer a special index is introduced into the spirit, which is transparent. In both these cases the index has to be set after one reading to make it ready for another.

In like manner every measuring instrument has its index.

Index-error. See ERROR.

Insolation.—Originally exposure to sunshine ; solarisation is also used in the same sense. It is now applied to the solar radiation received by terrestrial or planetary objects (Willis Moore).

The amount of solar-radiation which reaches any particular part of the earth's surface in any one day depends upon (1) the constant of solar-radiation, (2) the area of the intercepting surface and its inclination to the sun's rays, (3) the transparency of the atmosphere, (4) the position of the earth in its orbit. The following table quoted from Angot is taken from Willis Moore's *Descriptive Meteorology.*

Calculated Insolation Reaching Earth, assuming the mean coefficient of transparency of the atmosphere to be 0·6. (Angot).

Latitude.	January.	February.	March.	April.	May.	June.	July.	August.	September.	October.	November.	December.	Year.
N.													
90°	0·0	0·0	0·0	1·4	6·7	9·9	7·9	2·4	0·1	0·0	0·0	0·0	28·4
80°	0·0	0·0	0·2	2·7	7·5	10·3	8·5	3·8	0·5	0·0	0·0	0·0	33·5
60°	0·1	1·0	3·9	8·2	12·0	13·8	12·6	9·2	4·9	1·5	0·2	0·0	67·4
40°	3·3	5·7	9·4	12·9	15·3	16·2	15·6	13·5	10·2	6·6	3·8	2·7	115·2
20°	9·0	11·2	13·6	15·2	15·8	15·9	15·8	15·3	14·0	11·7	9·4	8·2	155·1
Equator	14·0	14·9	15·3	14·6	13·5	12·8	13·1	14·2	15·0	15·0	14·2	13·6	170·0
S.													
20°	16·8	15·9	13·9	11·2	8·8	7·7	8·3	10·5	13·1	15·3	16·6	17·0	155·1
40°	16·6	13·9	9·9	6·0	3·4	2·4	3·0	5·2	8·8	12·8	15·9	17·3	115·2
60°	13·4	9·2	4·4	1·3	0·1	0·0	0·1	0·8	3·4	7·8	12·3	14·6	67·4
80°	8·8	3·5	0·4	0·0	0·0	0·0	0·0	0·0	0·1	2·3	7·4	11·0	33·5
90°	8·3	2·1	0·0	0·0	0·0	0·0	0·0	0·0	0·0	1·0	6·5	10·5	28·4

The unit is the amount of energy that would be received on unit area at the equator in one day, at the equinox, with the sun at mean distance if the atmosphere were completely transparent. It is 458·4 times the solar constant, or in gramme·calories per minute 885, taking the solar constant to be 1·93.

Inversion. — An abbreviation for "inversion of temperature-gradient" (see GRADIENT). The temperature of the air generally gets lower with increasing height but occasionally the reverse is the case, and when the temperature increases with height there is said to be an "inversion".

There is an inversion at the top of a fog-layer, and generally at the top of other clouds of the stratus type. Inversions are shown in the diagram of variation of temperature with height in the upper air, p. 38, by the slope of the lines upwards towards the right instead of towards the left, which is the usual slope. In the troposphere inversions do not generally extend over any great range of height; the fall of temperature recovers its march until the lower boundary of the stratosphere is reached. At that layer there is generally a slight inversion beyond which the region is isothermal, so far as height is concerned. For that reason the lower boundary of the stratosphere is often called the "upper inversion". In some soundings with ballons-sondes from Batavia the inversion has been found to extend upwards for several kilometres from the commencement of the stratosphere.

It is important also to note that frequently in anti-cyclonic weather, and especially cold anticyclonic weather, there is often an inversion at the surface; the temperature increases upwards instead of decreasing.

Ion. — The name selected by Faraday for the component parts into which a chemical molecule is resolved in a solution by the electrolytic action of an electric current. Of the two component ions one is always electro-positive, and the other electro-negative. The electro-negative ions, consist of atoms of oxygen, chlorine or some other corresponding element or radicle, and the electro-positive ions consist of atoms of hydrogen, potassium, or some other metallic element or radicle. Each electro-positive ion is called a cation. It is charged with a definite quantity of positive electricity and travels with the electric current to the cathode, the conductor by which the current *leaves* the solution, while the electro-negative ion, called the anion, is charged with an equal quantity of negative electricity and travels against the electric current to the anode, the conductor by which the current *enters* the solution.

It is supposed that a solution which will conduct an electric current is ionised by the spontaneous dissociation of the components of its molecules and the consequent formation of free ions carrying their appropriate electric charges. In a solution, recombination and dissociation are constantly going on and the electric current causes the free ions charged with positive electricity to move slowly with the current and those charged with negative electricity to move against the current.

Similarly, a gas may conduct electricity to a less extent, but in the same way, as a solution when it contains free ions, which may be produced by the action of radio-active agents, ultra-violet light, very hot bodies, the combustion of flame and in other ways. The conduction of electricity through the atmosphere is now, therefore, attributed to the free ions which exist in it, and its capacity for conducting electricity is attributed to its ionisation.

The ions in the air may be atoms of hydrogen or oxygen, or they may be aggregates of those atoms with some other material.

A certain number of the ions in atmospheric air doubt-less arise from the radio-active materials in the soil. These materials give rise to an emanation, as it is called, which must gradually reach the surface through the pores of the soil. The supply will naturally depend on· the state of the soil, whether damp or dry, frozen or covered with snow, and presumably also on variations of the baro-metric pressure which promote or check the escape of emanation. Other ions must be produced by light from the sun. These will naturally chiefly arise at considerable heights above the ground, where sunlight is stronger and relatively richer in ultra-violet light than near the ground. In addition there seems to be some other powerful source at high altitudes, possibly some form of electrical radiation from the sun.

Ionisation.—See p. 322.

Iridescence or **Irisation,** words formed from *Iris,* the rainbow, to indicate the rainbow-like colours which are sometimes seen on the edges of clouds; tinted patches, generally of a delicate red and green, sometimes blue and yellow, occasionally seen on cirrus and cirro-cumulus clouds up to about 25° from the sun. They may be also seen at times on the edges of fracto-cumulus or strato-cumulus clouds. The boundary between the two tints is not a circle with the sun as centre, as in a CORONA, but rather tends to follow the outline of the cloud. They are probably not due to the refraction of light by water drops, which produces the colours of the rainbow, but to the diffraction of light scattered by the very small water drops, and are to be classed like the corona with the iridescence of the opal and the mother-of-pearl.

Diffraction-colours formed in artificial clouds in the

same way as in the corona, become more brilliant as the cloud gets older and the drops more uniform in size. Hence it seems probable that an iridescent cloud is an old cloud that has been drifting for some time.

Isabnormals. See ISANOMALIES.

Isanomalies.—This word is a combination of the prefix ISO- and the word ANOMALY, which, like the more common adjective *anomalous*, signifies departure or deviation from normal. The normals used for reference are obtained on various plans. Normals of temperature have been obtained by taking the general mean of the observed temperatures of successive parallels of latitude and thus assigning a normal temperature to each latitude ; isanomalies of temperature are then the departures of mean temperature for any place from the normal for its latitude; places that are relatively warm for their latitude have a positive anomaly, and places that are relatively cold for their latitude a negative one. Isanomalies are then lines on a map showing equality of departure of the average temperature of any place from the normal for its latitude.

There are, however, not many meteorological elements which can be said to have a normal value for latitude, and it is usual to employ as normals for any place the average or mean value for a long period of years.

In that case departures, or differences from the normal for the corresponding period, of the value for any one period, say a month or a year, are called ABNORMALS or abnormalities, and a chart showing equality of departure from the normal a chart of ISABNORMALS. Isabnormal is an objectionable compound because it is made up of a Greek prefix and a Latin body ; if the departures are to be called abnormals the lines of equal departure ought to be called equi-abnormals, so that the tendency is to use ISANOMALIES for lines of equal departure of a value from its long period average.

Isentropic.—Without change of ENTROPY (*q.v.*) generally equivalent in meaning to ADIABATIC.

Iso.—The prefix ISO- is the Greek equivalent of the Latin EQUI- and implies the setting out of lines on a chart or diagram to show the distribution of set values of some meteorological element. The words with this prefix can generally be interpreted 'by the reader on this basis: some examples are set out under the separate headings below.

Thus :—

·ISOBARS, from *baros,* are lines' on a chart showing equal barometric pressure.

ISOHELS, from *helios,* are lines showing equal duration of sunshine.

ISOHYETS, from *huetos,* are lines showing equal amounts of rainfall.

ISOPLETHS, from *plethos,* lines showing equal amounts of a meteorological element.

· The word *isogram* was recommended for this purpose by Sir Francis Galton.

ISOTHERMS, from *therme,* are lines showing equal temperatures.

Isobars.—If some of the air were removed from a room the pressure inside would be reduced and the pressure outside would force air through the windows and doors till the room was again filled with the normal amount of air. If over any area some of the air were by any means removed the pressure over that area would be reduced, and the pressure of the air in the surrounding districts would tend to force air into the region of deficient pressure. Such areas of deficient pressure are found to exist, but for the following reason the air does not actually flow into them. Anything moving above the surface of the earth will continue to move in a straight line if no force acts on it; but the earth in its rotation turns under the moving body; the moving body is therefore apparently deflected to the right in the Northern Hemisphere. This is true of a cannon-ball, and it is true of a moving current of air. Hence the wind does not actually blow into the area of low pressure; air from the North is deflected to the West side of the area, air from the West to the South side, and so on; the wind therefore instead of blowing straight in from all sides blows round an area of low pressure counterclockwise in the Northern Hemisphere. We thus have the apparent paradox of a force tending to push the air into the centre of the low pressure area while the air is actually moving round the centre at right-angles to the force that is acting on it. There are many examples of similar things in nature; the Earth's motion round the sun for instance; or the water in a basin when there is a hole in the centre from which the plug has been taken out; the slightest circular motion sets up a swirl, and the water moves round the basin at right-angles to the force of gravity which is tending to force it towards the hole.

In the case of an area of high pressure the air blows out from the high pressure, but it is deflected to the right as in the former case, with the result that the wind blows round the area of high pressure in a clockwise direction. In either case if you stand with your back to the wind the low pressure will be on your left hand, this is BUYS BALLOT'S LAW. In the Southern Hemisphere the reverse is the case.

If the observed heights of the BAROMETER (reduced to sea level) from a number of places are put on to a map and arrows are put in to represent the direction of the wind, we have a weather map which at first sight looks like a disordered collection of figures ; we may make it clearer, however, by drawing lines through places where the barometer stands at the same height ; thus we may draw one line through all places where the barometer stands at 1,015 mb., another through all places where it stands at 1,010, and so on. Such lines are called ISOBARS. It may happen that we cannot find any station where the barometer stands at say 1,015 mb., but if we find one where it stands at 1,016 and another where it stands at 1,014 we take it that the 1,015 line passes midway between the two stations. When the isobars are drawn in we can readily see the shapes of the areas of low and high pressure, and we see also that the wind blows in accordance with Buys Ballot's law. The areas of low pressure are called CYCLONES, DEPRESSIONS, or simply LOWS ; the areas of high pressure ANTICYCLONES, or HIGHS.

The isobars are analogous to contour lines on an ordinary map, the high pressures corresponding to the hills, the low pressures to the valleys. The moving air does not go straight from the highs to the lows, but it blows round the highs in a clockwise, and round the lows in a counter-clockwise direction. On the contours of the earth we may descend from a height of say 1000 feet to 500 feet by a gentle slope many miles in length, or in another place we may descend by a precipitous scarp ; in the former case a stream will run down sluggishly, in the second it will be a swift torrent full of rapids and waterfalls. So with the pressure ; we may travel a long way between a place where the barometer reads, say, 1020 millibars to another where it reads

1015 millibars, or we may have to go only a comparatively short distance. The steepness of the gradient on a map is measured by the distance between the contour lines ; the steepness of the barometric gradient is measured by the nearness of the isobars. The strength of the wind depends on the steepness of the barometric gradient, just as the velocity of the stream depends on the steepness of the slope, but the analogy is not quite perfect for the stream runs down the slope across the contour lines, whereas the wind blows nearly along the isobars with a slight inward curvature towards the low pressure. In the case of the wind close to the surface if the five-millibar isobars are 400 miles apart the barometric gradient is slight, and the wind will be about 10 miles per hour ; if the distance apart is 60 miles the gradient is steep, and the wind will be about 70 miles per hour. The wind calculated from the barometric gradient is called the GRADIENT WIND or, if no allowance is made for the curvature of the path of the air, the GEOSTROPHIC WIND ; it is in most cases the wind met with at or about 1500 feet ; nearer the surface, owing to the friction, the actual wind is less than the gradient wind. The gradient wind as stated depends principally on the distance apart of the isobars ; it is modified, however, to a small extent by the variations of density of the moving air and therefore by the height of the barometer and by the temperature ; a table is given on pp. 172–173 showing the geostrophic wind for various pressures and temperatures according to the formula of p. 136. The values are dependent upon the latitude and are given in the table for two latitudes 52° and 40°.

Further tables are given in the *Computer's Handbook* M.O. 223. Section II.

TABLE showing the distances apart in nautical miles of consecutive 10 mb. isobars corresponding with stated geostrophic wind-velocities at various pressures and temperatures in latitudes 52° and 40°.

NOTE.—The calculation of the geostrophic wind from the pressure gradient depends upon the density of the air and therefore upon the ratio of the pressure to the temperature. The figure for density of air is not generally available without a lengthy calculation, and in this table, which at best is only approximate, the distances apart in nautical miles on p. 173 are given for the pressures in the left hand compartment of the heading on this page and the temperatures corresponding thereto in the same horizontal line. The influence of humidity is disregarded.

Corrections:—For an increase of 1 mb. pressure SUBTRACT $\frac{1}{10}$ per cent. from the velocity; for 1a. ADD $\frac{1}{3}$ per cent.; for 1° in latitude SUBTRACT $1\frac{1}{3}$ per cent.

T|p.	·26	·27	·28	·29	·30	·26	·27	·28	·29	·30
Density g/m³	1,340	1,290	1,243	1,201	1,160	1,340	1,290	1,243	1,201	1,160
Pressure *p.*					Temperature θ.					
1,050 mb.	273	284	294	305	315	273	284	294	305	315
1,000 mb.	260	270	280	290	300	260	270	280	290	300
950 mb.	247	256	266	275	285	247	256	266	275	285

Geostrophic Wind Velocity.		Distances apart, in nautical miles, of consecutive 10 mb. isobars.										
		Latitude 52°.					Latitude 40°.				
m/s.	mi/hr.										
1	2·2	3,510	3,645	3,780	3,915	4,050	4,361	4,529	4,697	4,864	5,032
5	11·2	702	729	756	783	810	872	906	939	973	1,006
10	22·4	351	365	378	392	405	436	453	470	486	503
15	33·6	234	243	252	261	270	291	302	313	324	335
20	44·7	176	182	189	196	203	218	226	235	243	252
25	55·9	140	146	151	157	162	174	181	188	195	201
30	67·1	117	122	126	131	135	145	151	157	162	168
35	78·3	100	104	108	112	116	125	129	134	139	144
40	89·5	88	91	95	98	101	109	113	117	122	126
45	100·7	78	81	84	87	90	97	101	104	108	112
50	111·8	70	73	76	78	81	87	91	94	97	101

If we put down on the weather map besides the barometer readings and the wind arrows, the state of the weather
we shall see that in anticyclones it is usually fine, while
in the depressions it is rainy and cloudy on the East side,
and finer on the West side of each depression. The
weather in fact is intimately connected with the shape of
the isobars. As this is a most important fact in meteorology it will be well to consider a little more closely the
areas of high and low pressure.

A DEPRESSION is a part of the atmosphere where the barometer is lower than in the surrounding parts. (See Pl.
XI). The isobars round such an area are more or
less circular or oval, though there are often irregularities.
The size of a depression may vary enormously ; one may
cover only a part of an English county, another may fill the
whole space between our islands and the Arctic circle. Some
are much deeper than others ; a deep depression is one where
the barometer is very low near the centre ; a shallow depression is one where the barometer, though low near the
centre, is not very much lower than in the surrounding
districts. North of the Equator the wind blows round
the depression in a counter-clockwise direction, and the
steeper the barometric gradient, that is the deeper the
depression, the stronger is the wind. The sky is dull and
overcast on the east side of the depression, with rain near
the centre, especially heavy on the north-east side. Near
the centre in the region where there is an abrupt change
of wind direction from south on the east side, to north on
the west side of the depression, there is heavy rain and
often squalls. On the west side, in the region of northerly
or north-westerly winds, the cloud sheet is broken up into
detached clouds which get further apart, fewer, and less
rainy the further one goes from the centre.

Plate XI.
XIII   page 176

ANTICYCLONE.

DISTRIBUTION OF WEATHER, WIND, AND PRESSURE, 7 A.M. 17th NOVEMBER, 1915.

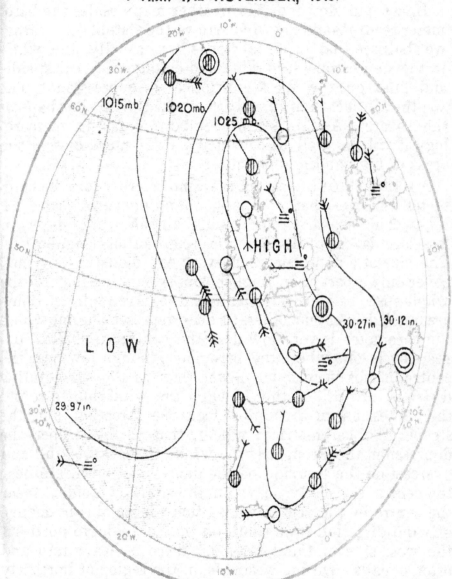

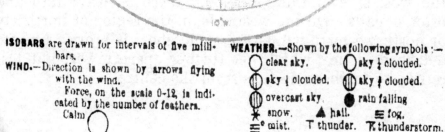

ISOBARS are drawn for intervals of five millibars.

WIND.—Direction is shown by arrows flying with the wind.

Force, on the scale 0-12, is indicated by the number of feathers.

Calm

WEATHER.—Shown by the following symbols :—

clear sky.   sky ¼ clouded.
sky ½ clouded.   sky ¾ clouded.
overcast sky.   rain falling
snow.   hail.   fog.
mist.   T thunder.   thunderstorm.

COL.

DISTRIBUTION OF WEATHER, WIND, AND PRESSURE, 7 A.M. 1st MAY, 1915.

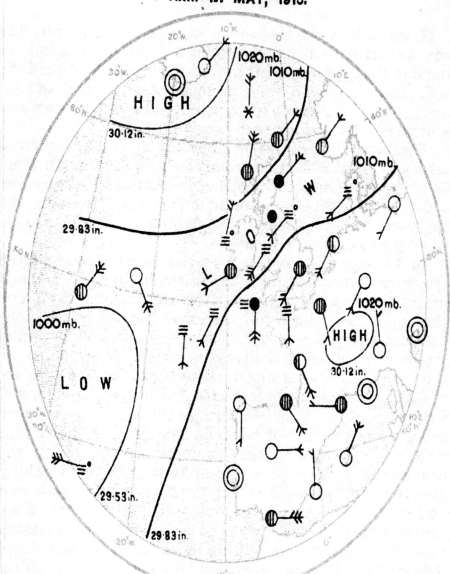

ISOBARS are drawn for intervals of ten millibars.

WIND.—Direction is shown by arrows flying with the wind.

Force, on the scale 0-12, is indicated by the number of feathers

Calm ○

WEATHER.—Shown by the following symbols :—

○ clear sky.	◐ sky ½ clouded.
◓ sky ¼ clouded.	◓ sky ¾ clouded.
◑ overcast sky.	● rain falling
✳ snow.	▲ hail.	≡ fog.
≡° mist.	T thunder.	⊼ thunderstorm

Wy. & S., M.O. Press, S.W. 7.

Ps. 1130. 26779. 464. 6000 1/18.

If we note a depression on a weather map for one day we shall usually find that on the map for the following day the depression has moved in an easterly direction; a depression seldom remains long in one place, and its drift is usually towards some point between north-east and south-east, though there are exceptions.

Since the air in front of a depression is coming from the south, and in the rear from the north, there will often be a great difference of temperature between the two sides. This is particularly noticeable in winter when the approach of a depression is heralded by warm, and its passing away by cold weather.

As the depression moves it carries its weather and wind system with it, so that an observer situated on its track would have the following sequence of weather :—The barometer begins to fall, the wind becomes southerly, the sky becomes overcast and the weather muggy, and in winter the temperature is well above the normal ; the clouds get thicker, the wind stronger, rain begins to fall ; as the centre approaches the barometer gets lower, the wind gets stronger and the rain heavier ; as the centre passes over there are often gusts of wind or squalls, with heavy rain, " clearing showers " ; the barometer ceases to fall and commences to rise ; the clouds show signs of breaking, and the wind changes round to the north or north-west and often blows more strongly than it did before the centre passed ; as the centre moves away the wind lessens, the rain ceases, or only occurs in showers, the sky clears. The rate at which these changes take place depends on the size of the depression and its rate of travel ; 24 hours is an ordinary time for such changes to be gone through, but it may be longer and it may be shorter. The above sequence of weather is a typical one, but there are many differences in individual depressions; some are rainy without much wind, others bring much wind, but not much rain.

The above typical sequence of weather will only be experienced by an observer who is on the track of the centre of the depression. One further south will have south-westerly winds at first, with dull weather, becoming rainy; the wind will gradually veer to the west when the centre is passing to the north, the barometer will begin to rise and the wind will veer further to the north-west as the centre passes away. An observer a long way from the track of the centre will perhaps only experience a slight fall of the barometer, with cloudy weather.

An observer north of the track will have south-easterly or easterly winds at first, with probably much rain; the wind will back to the north-east or north as the centre passes to the south. The winds on the north side of a depression are usually less strong than those on the south side, the isobars on the polar side being less crowded together than those on the equatorial side. Thus a depression passing on the south gives less wind, but probably more persistent rain, than one passing on the north. Gloomy days with an east or north-east wind, and rain all day, are usually due to depressions passing to the south of the observer. The easterly current on the north side of a depression frequently brings snow in winter.

If high clouds are visible they will frequently be seen to be moving away from the centre of low pressure; thus a south wind on the surface, with high clouds moving from the west, is a sure sign of the existence of a depression to the west.

Plate XIII.
XI page 174

DEPRESSION.

DISTRIBUTION OF WEATHER, WIND, AND PRESSURE,
6 P.M. 13th FEBRUARY, 1915.

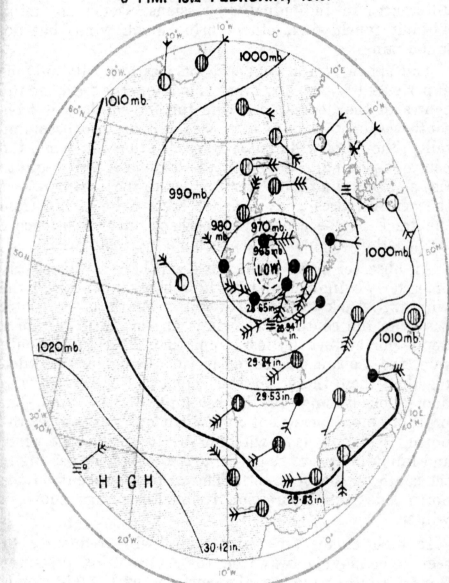

ISOBARS are drawn for intervals of ten millibars.

WIND.— Direction is shown by arrows flying
with the wind.

Force, on the scale 0-12, is indicated by the number of feathers.

Calm

WEATHER.—Shown by the following symbols :—

○ clear sky.   ◐ sky ½ clouded.
◑ sky ¼ clouded.   ◒ sky ¾ clouded.
◍ overcast sky.   ● rain falling
✳ snow.   ▲ hail.   ≡ fog.
≡• mist.   T thunder.   ℞ thunderstorm

Plate XIV.

V-SHAPED DEPRESSION.

DISTRIBUTION OF WEATHER, WIND, AND PRESSURE,
7 A.M. 8th OCTOBER, 1915.

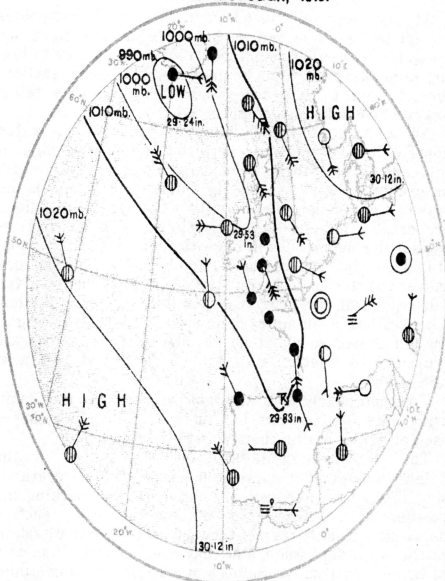

ISOBARS are drawn for intervals of ten milli-
    bars.

WIND.—Direction is shown by arrows flying
    with the wind.
        Force, on the scale 0–12, is indi-
    cated by the number of feathers.
        Calm ◯

WEATHER.—Shown by the following symbols :—
    ◯ clear sky.   ◖ sky ¼ clouded.
    ◐ sky ½ clouded.   ◑ sky ¾ clouded.
    ◉ overcast sky.   ● rain falling
    ✳ snow.   ▲ hail.   ≡ fog.
    ≡° mist.   T thunder.   ℞ thunderstorm

At times, especially in summer, very small depressions are apt to form ; several such depressions are sometimes seen on the weather map for the same day ; they follow the same laws as large depressions, but being shallow they do not usually occasion much wind; they bring heavy rains and thunderstorms in the summer.

An ANTICYCLONE, or high-pressure system, is the contrary to a depression ; here the barometer is high in the centre, the isobars are usually more or less circular or oval, they are also usually further apart than is the case in a depression, therefore the winds in an anticyclone are usually lighter. An anticyclone is not so small as the smaller depressions, though the large ones may equal it in size. It often covers a large area. An anticyclone moves but slowly and irregularly ; it may remain in the same position for many days, or even weeks, at a time. The weather in an anticyclone is usually fine and bright, though extensive cloud sheets may form, and fogs are prevalent in winter ; rain seldom falls, and persistent rain never.

The depression and the anticyclone are the main arrangements of isobars, but there are five other shapes each of which has its characteristic weather.

The SECONDARY DEPRESSION.—Sometimes in the neighbourhood of a depression, usually on its southern side, the isobars take a slight bend outwards, marking the position of a small centre of low pressure ; such a depression usually travels forward in the same direction as the main depression, and may even outstrip it in rate of travel. It usually produces much rain, and sometimes much wind. In the summer secondary depressions are

---

* Illustrations of the various types of isobars are given under the respective headings ANTICYCLONE, SECONDARY, &c.

often very shallow, and resemble the shallow depressions already noticed ; like them they occasion heavy rain and thunderstorms. When they are secondary to deep depressions they often cause a crowding together of the isobars on their southern side, and thus occasion strong winds.

The V-SHAPED DEPRESSION.—This is a further extension of the Secondary ; the isobars, instead of bulging out slightly, extend out a long way in the form of the letter V. The wind on the east side is from a southerly point, that on the west side from a northerly point, in accordance with Buys Ballot's law ; the east side is a region of cloud and rain, often heavy driving rain ; over the central line there is an abrupt change, very fine weather being experienced on the west side. As the V-shaped depression moves over any place the observer experiences southerly winds and driving rain, both wind and rain becoming stronger as the central line approaches ; as it passes over there is a sudden change of wind to a northerly point ; the rain stops, and the sky rapidly clears ; the central line is often a region of heavy squalls ; there is a marked fall of temperature with the passage of the central line. See Plate XV.

WEDGE OF HIGH PRESSURE.—Between two depressions there is often a region of high pressure where the isobars are shaped like an inverted V ; the high-pressure wedge usually extends from an anticyclone poleward between two depressions that are skirting the northern edge of the high pressure. The wedge moves forward in an easterly direction between the two depressions ; it is in fact merely the relatively high pressure between the depressions. The front of the wedge is often a region of extremely fine weather with northerly winds, rapidly becoming light as

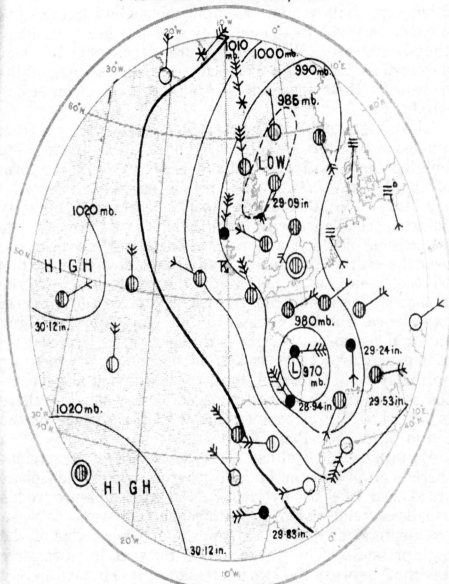

Plate XV XII page 176

SECONDARY DEPRESSION.

DISTRIBUTION OF WEATHER, WIND, AND PRESSURE,
7 A.M. 22nd FEBRUARY, 1915.

ISOBARS are drawn for intervals of ten millibars.

WIND.—Direction is shown by arrows flying with the wind.

Force, on the scale 0-12, is indicated by the number of feathers.

Calm

WEATHER.—Shown by the following symbols:—

clear sky.
sky ¼ clouded.
sky ½ clouded.
sky ¾ clouded.
overcast sky.
rain falling
snow.
hail.
fog.
mist.
thunder.
thunderstorm

Plate XVI.

WEDGE.

DISTRIBUTION OF WEATHER, WIND, AND PRESSURE, 7 A.M. 9th DECEMBER, 1915.

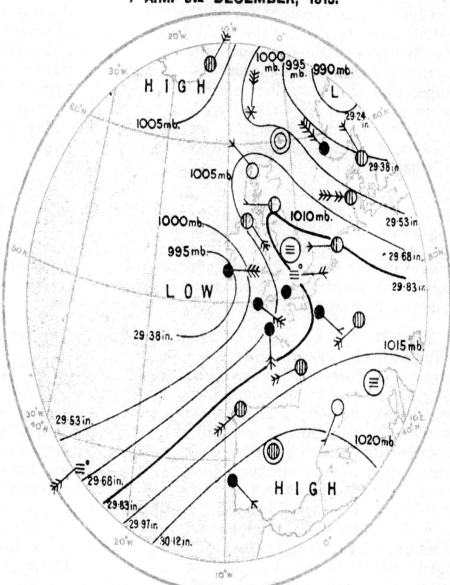

ISOBARS are drawn for intervals of five millibars.

WIND.—Direction is shown by arrows flying
with the wind.

Force, on the scale 0–12, is indicated by the number of feathers.

Calm

WEATHER.—Shown by the following symbols :—

○ clear sky.   ◐ sky ¼ clouded.

◑ sky ½ clouded.   ◕ sky ¾ clouded.

◉ overcast sky   ● rain falling

✳ snow,   ▲ hail.   ≡ fog.

≡° mist,   T thunder.   ℞ thunderstorm.

the central line approaches ; on the central line there is a calm ; after its passage the wind backs to the south-west, clouds begin to come up, and rain usually follows rapidly as the new depression approaches. After the passage of a depression, if the weather clears up very rapidly and the wind falls quickly, it is usually the sign of the approach of a wedge ; in such a case very fine weather may be forecasted for a few hours, followed again by bad weather. " It has cleared up too quickly to last."

The COL.—A col is a region between two anticyclones, and may be likened to a mountain pass between two higher peaks. Since the wind is blowing round the two anticyclones in a clockwise direction the col is a region where light airs from very different directions are brought into close proximity. This gives conditions for fog in cold weather, and for thunderstorms in hot weather.

STRAIGHT ISOBARS.— Occasionally the isobars run straight over a very considerable area. In these latitudes straight isobars usually have the lowest pressure to the North, and thus in accordance with Buys Ballot's law the winds are westerly. There may be a great diversity of weather in a region of straight isobars, for it must be remembered that the northern side extends to a low-pressure region and the southern side to an anticyclone ; therefore in the Northern region we get much cloud and some rain, in the Southern clear skies and fine weather.

Major Gold, D.S.O., Commandant of the Meteorological Section, G.H.Q.. makes the following comments, which fairly illustrate the difficulty of making positive statements about the relation of weather to isobars :

Straight Isobars.—If the anticyclone is a warm one, the Southern side, also, gets cloudy skies and rainy weather, see January 6th, 1916,

January 4th, 5th, 1914, January 2nd, 10th, 11th, 12th, 17th, 18th, 1910. Perhaps there is a seasonal variation in the weather in straight isobars. In January they nearly always seem to get rain right to the edge of the anticyclone. Straight W. to E. isobars usually mean cool or moderate temperature in Summer and rather mild in Winter. One gets also straight isobars running from S. to N. (See January, 1913 : not much rain but some cloud and mist). Thunderstorm weather when it is very warm to the South.

Also N. to S. straight isobars (January 2nd, 12th. 1911 ; December, 1913 ; squally. sno﹅, hail and sleet weather in winter. September 29th. 30th, October 2nd. 3rd, 4th, 1915 ; showery; thunder in Flanders). **Wedge** : when the dominant anticyclone is to the North, it is more stable than the wedge proper (which is very unstable as a rule) and gives N. winds on the E. side and E. winds on the W. side.

It is the business of the forecaster who has a weather map before him to note the arrangements of the isobars, and the positions of high and low pressure ; he must note whether the low-pressure systems are main depressions, secondaries, or V-shaped depressions ; he has to judge from the map the directions in which the disturbances are likely to travel, and, knowing the weather which each kind brings, to warn different districts what wind and what kind of weather they are to expect. In judging the direction of travel the meteorologist is guided by certain rules and by past experience ; a depression usually travels from some point between south-west and north-west to some point between north-east and south-east ; they frequently skirt the Western seaboard of Europe ; they do not pass through anticyclones ; when an anticyclone is situated to the West of these islands depressions do not come in from the Atlantic, but there is then a tendency for depressions to pass from North to South down our Eastern coasts. The meteorologist must also forecast what temperatures are likely ; in the region of Easterly winds on the North side of a depression cold weather is likely, with snów in winter; the approach of a depression from the west during a frost in winter is sure to bring about a thaw on the southern side of its path. The endless varieties of weather must, as far as possible, be foreseen by the meteorologist with the map before him.

The solitary observer who has no means of making a map may however recognise some of the signs of the approach of certain types of weather. Remembering BUYS BALLOT'S LAW, and watching his barometer, he may recognise the approach of a depression, and may even on many occasions roughly plot out its track ; he may often tell whether the fine weather is of an anticyclonic type, or whether it is the result of a wedge and therefore only transitory. In short, if he has a knowledge of the principles disclosed by weather maps and has a barometer he will be in a much better position than his neighbours to forecast the weather from local manifestations.

Isothermal—of equal temperature. An isothermal line is a line of equal temperature, and, therefore, is the same as isotherm.

Isothermal is frequently used in meteorological writings on the upper air for the so-called "isothermal layer" by which is meant the layer indicated in the records of all ballons-sondes, of sufficient altitude, by the sudden cessation of fall of temperature with height and generally by a slight INVERSION (see also GRADIENT) followed by practical uniformity of temperature. The layer is not really isothermal. Its temperature on the occasions when simultaneous soundings have been secured at different places shows a temperature-gradient in the stricter sense of difference of temperature at the same level, and an inspection of the diagram reproduced under BALLON-SONDE,

representing the results of a large number of soundings
in the British Isles, shows that the range of temperature
at the highest layer is greater than the range at the surface.
But it is also clear from the diagram that in each single
sounding the balloon reaches a region where the thermometer ceases to fall. To avoid the misconception which
the use of the word isothermal for this region would imply,
M. Teisserenc de Bort, who was largely instrumental
in its discovery, coined the word stratosphere, while he
gave the name of troposphere to the region below. These
names have now been generally adopted. The stratosphere has also been called the advective region, in
contradistinction with the convective region below it.

We are still without any effective explanation of the
origin of differences of temperature which are found in
the stratosphere ; they must probably be classed among
the most fundamental characteristics of the general
circulation of the atmosphere and among the primary
causes of the changes of weather, but hardly any light has
been thrown on the mechanism of the process.

Katabatic.—Referring to the downward motion of air
due to convection. A local cold wind is called katabatic if
it is caused by the gravitation of cold air off high ground ;
such a wind may have no relation to the distribution of
atmospheric pressure. See Bora and Breeze.

Khamsin.—A hot, dry wind which passes over the
Egyptian plain from the southward, forming the front of
depressions passing eastward along the Eastern Mediterranean, while there is an area of high pressure to the
East of the Nile in Middle Egypt.

Kilometre.—A length of one thousand metres, approximately five-eighths of a mile.

Lake.—The water that collects in a hollow or depression in the land's surface. In meteorology a lake serves the purpose of a huge rain-gauge, and, subject to some allowance·for lag and evaporation, indicates the variations in the collective rainfall of the area which it drains. For example, the Victoria Nyanza under the equator, apart from gradual fluctuations of level which in the last twenty years have followed closely the variations in the SUNSPOT-NUMBERS (*q.v.*), has a seasonal variation which is connected with the seasonal rainfall of the spring and early summer and of the late autumn in equatorial Africa. (see CLIMATIC TABLES).

Land-Breeze.—A light wind passing across a coast line from the land, seaward. It generally begins with the setting in of coolness in the evening and disappears with the advance of temperature over the land in the day time, or is replaced by a sea-breeze, and it is therefore regarded as a katabatic wind due to convection between the colder layer over the earth and a warmer layer over the sea. In sunny weather there is a large diurnal change of temperature in the land and hardly any in the sea, and the direction of the wind is regarded as alternating with the direction of the temperature-gradient along the level.

Lapse, from the Latin *lapsus*, a slip, a word suggested for use instead of gradient (which is from *gradus* a step) to denote the loss of temperature or pressure of the atmosphere with height. So that *lapse-rate*, or *lapse-ratio*, for temperature will be the fall of temperature per kilometre of height. A *lapse-line* will be a line representing the change of temperature with height. The word is connected with the word *labile* which means liable to slip, and applies technically to the peculiar state of equilibrium of an isentropic, or thoroughly churned atmosphere (see ENTROPY). The equilibrium is neither stable nor unstable, that is to say, if it is disturbed by slow mechanical process it will, when left to itself, neither go back to its original state nor go forward, but remain indifferent, in its displaced condition.

In these circumstances the air will have the greatest possible lapse-rate of temperature short of instability.

The lapse rate of temperature may change its sign and indicate an increase of temperature with height. This apparently always happens in and above a layer of fog, and not infrequently in and above other forms of cloud. In that case the lapse-line showing the change of temperature with height will have a slope to higher temperature upward, opposite from and therefore easily distinguished from the ordinary slope to lower temperature upward. We refer to that state as a *recovery*, instead of using the term "inversion of temperature-gradient" which is used at present and is often shortened to "inversion." Generally speaking, the recovery is only temporary in the journey upward and is followed by a relapse with perhaps a different lapse-rate, unless the point has been reached at which the fall of temperature with height ceases. That is the boundary between the stratosphere and the troposphere. We may call that point on the lapse-line the *lapse-limit* or TROPOPAUSE.

The shape of a lapse-line is a very important index of the condition of the upper air; it has often been determined by the results obtained with a ballon-sonde. The normal average shape has a lapse rather less than that of the isentropić atmosphere of saturated air, or almost one half of the "adiabatic gradient" for dry air.

The investigation of the air near the sea surface during fog off the Banks, carried out on the "Scotia," has shown that the effect of the mixing of the air of the surface over the cold water is to replace the normal lapse-line at the lower end by a line which shows a gradual recovery of temperature from the cold surface to the undisturbed condition at a kilometre more or less in height. In the lower, or colder, part the water-vapour is condensed in fog.

It would appear that in a region where convection is going on over an extended area there must be an isentropic lapse-rate, that the process of the gradual ascent of warmed air is a gradual formation of a thicker isentropic layer. An isentropic lapse-rate seems also to be indicated when mixing takes place in the surface layers owing to turbulence over water which is *not less warm* than the air in contact with it.

Lenticular.—In shape like a lens or lentil. The word is used to identify a cloud of characteristic shape formed by a large mass of clustered cloudlets which is apparently disposed horizontally, has well-defined edges, a pointed end and broad middle or base. Sometimes the cloud becomes thin in the broad part and gives one the impression of a horizontal bow or horse-shoe of cloud, foreshortened by being seen from a distant point underneath it.

Level.—A surface is level if it is everywhere at right-angles to the force of gravity which is indicated by the plumb-line. When a table is not level the force of gravity makes things roll towards the lower edge, but when we are considering areas so large that the curvature of the earth has to be allowed for, the words higher or lower have no meaning unless we can refer the heights to some "level" surface accepted as a datum. The accurate comparison of levels in different regions of the earth is a problem of the greatest refinement and delicacy. Part of the problem is to determine whether the level of the sea, apart from any disturbance due to waves, is the same all over the world or not. For example, it used to be a debatable question if a cut were made across the Isthmus of Panama from the Atlantic to the Pacific, whether the water would flow from the Atlantic to the Pacific or *vice versâ.* That question has doubtless been solved by the accurate levelling of the engineers of the Panama Canal. On land, levels can be set out with great accuracy by means of a spirit-level, but allowance has to be made for the curvature of the earth. Land-levels in Great Britain are referred to the ordnance datum which is the assumed mean level of the sea at Liverpool, and is 0·650 ft. below the mean level of the sea of the British Isles, and in Ireland to low water of spring tides in Dublin Bay, which is 21 ft. below a mark on the base of Poolbeg lighthouse. The datum in mariners' charts is usually "low water ordinary spring tides."

Tidal and river levels in Great Britain are usually referred to Trinity High Water (T.H.W.) 12·47 ft. above Ordnance Datum.

Lightning.—The flash of a discharge of electricity between two clouds or between a cloud and the earth. A distinction is drawn between "forked" lightning, in which the path of the actual discharge is visible, and "sheet" lightning, in which all that is seen is the flash of illuminated clouds and which is attributed to the light of a discharge of which the actual path is not visible.

Since the introduction of photography many photographs of lightning have been obtained, and in general character they cannot be distinguished from photographs of electric discharges of six inches or more in length which are obtained in a laboratory, but the varieties of form of lightning discharges are very numerous. Frequently a flash shows many branches, especially the upper part of a flash between the clouds and the earth. Among a collection of photographs thrown upon a lantern screen, Dr. W. J. S. Lockyer once interpolated a photograph of the River Amazon and its tributaries, taken from a map, and the photograph was accepted without comment as a picture of lightning.

No satisfactory evidence has yet been produced as to what limits or defines the portion of the atmosphere which is freed from electric stress by a discharge of lightning, nor how the path of the discharge is selected.

Lightning-conductors, which are metal rods leading from the salient points of buildings to conductors buried in moist earth, have been used since the time of Benjamin Franklin to protect buildings from damage by lightning. A good deal of attention was devoted to the method of operation of lightning-conductors, especially by Sir Oliver Lodge, whose lectures before the Society of Arts are the best source of information on the subject.

The chief use of conductors is supposed to be the relief of stress in the immediate neighbourhood of a building by the so-called silent or brush-discharges from its exposed points. These brush-discharges are often visible in snow storms as discharges from the yards and points of ships or from an ice-axe and other projecting points in high mountains. The phenomenon is known as Corposants, or St. Elmo's fire. For PROTECTION AGAINST LIGHTNING see p. 325.

Line-Squall.—A squall of wind, accompanied by rain or hail, associated with a sudden drop of temperature and the passing of a long line or arch of dark cloud. The sequence of events as represented on recording meteorological instruments is one of the most clearly defined and easily recognised of all types of weather. There is a sudden rise of the mercury in the barometer by about 2 mb. (less than ·1 in.), a veer of wind through about 8 points, a simultaneous fall of temperature as much as 5° to 10°C., or 10° to 20°F., a sudden squall of wind, sometimes of great violence, lasting for a few minutes.

The sequence of phenomena is represented by the sketches made by Mr. G. A. Clarke, of Aberdeen Observatory, with the accompanying records, which are reproduced in figure 1. The four sketches of the line of dark cloud are made at intervals of 2 minutes, and the set represent 6 minutes in the life-history of the cloud.

The line of the squall, which is marked locally by the line or arch of the cloud, often extends across the country for hundreds of miles and represents the sudden transition from a southerly wind to a westerly wind, or from a southerly type of weather to a westerly type. The cloud appears to be due to convection between the cold westerly current and the warmer southerly current; the squall is therefore probably katabatic in its origin, and its violence on the actual passing of the cloud accounted for in that way; it represents the dash forward of a breaking wave, or more strictly speaking, of the water of a broken wave.

The phenomenon has been studied in the Meteorological Office during the past 10 years. A short account of the results of the investigations is given in Shaw's *Forecasting Weather.*

Line Squall : Figure 1.

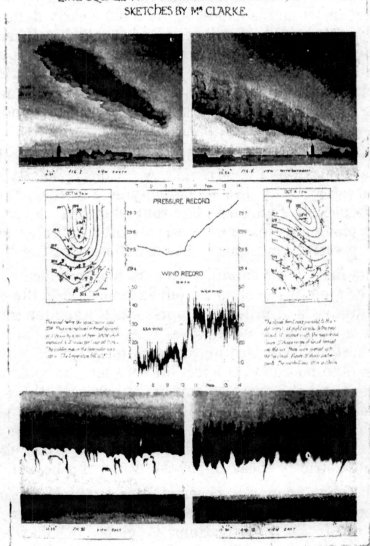

Line squalls frequently occur at the time of the passage of the TROUGH of a deep depression when the transition from southerly wind to westerly wind takes place suddenly. They also occur as a preliminary to a thunder-storm, and in such cases the wind of the squall is sometimes very destructive. They form the most serious danger to aircraft; at the same time, their characteristics lend themselves to forecasting with unusual precision provided their existence is once identified, because the line travels across the country with a very definite velocity.

Special arrangements are therefore made to obtain notifications of the passage of a line squall over the stations at the outside edge of our area.

Liquid.—The name given to a class of fluids. The peculiar property of a liquid is that a limited quantity poured into a sufficiently large vessel forms a definite and permanent layer with a free surface. Gases can also be poured from one vessel to another, but unlike liquids the boundary between the heavy gas at the bottom and the lighter gas above it is obliterated in time and a complete mixture of gases results; with a liquid the well defined surface of separation remains. Liquids are of all degrees of mobility from pitch which moves only inches in a month, through the stages of treacle, and glycerine, which visibly move, but take time, to water or ether which move at once on tilting and can be " shaken up."

Low, used to denote a region of low pressure, in the same way as HIGH is used for the region of high pressure : a depression. See also ISOBARS.

Lunar dependent upon *luna*, the moon ; thus a

lunar rainbow is a rainbow formed by the rays of the moon, a lunar cycle a cycle dependent upon the moon's motion. A month is really, from its name, a lunar cycle, but the introduction of a calendar month makes it necessary to draw a distinction between it and the lunar month, which is the period from new moon to new moon. In astronomy it is called the synodic month, and is equal to 29·5306 days. The endeavour to bring the month or the revolution of the moon round the earth into relation with the year or the revolution of the earth round the sun, has given rise to the differences of calendar which have been or are in use.

Mackerel Sky.—A sky covered with cirro-cumulus clouds arranged in a somewhat regular pattern, and showing blue sky in the gaps. See CIRRO-CUMULUS and CLOUDS.

Magnetic Needle.—A strip of steel permanently magnetised and provided with an agate cup for balancing on a point, like the needle of a compass. See COMPASS.

Mammato - cumulus. — When low clouds have rounded projections, or pap-like protuberances, from their under surface the term mammato-cumulus is applied to them. They are appropriate to the disturbed atmospheric conditions which accompany the close of a thunderstorm. An example is given in the accompanying illustration, obtained by Captain Cave at Ditcham Park. They do not occur often in England and never persist for long. Their relation to cumulus clouds in the ordinary sense is not

Mammato Cumulus (Festoon Cloud) after thunderstorm in August, 1915.

This photograph is reproduced in illustration of the commotion which occurs in the atmosphere in the various stages of a thunderstorm. It may be taken as the sequel to the illustration of the Cumulo-Nimbus cloud shown in figure 1 reproduced under CLOUD. The cumulo-nimbus is a thundercloud approaching, the mammato cumulus a thunderstorm receding.

apparent. Both are bulging clouds, but in these the bulging is downward, while in ordinary cumulus it is upward.

Mares' tails.—A popular term used to describe cirrus cloud, in which the thread-like filaments are arranged in the form of fans or plumes. See CIRRUS.

Maximum.—The highest reading of an instrument during a given period. The context generally shows the period to which reference is made. An instrument, like a maximum thermometer, is often designed for the purpose of giving the highest reading that has occurred since it was last read. The term "absolute maximum" is also used, the meaning of which is generally clear from the context, but see ABSOLUTE EXTREMES.

Mean.—The mean value of a set of values is the number formed by adding all the individual values together and dividing the sum by the number of values. In some cases there is an ambiguity unless the context makes it clear how the values are classified. For example, the mean temperature of the atmosphere lying over a certain place might indicate the arithmetical mean of the temperatures taken at equal intervals of height, or at equal intervals of pressure, going upwards. See also AVERAGE.

Meniscus.—The curved upper surface of liquid in a tube. If the tube is of narrow bore the curvature is pronounced, and in estimating the height of the liquid column, allowance must be made for it. In the case of

water, the meniscus, when viewed horizontally against
the light, appears as a dark belt. The upper edge
represents the highest point to which the water is drawn
up against the glass, and the lower edge the lower part
of the surface out in the middle of the tube. When the
tube is broad like the measuring glass of a raingauge, the
bottom edge should be used in reading; but in narrow
tubes the mid-point would be more suitable. Mercury
has a convex upper surface and in the case of the barometer the index is adjusted to the top of the meniscus.

Mercury.—Mercury is a metallic element of great
value in the construction of meteorological instruments.
In the mercurial barometer its great density enables the
length of the instrument to be made moderate, while the
low pressure of its vapour at ordinary temperatures makes
possible a nearly perfect vacuum in the space above the
top of the barometric column. In the mercury thermometer there is no risk of condensation in the upper end
of the stem, as in the case of the spirit thermometer.

Specific gravity = 13·5955 at 273a.
Specific heat   = 0·0335 at 273a.
Freezing point = 234·2a.

Meteor.—A meteor, or shooting star, is a fragment of
solid material entering the upper regions of the atmosphere from outer space and visible by its own luminosity.
The luminosity is attributed to incandescence due to the
compression of the air in front of the meteor. (See
ADIABATIC.) A large meteor may leave a luminous trail
that persists for half-an-hour or longer.

Accurate determinations of the track of the meteor by reference to the constellations and of the different positions of the trail, by observers in different parts of the country, may enable the height of the streak, and the velocity of the lofty air currents containing it to be determined. From the results it has been conjectured that the height to which the atmosphere extends with sufficient density to retard the speed of meteors is 300 k. (188 miles).

Meteorograph.—A self-recording instrument which gives an automatic record of two or more of the ordinary meteorological elements. Of late the term has been more generally applied to the instruments that are attached to kites or small balloons and sent up to ascertain the pressure, temperature and humidity of the upper atmosphere.

Meteorology.—The science of the atmosphere. The word "meteor" from which the name is derived has now acquired a restricted meaning. It can be, and sometimes is, used for any atmospheric phenomenon.

Metre.—The unit of length in the metric system. 1 metre $= 39 \cdot 37$ inches $= 3 \cdot 281$ feet.

Microbarograph. — An instrument designed for recording small and rapid variations of atmospheric pressure. It consists of an airtight reservoir of ample size containing air, and the difference of the external atmospheric pressure and the internal pressure in the reservoir is made to leave a record on a drum driven by clockwork. The reservoir is well protected from changes of temperature by a thick covering of felt or other non-conducting material, and it is also provided with a small leak, the magnitude of which can be adjusted. If the external pressure changes slowly the leak allows the internal pressure to follow it closely, but as the leak is small, the internal pressure cannot adjust itself rapidly to any sudden changes in the external pressure, and consequently a record of such changes is obtained.

Millibar.—The thousandth part of a BAR, which is the meteorological unit of atmospheric pressure on the C.G.S. system. Since the " bar " is equal to a pressure of one megadyne per square centimetre, *i.e.*, to 1,000,000 dynes per square centimetre, a millibar is equivalent to 1,000 dynes per square centimetre.* The millibar has been in general use in the Meteorological Office since May 1st, 1914. The principal advantage of using a unit of this type is that a statement of atmospheric pressure as a certain number of millibars is perfectly definite. According to the older practice that a separate unit had to be used for *length* in reading the height of the mercury in the barometer, generally the inch or the millimetre, but this

---

* It should be explained here that a megadyne is a measure of force. The dyne is the unit force of the C.G.S. system of units, and stands for the force which produces unit acceleration in one gramme. As the force of gravity is the most familiarly known of all forces, we may say tha the force of one dyne differs but little from the weight of a milligramme, and a megadyne stands in the same relation to the weight of a kilogramme. The precise numerical relation is dependent upon locality, because the weight of a body, that is, the force which gravity exerts on it, depends upon latitude and the distance from the Earth's centre. At sea-level, in latitude 45°, the gramme weighs 980·6 dynes, the kilogramme 0·9806 megadynes.

length is not a measure of the atmospheric pressure until the density of the mercury, the temperature of the scale and the value of gravity at the place are allowed for. The "millibar" on the other hand can only be used for *pressure.* If a barometer graduated in the C.G.S. system is set up at any place, there is a definite temperature called the *fiducial temperature* at which the scale reading of the mercury column gives the pressure of the air in millibars; a correction must be applied to the reading when the temperature of the instrument is not the fiducial temperature. (See *Observer's Handbook.*)

1,000 millibars are equivalent to the pressure of a column of mercury 750·1 millimetres (29·531 inches) high at 0° C. (273a.) in latitude 45°.

Millimetre. — The thousandth part of a metre. 25·4 mm. = 1 inch.

Minimum.—The opposite of maximum. See MAXIMUM.

Mirage.—The image of an object which is seen displaced, upwards or downwards, usually vertically, by the REFRACTION of the rays of light in their passage through layers of air of different densities near the ground. Where the density of the layers of air decreases, from the ground upwards, more rapidly than the normal rate, as it does when the ground is covered with a layer of very cold air, the rays of light are bent towards the earth and the image is therefore seen raised above the object, which may even be below the horizon at the time.

If the density increases rapidly upwards at the ground, as it does over highly heated deserts, the rays are bent upwards and the image is formed below the object. In its commonest form Mirage has the appearance of a sheet of water, often surrounded by banks, reeds and other objects. In this case what appears to be a sheet of water is the image of the sky behind the object at which the observer is looking, the rays of light being totally reflected from the layer of heated air which is in contact with the ground. The banks, reeds, &c., are the images of various objects, repeated with more or less distortion by being viewed through layers of air of different and varying density, so that a dark stone appears as though it were an upright stake, or plant, and so on. Hills situated at a short distance away may appear as detached masses floating on this lake-like surface, their lower portions being invisible under the conditions prevailing. In the same way dark stones or gravel capping a gentle roll of the ground in the desert may present the appearance of a distant vertical cliff of considerable height. Mirages may often be seen over smooth road surfaces on calm hot days in England, especially over tarred roads. They simulate pools of water on the roadway in which surrounding objects are reflected.

Mist.—Cloud at the level of the ground, consisting of minute drops of water suspended in the air. Mist occurs most frequently in the British Isles in the autumn or winter, especially in still weather. A calm autumn or winter night that commences by being clear will usually become misty towards morning if the air is damp, because the nocturnal cooling lowers the temperature of the air below its dew point. At such times hill tops may have clear weather, while valleys only a few hundred feet below are covered with a dense blanket of mist.* In wet weather, on the other hand, the clouds may be so low as to cover the hills and produce mist on them while the plains below experience clear weather. (SCOTCH MIST—see p. 340.)

Mistral.—A strong dry, cold wind that is experienced on the Mediterranean coast of France. It blows from the north-west.

Mock Sun.—An image of the sun, sometimes very brilliant, that occurs most frequently at a distance from the sun equal to the radius of the ordinary HALO, *i.e.*, 22°.

Mock Sun Ring.—A colourless HALO passing through the sun parallel to the horizon, hence it is also called the Horizontal Circle. On it are situated most of the MOCK SUNS.

Monsoon.—The term is applied to certain winds which blow with great persistence and regularity in opposite directions at different seasons of the year. The monsoon winds are confined to tropical regions, and are most marked on the shores of India and China, where there is a south-west monsoon in the summer months and a north-east monsoon in the winter months. The term is also applied to the rainy season of India which sets in with, and is governed by the monsoon wind that blows from the south-west or west in the summer on the south and west coasts of India.

Moon.—The only satellite revolving round the earth. The possibility of its influencing the weather has often

---

* See reproduction of a photograph of Valley-fog under CLOUDS.

been advanced, but never demonstrated by means of statistical evidence to the satisfaction of meteorologists. The brilliance of the moon is due solely to the sunlight falling upon it. Telescopes show a rugged and clear cut landscape very different from what would be visible if the surface were hot enough to radiate a considerable quantity of heat across a quarter of a million miles to the earth. One of the many fallacies connected with the moon is that its rays are injurious to plants, but no doubt this arose simply because nights of ground frost, harmful to vegetation, are almost always clear ; and so it happens that with the moon suitably placed, the damage is done on the occasions when it is visible and not when it is hidden by cloud. An explanation of the moon's apparent influence in scattering clouds is·given in the *Quarterly Journal of the Royal Meteorological Society*, vol. 28, under the title of " La lune mange les nuages," and in Shaw's *Forecasting Weather*, p. 175. For a note on the supposed connexion of the weather with the moon, see PHASES OF THE MOON.

Nadir. See ZENITH.

Nephoscope. — An instrument for measuring the motion of clouds. A description of the different forms and methods in use is given in the *Observer's Handbook*. A *Camera Obscura* is a very useful form of nephoscope.

Nimbus.—Ragged clouds of indefinite shape from which rain or snow is falling. See CLOUD.

Normal.—The name given to the averages of any meteorological element such as pressure, mean tempéra- ture, maximum temperature, minimum temperature, duration of sunshine, velocity of wind, taken for a sufficient number of cases to form a satisfactory basis of reference, and thus obtain the *difference from normal* which is the excess or defect of a particular example above or below the normal.

Thirty-five years form a very good period for satisfactory normals, but shorter periods have to be used if the figures for 35 years are not available.

The formation of a set of normals for all the stations in its region is the first duty of a National Meteorological Institute in respect of climate, and in this respect the Russian and Indian Governments have set a laudable example in the Climatological Atlases which they published almost simultaneously. In this country we have published successive editions of normals of instrumental observations for 30 Telegraphic Reporting Stations and for about 150 Climatological Stations (Temperature and Rainfall), many of which date back for 40 years, and about 80 Sunshine Stations with records for 30 years. Monthly maps showing those climatological normals have also been published as an appendix to the *Weekly Weather Report*, M.O. 214A, Appendix 4. A selection of these maps is given in *The Weather Map*.

The non-instrumental observations, as wind, fog, snow, &c., can also be usefully summarised in the form of FREQUENCY normals but this is less often done.

Observatories with self-recording instruments furnish material for an elaborate series of normals which are most effectively represented by isopleths, of which a number are given in *The Weather Map*, pp. 72 to 87.

As an example of normals expressed in figures, we give the hourly normals for wind velocity at Kew Observatory, and the monthly normals for a number of stations in England and France.

Table of Normal Hourly Velocities of the Wind in
month at Kew Observatory

Hour.	Before noon.											
	1	2	3	4	5	6	7	8	9	10	11	12
	Metres per second.											
Jan. ...	3·3	3·3	3·3	3·3	3·4	3·4	3·3	3·4	3·5	3·8	4·2	4·3
Feb. ...	3·3	3·3	3·3	3·3	3·3	3·3	3·3	3·4	3·8	4·1	4·7	4·9
March ..	3·1	3·1	3·0	3·1	3·1	3·1	3·3	3·6	4·3	4·7	5·1	5·2
April ...	2·7	2·7	2·5	2·6	2·6	2·8	3·3	3·8	4·3	4·7	5·0	5·2
May ...	2·3	2·3	2·2	2·2	2·2	2·6	3·2	3·6	4·0	4·3	4·7	4·7
June ...	2·1	2·0	2·0	1·9	2·1	2·5	3·0	3·3	3·6	3·8	4·2	4·2
July ...	1·9	1·8	1·8	1·8	1·8	2·2	2·6	3·0	3·4	3·7	3·9	4·0
August.	2·0	1·9	1·9	1·9	1·9	2·1	2·5	3·1	3·5	3·8	4·1	4·2
Sept. ...	1·3	1·8	1·9	1·9	1·8	1·9	2·1	2·6	3·1	3·5	3·9	3·9
Oct. ...	2·4	2·4	2·4	2·4	2·4	2·5	2·6	2·7	3·2	3·6	4·2	4·3
Nov. ...	3·0	3·0	3·0	3·0	3·0	2·9	2·9	3·0	3·3	3·4	4·0	4·2
Dec. ...	3·4	3·4	3·3	3·4	3·4	3·4	3·4	3·5	3·6	3·7	4·1	4·3

This table was prepared to furnish a reply to a question as to the
best time of year for learning to fly on a machine of small power.
The reply given by the figures is that, *on the average*, the wind is
strongest from 11 a.m. to 4 p.m. in March and April, lightest from
midnight to dawn in June, July, August and September. September

metres per second for each hour of the day, for each (averages for 30 years 1881–1910).

13	14	15	16	17	18	19	20	21	22	23	24	Day	
				After noon.									
				Metres per second.									
4·3	4·3	4·1	3·8	3·8	3·7	3·7	3·7	3·6	3·4	3·4	3·4	3·7	Jan.
5·0	4·9	4·7	4·4	4·0	3·8	3·8	3·6	3·6	3·4	3·4	3·3	3·8	Feb.
5·2	5·2	5·1	4·9	4·5	3·9	3·7	3·5	3·5	3·3	3·2	3·1	3·9	March
5·2	5·2	5·2	5·1	4·8	4·3	3·8	3·4	3·3	3·0	2·9	2·7	3·8	April
4·8	4·7	4·7	4·7	4·5	4·1	3·6	3·1	2·9	2·6	2·5	2·4	3·5	May.
4·2	4·3	4·3	4·3	4·2	3·9	3·4	2·9	2·7	2·5	2·3	2·1	3·1	June
4·1	4·2	4·1	4·1	3·9	3·6	3·2	2·7	2·4	2·2	2·1	2·0	2·9	July.
4·3	4·3	4·3	4·2	4·0	3·6	3·0	2·6	2·5	2·3	2·2	2·1	3·0	August
4·0	4·1	3·9	3·7	3·4	2·8	2·5	2·4	2·3	2·2	2·0	1·9	2·7	Sept.
4·3	4·2	3·9	3·5	3·1	2·9	2·7	2·6	2·6	2·6	2·5	2·4	3·0	Oct.
4·3	4·2	3·9	3·5	3·4	3·3	3·3	3·2	3·2	3·1	3·0	3·0	3·3	Nov.
4·3	4·2	3·9	3·7	3·6	3·6	3·6	3·5	3·6	3·5	3·4	3·5	3·6	Dec.

on the whole, is the best month, July the next best, March the worst. But in view of the seasonal frequency of strong winds shown in the diagrams on pp. 281 to 285, the answer does not seem complete. For such questions FREQUENCIES give better answers than NORMALS. A similar table giving the values for the top of the Eiffel Tower, Paris (300 metres high), will be found on p. 287.

† TABLE OF WIND velocity in metres per sec. for each month of the year.

	Averages for	January	February	March	April	May	June	July	August	September	October	November	December	Mean Velocity for the year.
Kew	1881–1900	3·5	3·7	3·8	3·7	3·4	3·0	2·9	3·0	2·7	2·9	3·4	3·5	3·29
Dunkirk ...	1882–1900	6·5	6·5	6·9	6·4	6·2	5·6	5·6	5·7	5·4	6·1	6·0	6·4	6·11
Falmouth ...	1881–1900	5·4	5·4	5·1	4·8	4·3	4·0	4·2	4·2	4·0	4·5	5·1	5·4	4·70
Jersey ...	1895–1907	7·7	7·5	7·4	6·9	6·5	6·1	5·6	6·3	6·5	7·0	7·7	7·9	6·93
Paris (Bureau Centrale Météorologique).	1889–1908	2·4	2·5	2·5	2·4	2·2	2·2	2·0	2·0	1·8	1·8	2·0	2·2	2·17
Paris (Eiffel Tower).	1890–1909	10·2	9·8	9·4	8·7	8·3	7·6	7·4	8·0	8·2	9·3	9·2	9·9	8·83
Langres ...	1891–1907	5·2	5·1	5·2	4·6	4·7	4·0	3·9	3·8	4·1	4·6	4·6	4·9	4·56
Angers ...	1893–1908	6·0	5·8	6·1	5·7	5·6	5·4	5·4	5·5	5·1	5·0	5·0	5·5	5·51
Lyons ...	1881–1900	3·2	3·5	4·1	4·0	3·6	3·2	3·1	2·9	2·9	3·2	2·9	3·0	3·30
St. Martin de Hinx.	1879–1889	2·7	3·4	3·5	3·9	3·3	3·3	2·8	2·7	2·5	2·7	2·8	3·0	3·05
Perpignan ...	1881–1900	4·9	4·6	4·6	4·7	3·8	3·6	3·3	2·9	2·7	2·9	3·0	4·3	3·77

† From " Études sur Le Climat de la France," by A. Angot. The values for Kew and Falmouth have been corrected for the factor of the anemometer.

Observer, in meteorology, is a person who undertakes, in co-operation with others at a réseau of stations, to make regular simultaneous records of the weather upon an organised plan. Good observing requires punctuality and accuracy, and therefore skill, in reading and setting instruments, and intelligence in noting occurrences which are worth recording, though they are not in the prescribed routine. The best observer is one who is personally interested in scientific work on a co-operative basis. The work of the observers for the Weather Map is partly represented by the four maps of the gale of December 27–28, 1915, which face *Weather Map*, p. 88, and which show also the work of the compiler and map-maker at the Central Office. The work of the telegraphist is also necessary, but if that is perfect it makes no show at all on the maps. If it is not perfect the map at once bears evidence of the imperfection.

Ombrometer.—Another name for RAINGAUGE.

Orientation from *Oriens* (Lat.), the rising of the sun — the East. The direction of an object referred to the points of the compass. The meaning is much the same as the meaning of '*azimuth*' except that the azimuth is more particularly referred to the meridian line.

The exact orientation of a position is generally best made out by the aid of an ordnance-map, identifying the position and the bearings of some prominent landmarks visible from it. Churches in England are usually oriented East and West, but the orientation is not always very exact.

Orographic Rain is produced by the forced ascending currents due to mountains. A horizontal air current striking a mountain slope is deflected upwards, and the consequent DYNAMICAL COOLING produces rain if the air contains much aqueous vapour. The dynamics of the process is not altogether free from difficulty, as the lifting of the air requires a certain amount of energy. If the mountains extended to the boundary of the troposphere the air would presumably go round, and not over the mountain. On the analogy of flowing water we might expect the air to go round any mountainous obstacle instead of over it. It does sometimes, but not always.

Ozone is an allotropic form of oxygen for which the chemical symbol is O_3. It is produced by passing electrical sparks through oxygen, or by the action of cathode or ultra-violet rays. There is generally at least a trace of it in pure atmospheric air. The quantity is usually estimated by the depth of the colour of so-called ozone papers exposed for a given time. Some observers have described a powerful influence exerted by ozone in increasing the transfer of electricity between the atmosphere and the ground.

Pampero.—A name given in the Argentine and Uruguay to a severe storm of wind, with rain, thunder and lightning. It is a LINE SQUALL, with the typical arched cloud along its front. It heralds a cool South-Westerly wind in the rear of a DEPRESSION ; there is a great drop of temperature as the storm passes.

Paranthelion.—A mock sun (see HALO) appearing on the MOCK SUN RING at about 60° from the ANTHELION.

Paraselenae.—Mock moons, *i.e.*, images of the moon, occurring most often at certain points on the ordinary halo of 22° radius. Like parhelia or mock suns they are probably formed by the reflection of light from the surfaces of the snow-crystals in cirro-nebula.

Parhelia or mock suns. Images of the sun occurring in connexion with solar halos. See MOCK SUN.

Pentad a period of five days. Five-day means are used in meteorological work, as five days form an exact sub-division ($\frac{1}{73}$rd) of the ordinary year, an advantage not possessed by the week.

Periodical.—Recurring at regular intervals. Periodical variations of meteorological elements generally have a period of one day, or one year, corresponding with the rotation of the Earth and its annual progress round the sun. Many attempts have been made to identify the variations of rainfall and other meteorological elements with a period of years. Thus the period of the frequency of sunspots, about 11 years, has been regarded with some favour, as a meteorological period. A period of 19 years has been suggested with regard to the climatic elements of Australia and the wandering of the anticyclones of the southern tropical belt. Thirty-five years make up the period which seems to fit in best with the variations of climate suggested by Brückner in his examination of the records of rainfall, lake levels, floods, droughts, and other experiences going back in time as far as possible.

A period of three or four years is indicated for a recognisable oscillation in barometric pressure.

The fluctuations of the yield of the wheat harvest between 1885 and 1905 were shown in the Meteorological Office to be represented with curious fidelity by a combination of oscillations with a common point of mean value, so that the crops appeared to repeat themselves numerically after 11 years.

Professor Turner has suggested that these periods may possibly be fractional periods of the period of revolution of the swarm of leonid meteors, which is about $33\frac{1}{3}$ years.

Up to now there has not been sufficient material for a proper critical examination of these various suggestions. Moreover it is probable that the question cannot be dealt with separately for a small part of the earth's surface when the primary causes are external to the earth's atmosphere. Some method must be found for determining the change in the atmosphere as a whole, and then perhaps some particular feature like the trade winds may be found to form a sort of "pulse" of the circulation and thus act as an indicator of the atmospheric changes. If so, the process of examining for periodic changes will be so much simplified as to offer a very promising field of meteorological inquiry.

Persistence, a term used by Hon. R. Abercromby, the repetition of meteorological conditions or what may be called moods of weather. For several months the distribution of pressure may be of the same general type, with temporary interruptions. In N.W. Europe cyclones generally arrive from the Atlantic and pass eastwards, alternating with relatively high pressure in connexion with a persistent anticyclone to the south. If the path along which the centres of the lows travel remains the same, the alternation of cyclonic and anticyclonic weather persists. If, on the other hand, the Scandinavian high pressure develops in area and intensity, the path of depressions may be to the southward of our islands, and easterly weather becomes persistent.

On the other hand, the development of high pressure over Greenland, extending southward over the Atlantic, gives a northerly type of weather which is sometimes persistent for a season.

Persistent rain.—For some reason which cannot be explicitly stated rain generally lasts for only a few hours;

looking over the published results for the observatories of the Meteorological Office for the year 1912 we find the longest sequences of hours with rain are as follows :—

Longest Periods of consecutive hours of rainfall 1912.

	Valencia.	Kew.	Eskdalemuir.
	Number of hours.	Number of hours.	Number of hours.
January	22	9	24
February	19	6	11
March	15	5	16
April	16	3	6
May	13	6	9
June	19	9	11
July	12	7	10
August	14	9	13
September	28	15	19
October	9	8	29
November	8	5	11
December	14	6	19

At Kew Observatory in the past ten years rain extending over 25 consecutive hours was recorded three times viz., 1906, November 7th–8th ; 1914, March 8th–9th, and 1915, May 13th–14th.

The table does not fully represent all that the inspec tion of the published figures suggests, for example, in August, at Valencia, only one fine hour intervened between two spells of eleven and twelve hours respec tively, and at Valencia, too, though April had a longe spell of rain than March, there were 228 rain-hours in

March as compared with April's 47. At Eskdalemuir, a moorland station in Dumfriesshire, in the last three days of March only 28 hours out of the 72 were free from rain.

A twelve-hour rain is exceptional at an inland station like Kew, on the eastern side of Britain, but it does occur sometimes. In June, 1903, there was a run of thirty hours, separated by only one rainless hour from a preceding run of twenty hours, and that again by two rainless hours from another run of seven hours, so that there was nearly continuous rain for sixty hours at a stretch. In the same month Valencia had no spell of more than eleven consecutive hours of rainfall, though two separate fair hours broke up a spell of twenty-five hours' rain. The persistence of rain in particular localities on special occasions is a subject of great interest which is not at all understood. In it lies the explanation of local floods which are sometimes of the most extensive character, such as those of East Anglia in August, 1912, and in Eastern Ireland in August, 1905. Snowstorms are often similarly localised. In a similar way there is considerable difference in the succession of days of rain. Sometimes it rains with very little meteorological provocation, and, on the other hand, the meteorological conditions which are recognised as favourable for rain are sometimes productive of very little. The longest spell of consecutive days of rain at Kew in the 45 years 1871—1915 was one of 36 days which occurred in 1892 from September 16th to October 21st. Two spells in 1891 were nearly as long, viz., one of 31 days from September 26th to October 26th, and one of 34 days from November 7th to December 10th. See DURATION OF RAINFALL p. 303.

Phases of the Moon : The appearances of the moon by custom restricted to the particular phases of *new* *moon*, when nothing is visible, *first quarter*, when a semicircle is visible, with the bow on the West, *full moon*, when a full circle is visible, and *last quarter*, when a semicircle is visible with the bow on the East. These changes of phase are due to the fact that the moon in its monthly course round the earth, is at one time between us and the sun, while at another time we are between it and the sun. In the first case the half of the moon illuminated by the sun is turned directly away from us, and it is the period of new moon, in the second it is directed towards us, and the moon is full. At first quarter half the side of the moon facing us is lit up, and the remaining part will gradually become so ; at last quarter the appearance is similar, but the bright portion is diminishing.

It is a common practice of immemorial antiquity to associate changes in the weather with the phases of the moon ; but it must be remembered that, before the days of the cheap press and the daily newspaper, the phases of the moon were the shepherd's calendar, and the only means of marking intervals of time greater than a day and less than a year. There are about twelve and a half lunar months in a year, and the adjustment of the time-keeping of the moon to the daily and annual periods of the earth is a scientific question of great complexity and long history.

For conditions of weather that are of too long duration to be associated with a day, and too short to fill a year, the phases of the moon afford the only natural method of time-keeping, so the primary classification of such events as spells of weather must necessarily count in phases, or weeks.

Although we have now progressed beyond that stage and can use decimals in our reckoning, we are not altogether free from ancestral habits. If the sun happens to be shining we are accustomed to refer to the occurrence as "a fine day." It would be regarded as pedantic to speak of a fine hour or a fine minute, but the fine day is sometimes over in an hour, and is replaced by a wet day.

A well-known meteorological authority asserts, from his experience as a sailor, that weather changes set in with the "turn of the tide." It is possible that there may be also in this case some association with a single epoch of events which are really distributed over some hours, but no statistical inquiry has been made into the matter.

Phenology.—The study of the sequence of seasonal changes in nature. All natural phenomena are included, seed-times, harvests, flowering, ripening, migration, and so on, but often in practice the observations are limited to the times on which certain trees and flowering plants come into leaf and flower each year, and to the dates of the first and last appearance of birds and insects.

A phenological report is published each year by the Royal Meteorological Society.

Pilot balloon.—A small free balloon, the motion of which gives information concerning the wind currents aloft. Toy balloons, having a diameter of about 18 inches when inflated, are often used, but a rather larger size is preferable; they are filled with hydrogen and released, and their progress measured by means of a specially designed theodolite. If two theodolites are used at some distance apart the trajectory of the balloon can be completely determined, but one theodolite may be used if the rate of ascent of the balloon is known, assuming this to be uniform. Pilot balloons have shown that the wind, at a height of 1,500 feet, is usually in close agreement with the GRADIENT WIND. An East wind is often shallow, and there is a REVERSAL of wind direction on many occasions, the upper wind being Westerly ; on some occasions, however, the East wind is maintained up to great heights, though it seldom increases in velocity above 3,000 feet, at which height an East wind is usually at its maximum. Winds from other than Easterly directions may increase up to 30,000 feet or so, but still higher, when the STRATOSPHERE is reached, there is a decrease in velocity. In the first 3,000 feet there is usually a VEERING of the wind with height, whatever the direction of the wind. Sometimes great changes in direction occur at various heights ; these are usually veerings. When this is the case the velocity falls off near the level of the change, and when the direction is reversed there is generally a region of calm between the opposite currents. During the approach of depressions from the West a Southerly surface-wind changes to a Westerly wind in the upper air. In anticyclonic weather there is sometimes very little wind up to the greatest heights reached, and what little there is varies in direction from one level to another. Ordinary pilot balloons are sometimes followed to heights of four or five miles ; to reach greater heights larger balloons must be used, such as those used for sending up recording instruments (BALLONS-SONDES).

Instructions for observations with pilot balloons and for calculating the results are given in the *Computer's Handbook.*

Pluviograph.---A self-recording rain-gauge ; the rise of the water in the gauge is recorded by means of a pen attached to a float. Some form of device by which the gauge automatically empties itself when the water reaches a certain height is often employed.

Pluviometer.—A rain-gauge (*q.v.*).

Pocky Cloud.—Cumulus cloud, with a festooned appearance on the under side. See MAMMATO-CUMULUS.

Polar.—Occurring in the regions of the north and south pole. The meteorology of these regions is of a special type caused by the continuous presence of the sun above the horizon during a long period of the year, and its absence during an equal period. This makes the diurnal range of temperature small. The seasonal change on the other hand is large, extremely low temperatures during the long night being followed by less severe cold in the time of continuous daylight, when the thermometer often rises above the freezing point. The snowfall has always been found to be moderate; the great quantity on the ground represents the accumulated fall of many years because there is no loss except by evaporation and that is very slight at the very low temperature. Auroræ, as well as optical effects due to the presence of ice crystals in the air, are of common occurrence. In the south polar regions a spot has been found where the normal velocity of the wind is beyond the limit of gale. Both poles are separated from the equatorial regions by a great circumpolar whirl of prevailing westerly winds, and regions of relatively low pressure. These features are especially marked in the southern hemisphere.

Pole.—The geographical poles lie at the extremities of the axis of rotation of the earth. The magnetic poles are at some considerable distance from the geographical poles.

Potential as applied to energy indicates the energy which is due to the position of a body. In considering the total amount of energy available, in any case we must consider not only the position but the quantity of working substance that is collected there. If we wish to consider the influence of the position alone we must limit our ideas to a particular amount of the working substance. We naturally choose the unit measure as the amount for this purpose, and the potential energy of unit quantity is called the *potential at the point.* Thus, the electrical potential at any point in the atmosphere is the amount of energy which one unit of electricity possesses in virtue of its position at the point. Similarly, the gravitational potential or geo-potential at any point above the earth's surface is the potential energy of a unit quantity of material, a gramme or a pound, placed there.

Potential temperature.—The temperature which a specimen of air would acquire if it were brought down from the position to mean sea-level under ADIABATIC conditions.

Precipitation.—See p. 329.

Pressure.—Force per unit of area exerted against a surface by the liquid or gas in contact with it. The pressure of the atmosphere, which is measured by means of the barometer, is produced by the weight of the overlying air. The pressure exerted by the wind is generally very small in comparison. That due to a wind of force 6 is approximately one-thousandth part of the pressure of the atmosphere.

Prevailing winds.—When a station experiences wind more often from a certain direction than from others, that wind is termed the prevailing wind. The best example is the trade wind, which blows from the N.E. at many places between the equator and 30°N. Lat. with great regularity, and from the S.E. in the corresponding belt south of the equator. In latitudes 40° to 60°, north or south of the equator, westerly winds are very common and form circumpolar whirls. These are best developed in the southern hemisphere, where there is less land. For England and the neighbouring portion of Europe the best guide to the prevailing winds in different parts is the average distribution of pressure shown in the maps of Mean Pressure in the *Monthly Weather Report* and its *Annual Summary*. The prevailing direction is between S.W. and W. : there is more southing in the western districts than in the eastern. In monsoonal regions the prevailing winds are in opposite directions at different seasons, and in others there may not be a favoured direction. In all cases a long series of observations is required to make sure of the normal conditions.

Probability.—When the occurrence of an event is *apparently* doubtful, but under similar circumstances has happened before, more often than not, we speak of it as " probable." Mathematically, the probability is represented by the fraction obtained by dividing the number of times that the event has happened by the total number of times that the circumstances have arisen. It is a quantity that must lie between 0 and 1, and is usually denoted by the letter p. It should be clear from the definition that the probability, of the event failing to happen, when added to the probability that it will happen, must make 1. For example, we may consider the probability that to-morrow will be fine if to-day is wet. Out of a number N of occasions of wet days we count the number *n* when the following day was fine, and the probability·of a fine day to-morrow is *n/N*. It may be called the *random probability* because the occasions are simply chosen at random without any guiding principle. It is, of course, necessary to deal with a large number of observations before a reliable value for the probability is obtained.

It will·be noticed that in this sense probability is directly determined by the *frequency* of occurrence, so that the facts represented in tables of frequency can be equally well represented by tables of probability.

When we have no guide as to the expectation of an event except the number of times that a similar event has occurred previously, and we express the probability as a fraction $1/n$ with 1 as numerator, we may say that the *random chance* of the occurrence is one in *n* or that the *odds against* the occurrence are *n*–1 to one.

Prognostics.—Signs of coming weather. Some of them are dealt with under SHEPHERD OF BANBURY and WEATHER MAXIMS. There is a widespread belief that certain animals are in some way aware of the approach of wet weather, and behave in some special manner in consequence, but this seems unlikely. There is no reason for supposing that they can feel anything beyond the changes of temperature, moisture, wind, &c., in the air surrounding them, and changes in these are followed by a great variety of weather. Perhaps the most valuable instrument for prognostication is the barometer. Regions of high and low pressure have fairly definite weather associated with them, and mostly move across our islands from the west or south-west. A southerly wind, therefore, with a pronounced fall of the barometer, as an example, is a fairly reliable indication of an advancing depression, and therefore of rain. A gradual dimming of the clear blue of the sky, and the formation of a thickening sheet of high cloud, which often forms halos round the sun and moon, shows that the stormy area is not far off. By the application of BUYS BALLOT'S LAW (*q.v.*), it can be seen that the wind will generally veer towards west if the low pressure is going to pass on the north side of the observer, but will back if it is going to cross on the south side. In fine weather the wind often drops at night on the ground, while continuing to blow a few hundred feet up. It follows, therefore, that brisk motion of the lower clouds on a still sunny morning indicates a wind which may be expected down below during the middle of the day.

Psychrometer, the name given to the dry and wet bulbs as forming an instrument for *measuring coolness;* the combination of a thermometer having its bulb coated with wet muslin and an ordinary thermometer used for estimating the dampness of the air, by observing the difference between the readings of the two thermometers. In dry air evaporation takes place freely and cools the wet bulb. The cooling for a given temperature of the dry bulb depends principally upon the dryness of the air, or its absorbing power for moisture. In the aspiration psychrometer a fan is used so as to produce a draught of definite speed past the instrument.

Pumping.—Unsteadiness of the mercury in the barometer caused by fluctuations of the air pressure produced by a gusty wind, or due to the oscillation of a ship.

Purple Light.—A parabolic glow of colour varying from pink to violet appearing vertex upwards in the western sky at a considerable elevation above the point of sunset after the sun has passed below the horizon. It is a DIFFRACTION glow similar to the white glow round the sun during the day, which is caused by the interference of light scattered by particles of many sizes; as the sun sets, its light reaches only the more uniform particles of the upper atmosphere, and the coloration becomes purer, culminating in the coloration of the margin. In very clear weather a second, fainter purple light may follow the first. (See also BLUE OF THE SKY and TWILIGHT).

Pyrheliometer.—An instrument for measuring the radiant heat received from the sun. In the form of instrument devised by Ångström there are two metal strips, one of which receives the solar heat, while the other is warmed by means of an electric current. The current required to give equal heating of the two strips depends upon the intensity of the sun's rays, and when measured gives the amount of heat received.

Radiation.—See p. 330.

Rain is produced by the condensation of the aqueous vapour in the atmosphere. Each cubic foot, or cubic metre, of air is capable of holding a certain definite amount of water in the form of vapour; the amount depends greatly upon the temperature, being large when the temperature is high, and small when it is low. The water vapour is mixed with the air in varying proportions, and when the temperature of the mixture falls sufficiently a point is reached where the vapour is condensed into fine particles of water, and a cloud is formed. As the cooling continues more water is condensed to form larger drops which fall as rain. The cooling which produces rain is probably dynamical. See ADIABATIC and PERSISTENT RAIN : also DURATION OF RAINFALL, p. 303, and RAINDROPS, p. 334.

Rainband.—A dark band in the solar spectrum on the red side of the Sodium D lines, due to absorption by water vapour in the Earth's atmosphere. It may be best seen when the spectroscope is pointed at the sky rather than directly at the sun. The band is strengthened with increase of water-vapour, and also when the altitude of the sun is low, and his light has to shine through a greater thickness of air. It is of doubtful value as a PROGNOSTIC of rain.

Rainbow.—A rainbow is seen when the sun shines upon raindrops, or indeed upon spherical drops of water produced by a waterfall or by any other means. The drops may be at any distance from the observer, but the centre will always be exactly opposite the sun, and the angular diameter of the circle for each colour is invariable. When sunlight falls upon a drop of water it is reflected and refracted in all directions, but there are certain directions in which the light is much more intense than in others. An observer therefore looking at the drops in general will see some of them much better than others, and those drops which show up will lie in that particular direction in which they reflect the greatest amount of light. But the particular direction is different for each colour, and hence the rainbow consists of a series of rings of different colours. A similar explanation applies to the secondary bows. In the primary bow the red is outside. A rainbow is usually circular, the head of the observer being the centre of the circular arch, but a horizontal rainbow can be seén when the sun's rays from behind the observer fall on drops of dew on the grass, or gossamer threads of a meadow. In that case the bow is not circular.

Rain-day.—A day on which more than a certain specified amount of rain has fallen. It has been usual in the past to measure rainfall in hundredths of an inch, and ·01 inch has been the specified quantity, a day on which ·005 inch, or more, fell, counting as a rain-day.

Rainfall—water which falls from the atmosphere. The term is very commonly taken to include snow and hail. Precipitation is the proper inclusive term.

The measurement of a definite amount of rain, say, fifteen millimetres, 15 mm., means that if all the water had remained where it fell and not soaked in or run off, the depth of water on the ground would be 15 mm. An inch of rain is equivalent to 101 tons per acre ; a millimetre to a kilogramme per square metre, 6r one thousand metric tons per square kilometre.

Raingauge.—An instrument for measuring the rainfall. All the rain which falls on a definite area, generally a circle of either five or eight inches in diameter, is collected into a glass vessel, which is graduated to give the amount of rain.

Rain-spell.—According to the definition of the British Rainfall Organization, a rain-spell is a period of more than fourteen consecutive days, every one of which is a rain-day. On a general average, one or two such periods fall to the lot of most stations in the British Isles within the year.

Réaumur—Réne Antoine Ferchault de, d. 1757,

whose name is given to a scale of temperature now almost obsolete. On it the freezing point of water is zero, and the boiling point 80°.

Reduction, as applied to meteorological observations, generally means the substitution for the values directly observed of others which are computed therefrom and which place the results upon a comparable basis. Thus reduction to sea-level in the case of barometer readings, means estimation according to certain rules of the value which the pressure would have at a fixed level lower than that of the place of observation, and the reduction of a set of mean values extending over a regular series of years to a uniform or normal period indicates a similar procedure based upon comparison with neighbouring stations.

Reduction to Sea Level.—Both temperature and pressure are "reduced to sea level" before they are plotted on charts. To reduce mean temperature to sea level 1° F. is added for each 300 feet in the elevation of the station; 1a for 165 metres; other rates are used for maximum temperature and minimum temperature (see *Computer's Handbook,* Introduction, p. 11). This reduction is regarded as necessary in forming maps of ISOTHERMS of regions with a considerable range of level, otherwise the isotherms simply reproduce the contours; but it reduces the practical utility of the maps because the addition of ten or twelve degrees to the temperature actually observed gives an entirely false idea of the actual state of things in the locality represented.

The same objection does not apply to the reduction of pressure to sea level because the human organism has

M.O Form 4110 a

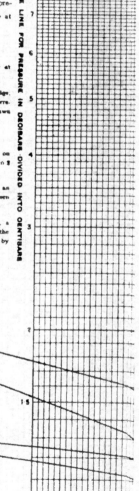

DIAGRAM for obtaining HEIGHT DIFFERENCES from PRESSURE-DIFFERENCES for different TEMPERATURES of the air-column from the formula

$$H - H_o = 067.4\ T \log_{10} \frac{p_o}{p}$$

where H is the height in kilometres, T is the temperature on the absolute scale, and p is the pressure measured in any units, but preferably in millibars. H_o and p_o are corresponding values of H and p at any definite height, usually ground level.

The process of using the diagram is as follows —

1. Find the point on the diagram corresponding with the pressure at ground level at the starting point.

2. By means of a parallel ruler, or of a set square and straight edge, set out a line parallel to the line on the temperature protractor that corresponds with the temperature of the lowest kilometre of the air column, drawn from the starting point.

3. Carry the line as far as the first kilometre.

4. Carry on from the point reached with a parallel to the line on the protractor corresponding with the temperature of the column from 1 to 2 kilometres, and so on.

5. When the top of the square has been reached, drop down along an ordinate to the base and begin again, until the given pressure-difference has been extracted, then add together the heights traversed.

There are two protractors for temperature, for the one marked A, a kilometre of height is represented by 5 cm. (2 of the large divisions of the height scale), for the other marked B a kilometre of height is represented by 12·5 cm. (5 of the large divisions).

A.

300 a.

200 a.

B.

300 a.

200 a.

GHT
RENCES

For protractor A 1 kilometre is represented by 2 large divisions
For protractor B 1 kilometre is represented by 6 large divisions

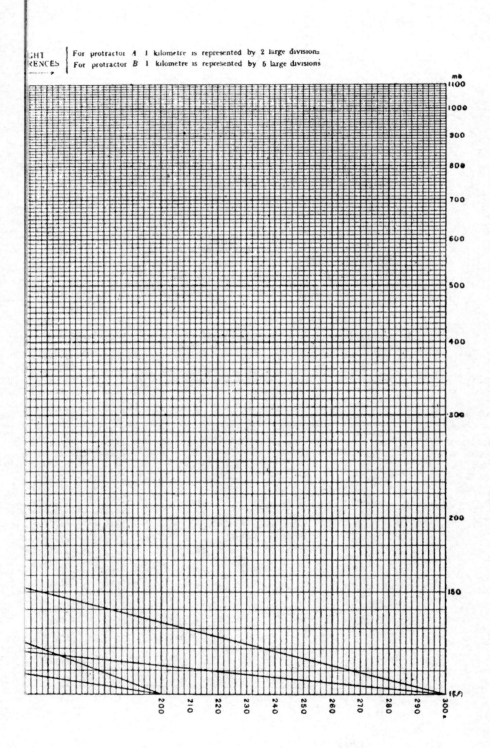

no such separate perception of pressure as it has of temperature.

The *reduction of pressure to sea level* is carried out in accordance with the general rule for the relation of difference of pressure to difference of height. This goes according to the equation

$$h - h_0 = kT \left(\log_{10} p_0 - \log_{10} p \right)$$

where h, p, h_0, p_0 are corresponding values of height and pressure, T is the absolute temperature, and k, a constant which is numerically equal to 67·4 when the height is to be given in metres, or to 221·1 when the height is to be given in feet. This equation is derived from the direct expression of the relation of pressure and height

$$g \rho \, dh = - \, dp.$$

The best way of working the equation is to use what is called semi-logarithmic paper, that is squared paper which is ruled in one direction in equidistant lines representing equal steps of height, and in the other direction according to the logarithm of the numbers indicated on it, like the graduation of a slide-rule. The relation between height and pressure for any one temperature is represented by a straight line that has a slope that can be calculated when k is known. The regular course is to find the proper point for the height and pressure of the starting point, and travel along the line of proper slope for the temperature so long as that temperature can be accepted, say for half a kilometre. When the half kilometre is reached adjust the slope for the mean temperature of the next half kilometre, and so on until the observed difference of pressure has been traversed. If the line reaches the boundary of the ruled paper, the vertical line or the horizontal line as the case may be, begin again on the other side of the ruling.

It will be seen that to make an accurate determination of the height the temperature of each stage must be known. If there are no actual measurements for the occasion an approximation may be made by using mean values either for the initial temperature or the lapse of temperature with height.

To simplify the process of obtaining the height differences from pressure differences semi-logarithmic paper is provided at the Meteorological Office ruled with the slope lines for given values of the temperature, so that with a parallel ruler the composite line for any particular determination can be easily drawn. A reduced copy of the form is shown in the figure.

The humidity of the air makes very little difference to the computation of height in our latitudes where temperature and moisture do not reach tropical figures. The best way for allowing approximately for humidity, which diminishes the density under standard conditions, is to regard the temperature as increased by one tenth of a degree for each millibar of water-vapour-pressure in the atmosphere.

Refraction.—The name applied to the bending to which rays of light are subjected in passing from one medium to another of different optical density. It plays an important part in many optical phenomena in the atmosphere; MIRAGE, HALOS, and RAINBOWS are refraction phenomena, the colours of the two latter being due to the fact that rays of different colours suffer a different amount of bending. Another refraction effect is that the apparent ALTITUDE of a heavenly body is greater than its real altitude because the rays of light entering the atmosphere are passing from a less dense to a more dense medium, and their final direction is nearer the vertical than their original direction.

Registering balloon.—A small free balloon carrying with it a light meteorograph and sent up to ascertain the temperature, humidity, &c., of the air. See BALLON SONDE.

Regression Equation.—See p. 339.

Relative Humidity.—All natural air, unless it is artificially dried, contains more or less water in the form of vapour. For each temperature there is a fixed and definite limit to the amount of water in a definite volume of air, such as a cubic foot or a cubic metre. Air which contains this full amount is called saturated air. The actual amount that can be present in a given volume depends on the temperature, and increases rapidly as the temperature rises. The relative humidity is the ratio of the amount that is present to the maximum amount that could possibly be present. This ratio is expressed as a percentage, so that saturated air, at whatsoever temperature it may be, always has a relative humidity of 100. Thus a relative humidity of, say, 75 means that a certain volume of air is holding in the form of vapour 75 grammes or ounces of water, whereas it is capable of holding 100 grammes or ounces. When saturated air is cooled by any means it ceases to be able to hold all the water in an invisible form, and fine water drops appear forming a fog or cloud.

From an analysis of upwards of 100,000 hourly readings at the observatories of the Meteorological Office during the three years 1907, 1908, 1909, it appears that on the average out of one thousand observations at every hour of the day or night throughout the year the frequencies of specified values of relative humidity are as follows :—

TABLE OF FREQUENCIES OF OCCURRENCE OF SPECIFIED VALUES OF RELATIVE HUMIDITY REFERRED TO A TOTAL OF ONE THOUSAND HOURLY OBSERVATIONS.

Relative Humidity.	Aberdeen.	Valencia.	Falmouth.	Kew.
	Frequency.			
100	1	14	0·2	1
95 to 99	45	186	104	76
90 to 94	150	191	213	171
80 to 89	378	335	328	321
70 to 79	270	217	234	206
60 to 69	119	51	102	135
50 to 59	33	5	18	71
40 to 49	4	1	1	17
30 to 39	0·2	0	0	2
Total ...	1000	1000	1000	1000

See also ABSOLUTE HUMIDITY, p. 290.

Reversal.—A large change (more than 90°) in direction between the surface current and the wind in the upper air. Reversals are most common with Easterly surface winds, and least common with Westerly. A reversal may take place quite close to the ground, or anywhere up to 15,000 feet or more. The most permanent case of a reversal is over the TRADE WIND, where the North-Easterly surface current is replaced by a South-Westerly current in the upper air.

When an eruption of the Soufriere in St. Vincent takes place, the dust, carried by the upper current, falls in Barbados, though it lies 100 miles to windward of St. Vincent (see PILOT BALLOON).

Ridge.—An extension of a "high" area shown on a weather chart, corresponding to the ridge running outwards from a mountain system. It is the opposite of a trough of low pressure.

Rime.—Ice crystals, like small needles, which form on trees and buildings in foggy, frosty weather. The needles point to the direction of the wind, and, in favourable situations, the summit of Ben Nevis for example, may accumulate and form large and heavy masses of ice.

River.—Geographically a river is simply the flow of water from the higher levels of the land to lower levels and is thus, in meteorology, only part of the great circulation of water through evaporation and condensation; but, from the point of view of climate, the variations of river-level are interesting and important as they represent the result of meteorological causes operating over a large region. The seasonal variation is often different from what might be expected, for example, the River Thames is at its highest in February, four months after the normal period of greatest rainfall. The great historic example of seasonal variation of river-flow is that of the Nile, upon which the fertility of lower Egypt depends; its annual rise begins at Assuan in June and reaches its maximum in the beginning of October. The Tigris and Euphrates, like most Continental rivers, show their rise in the spring with the melting of the snow in the regions of the head waters.

See CLIMATIC SUMMARIES appended to *The Weather Map.*

Roaring Forties.—The belt between latitudes 40° and 50° South latitude,' characterised by prevailing boisterous Westerly winds.

St. Elmo's Fire.—Brush-like discharges of electricity sometimes seen on the masts and yards of ships at sea during stormy weather; it is also seen on mountains on projecting objects. It may be imitated by bringing a sharp pointed object, such as a needle, near a charged Leyden jar.

Saturation.—When applied to the air this term indicates that all the moisture possible as water vapour at that temperature is present. A reduction of temperature would lead to the condensation of some of it to liquid drops, while a rise of temperature would make the air " dry " and enable it to take up more.

Screen.—In order to allow thermometers to indicate as nearly as possible the temperature of the air, and therefore to avoid the disturbing effect of the sun's rays and of neighbouring objects, louvred screens are used which allow of a free circulation of the air. The pattern used at the Meteorological Office observatories is a modification of that designed by Thomas Stevenson, C.E., one of the founders of the Scottish Meteorological Society. It is known in this country as the Stevenson screen, on the continent as the English screen.

Scud.—A word used by sailors to describe small fragments of cloud that drift along underneath nimbus clouds. The meteorological term is fracto-nimbus (Fr. Nb.). See CLOUDS.

In mountainous districts, after the passage of a depression, nimbus often breaks up into scud, which may persist with sunny weather for many hours.

Sea-breeze.—A breeze that blows from the sea during the day in fine weather and drops at night (see BREEZE).

In bright weather the warmed air over the land-surface rises, and there is an inrush of the cooler air from the sea to take its place ; at night, when the temperatures are more or less equalised, the wind dies away.

Sea-Level.—The level surface which the sea would have if the waves were smoothed out. Mean sea level (M.S.L.) is the mean position occupied by this surface during the whole year. In England M.S.L. is an arbitrary level at Liverpool. See LEVEL.

Seasons.—In meteorology the seasons are taken to be as follows :

1. Spring   ...   March, April, May.
2. Summer   ...   June, July, August.
3. Autumn   ...   September, October, November.
4. Winter   ...   December, January, February.

If an element is described as having simply a seasonal variation, it implies that it goes through its changes in a period of one year.

The selection of months to represent the seasons according to the farmer's year is guided by the consideration that each season shall comprise three months. The uniformity in length opens the way for some paradoxical cases. The warmest week of summer may be in the spring, late May, or in autumn, early September, and the coldest week of winter may be in the autumn, late November, or spring, early March. From the point of view of weather, we have in this country about five months of moderate winter weather between October and

April, and four months of summer weather from the middle of May to the middle of September, a short spring and a short autumn; but the seasonal variations are not nearly so large here as they are in continental countries, and the change from winter to summer and *vice versâ* is much less abrupt.

NORMAL TEMPERATURES AT SEA-LEVEL OF EACH WEEK OF THE SEVERAL SEASONS FOR ENGLAND SOUTH-EAST.

Week No.	Winter.	Spring.	Summer.	Autumn.
	a.	a.	a.	a.
1	278	278	287	288
2	78	79	87	87
3	78	79	88	87
4	77	80	89	86
5	77	80	89	85
6	77	81	89	84
7	77	81	89	83
8	77	82	89	82
9	78	83	89	82
10	78	83	89	81
11	77	84	89	80
12	77	85	89	79
13	77	86	88	79
Mean	277	282	289	283

RAINFALL IN MILLIMETRES.

	mm.	mm.	mm.	mm.
England, S.E.	172	131	160	216
Scotland, N.	413	251	268	396

The seasonal changes for England South-East, are set out in the accompanying table of *normal temperatures* for each week of the year, to which the seasonal rainfall of Scotland North, as well as of England South-East, has been added. The temperatures are given only to the nearest whole degree of the absolute scale, so that minute differences are not apparent.

If we allow for winter the temperatures 277, 278, 279, *i.e.*, from 39° F. to 43° F., and for summer the temperatures 287, 288, 289, *i.e.*, from 57° F. to 61° F., we see from the table that winter temperatures last from the 12th week of autumn (middle of November) to the 3rd week of spring (middle of March); then come ten weeks of slow transition, a degree each fortnight, to summer temperature in the first week of summer (beginning of June); the summer temperatures last until the third week of autumn, about the 21st September, then there are eight weeks of rapid transition of a degree each week until winter temperature is reached in the middle of November.

Some interesting particulars of the temperature of the several seasons in the British Isles are given in *Temperature Tables of the British Isles*, M.O. Publication 154 (1902). Diagrams are given for the daily temperature at four observatories: Aberdeen, Valencia, Falmouth and Richmond (Kew Observatory), and they show a lag of temperature behind the Sun very similar to that noticed in the diurnal changes of temperature which are figured in the same volume.

For rainfall in the South-East of England autumn is the rainy season with 216 mm., compared with 131 mm. in the spring, while in the North of Scotland winter is the rainiest season though spring is again the driest.

In considering the seasonal variations of rainfall it is

important to distinguish between the day rainfall and the night rainfall. We may contrast the two from the summary of forty years' observations at Kew Observatory.

	Average Daily Rainfall.			
	A.M.		P.M.	
—	Midt. to 6 a.m.	6 a.m. to Noon.	Noon to 6 p.m.	6 p.m. to Midt.
	mm.	mm.	mm.	mm.
January	0·37	0·37	0·36	0·36
February	0·38	0·35	0·34	0·29
March	0·31	0·30	0·32	0·34
April	0·33	0·34	0·39	0·30
May , ...	0·34	0·35	0·42	0·26·
June	0·43	0·45	0·54	0·51
July	0·39	0·42	0·67	0·48
August	0·36	0·42	0·59	0·42
September	0·49	0·37	0·43	0 46
October	0·59	0·57	0·60	0·50
November	0·49	0·40	0·48	0·49
December	0·46	0·38	0·41	0·40

It will be seen that there is a maximum in October for each of the four quarters of the day, but the October maximum for the afternoon and for the evening is a subsidiary one. The maximum for the whole year belongs to the afternoon in July, when the figure 0·67 is reached.

The reader is recommended to draw "isopleths" on this table, that is, lines of equal rainfall, ·60 mm., ·55 mm., ·50 mm., ·45 mm., ·40 mm., ·35 mm., and ·30 mm. He will find the grouping of the rainy and of the dry parts of the day in different months of the year very suggestive.

The idea of four seasons in agriculture appropriate to these islands, the winter for tilling, the spring for sowing and early growth, the summer for maturing and harvesting and the autumn for clearing and preparing, depends upon the peculiarity of our climate. Where the land is ice-bound in winter or rainless in summer another distribution has to be made.

Between the tropics there is nothing that can properly be called summer and winter; the seasons depend upon the weather and rainfall, and not upon the position of the sun, and the periods of growth are adjusted accordingly. In India, or the north-western part of it, the divisions of the year are the cold weather, the hot weather, and the rains.

It is curious, for example, that the period for growing wheat in Western Australia is locally the winter period, and coincides in actual time with our own, which is a summer period.

Secant.—In a right angled triangle the ratio of the hypotenuse to one side is the secant of the angle between the two. See SINE.

Secondary.—A small area of low pressure accompanying a larger "primary" depression. The secondary may develop into a large and deep cyclone, while the primary disappears. See ISOBARS and *Plate XII.*

Seismograph.—An earthquake recorder, or instrument for automatically recording the tremors of the earth.

Serein.—Fine rain falling from an apparently clear sky. It happens very rarely.

Shamal.—From an Arabic word originally meaning "left-hand" and thence "North" used to denote the North-Westerly winds of summer over the Mesopotamian plain. See *The Weather Map*, p. 60.

Shepherd of Banbury.—The nominal author of "rules to judge the changes of the weather." The following is taken from "The Complete Weather Guide," by Joseph Taylor, 1814 :—

"Who the shepherd of Banbury was, we know not; nor indeed have we any proof that the rules called his were penned by a real shepherd : both these points are, however, immaterial : *their truth is their best voucher.* Mr. Claridge (who published them in the year 1744) states, that they are grounded on forty years' experience, and thus, very rightly, accounts for the presumption in their favour. ' The shepherd,' he remarks, ' whose sole business it is to observe what has a reference to the flock under his care, who spends all his days, and many of his nights in the open air, under the wide-spread canopy of Heaven, is obliged to take particular notice of the alterations of the weather ; and when he comes to take a pleasure in making such observations, it is amazing how great a progress he makes in them, and to how great a certainty he arrives at last, by mere dint of comparing signs and events, and correcting one remark by another. Every thing, in time, becomes to him a sort of weather-gage. The sun, the moon, the stars, the clouds, the winds, the mists, the trees, the flowers, the herbs, and almost every animal with which he is acquainted, all these become, to such a person, instruments of real knowledge.' "

The rules enumerated are typical of all rules based on experience of the weather ; what of truth or error there is in them the reader may judge ; they are as follows :—

I. SUN.—*If the sun rise red and fiery*—Wind and rain.

II. CLOUDS.—*If cloudy, and the clouds soon decrease*—Certain fair weather.

III. *Clouds small and round, like a dapple-grey, with a north-wind* —Fair weather for two or three days.

IV. *If small Clouds increase*—Much rain.

V. *If large Clouds decrease*—Fair weather.

VI. *In Summer or Harvest, when the wind has been South two or three days, and it grows very hot, and you see Clouds rise with great white Tops like Towers, as if one were upon the*

Top of another, and joined together with black on the nether side—There will be thunder and rain suddenly.*

VII. *If two such Clouds arise, one on either hand*—It is time to make haste to shelter.

VIII. *If you see a Cloud rise against the Wind or side Wind, when that Cloud comes up to you*—The Wind will blow the same way that the Cloud came. *And the same Rule holds of a clear Place, when all the Sky is equally thick, except one Edge.*

IX. MIST.—*If Mists rise in low Grounds, and soon vanish*—Fair Weather.

X. *If Mists rise to the Hill-tops*—Rain in a Day or two:

XI. *A general Mist before the Sun rises, near the full Moon*—Fair Weather.

XII. *If Mists in the New Moon*—Rain in the Old.

XIII. *If Mists in the Old*—Rain in the New Moon.

XIV. RAIN.—*Sudden Rains never* last long : *but when the Air grows thick by degrees and the Sun, Moon and Stars shine dimmer and dimmer,* then it is like to rain six Hours usually.

XV. *If it begin to rain from the South, with a high Wind for two or three Hours, and the Wind falls, but the Rain continues,* it is like to rain twelve Hours or more, and does usually rain till a strong North Wind clears the Air. *These long Rains seldom hold above twelve Hours, or happen above once a year.*

XVI. *If it begins to rain an Hour or two before Sunrising,* it is likely to be fair before Noon, and to continue so that day ; *but if the Rain begins an Hour or two after Sunrising,* it is likely to rain all that day, except the Rainbow be seen before it rains.

XVII. WINDS.—*Observe that in eight Years' Time there is as much South-West Wind as North-East, and consequently as many wet Years as dry.*

XVIII. *When the Wind turns to North-East, and it continues two*

---

* See photograph of Cumulo-Nimbus under CLOUDS.

Days without Rain, and does not turn South the third Day, nor Rain the third Day, it is likely to continue North-East for eight or nine Days, all fair ; and then to come to the South again.

XIX. *After a Northerly Wind for the most part of two Months or more, and then coming South,* there are usually three or four fair Days at first, and then on the fourth or fifth Day comes Rain, *or else the Wind turns North again,* and continues dry.

XX. *If it turns again out of the South to the North-East with Rain, and continues in the North-East two Days without Rain, and neither turns South nor rains the third Day.* it is likely to continue North-East two or three months.

XXI. *If it returns to the South within a Day or two without Rain, and turns Northward with Rain, and returns to the South in one or two Days as before, two or three times together after this sort,* then it is like to be in the South or South-West two or three Months together, *as it was in the North before.*

The winds will finish these turns in a fortnight.

XXII. *Fair Weather for a Week with a Southern Wind* is like to produce a great Drought, *if there has been much Rain out of the South before. The Wind usually turns from the North to South with a quiet Wind without Rain; but returns to the North with a strong Wind and Rain. The strongest Winds are when it turns from South to North by West. When the North Wind first clears the Air, which is usually once a Week,* be sure of a fair Day or two.

XXIII. SPRING AND SUMMER.—*If the last eighteen Days of February and ten Days of March be for the most part rainy,* then the Spring and Summer Quarters are like to be so too ; and I never knew a great Drought but it entered in that Season.

XXIV. WINTER.—*If the latter End of October and Beginning of November be for the most part warm and rainy,* then January and February are like to be frosty and cold, except after a very dry Summer.

XXV. *If October and November be Snow and Frost,* January and February are likely to be open and mild.

The CORRELATION COEFFICIENTS (*q.v.*) for one or two of the above rules have been worked out, but they are disappointing :—

XXIII. For 38 years, S.E. England, between rainfall of last 18 days of February and first 10 days of March, and spring rainfall, the correlation coefficient is + 0·14 ; between the rainfall for the same period and summer rainfall, + 0·07.

XXIV. For 64 years at Greenwich, between October–November temperature and that of the following January–February, + 0·05 ; between October–November temperature and that of the following December–January–February–March, + 0·25.

None of these values indicates a connection of any significance ; in the case of XXIV. the Shepherd's proposition is negatived.

Silver Thaw.—An expression of American origin. After a spell of severe frost the sudden setting in of a warm damp wind may lead to the formation of ice on exposed objects, which being still at a low temperature cause the moisture to freeze upon them and give rise to a "silver thaw."

Simoon.—A strong, hot wind, accompanied by clouds of dust, experienced in the Sahara and the Arabian desert. It is probably due to convection movements similar to those in thunderstorms, but there are no clouds, rain or thunder and lightning ; this is probably owing to the extreme dryness of the air over the desert.

Sine.—The ratio of the vertical height of a distant object to the distance of its top from the observer is the same for all objects which have their tops in the same line of sight. It is one method of specifying the angles which the objects "subtend" at the eye of the observer, which could also be specified by the ratio of the vertical height to the horizontal distance of its foot (tangent), or by the ratio of the horizontal distance of the foot to the distance of the top from the observer (cosine). The values of these ratios are of great importance in surveying, and are called the trigonometrical ratios of the angles. They are formally defined as follows :—

Let AB be a line drawn from the observer to the top of the distant object, BC the vertical, AC the horizontal. Then ABC is a right angled triangle with C as the right angle.

The sine of the angle A (sin A) is the ratio BC to AB.
The cosine of the angle A (cos A) is the ratio AC to AB.
The tangent (tan A) is the ratio BC to AC.
The secant (sec A) is the ratio of AB to AC.
The cosecant (cosec A) is the ratio AB to BC.
The cotangent (cot A) is the ratio AC to BC.

If the angle is greater than a right angle some of these ratios are negative, and the following convention is adopted. A positive angle is measured from AC in the direction opposite to the motion of a watch hand. The line AB is always counted positive, AC is positive if C falls on the right of A, negative if C falls on the left, and BC is positive if B falls above AC, and negative if B is below AC. Thus if the angle is between 90° and 270° AC is negative, and if between 180° and 360° BC is negative.

Sine Curve.— This curve is obtained by plotting, against horizontal distances representing angles, vertical ordinates representing their SINES. Its simplest equation is $y = a \sin x$, the more general equation $y = a \sin (x - a)$ represents the same curve shifted forwards through a distance corresponding to the angle a. The importance of the curve in Meteorology is due to the fact that it represents the simplest form of PERIODIC variation ; its shape, in fact, is that of the conventional " wave." The diurnal and annual march of temperature, for example, would, in so far as they depend only on solar altitude, each be represented by a sine curve, and are so represented in theoretical work. Any periodic variation, however complex, can be represented by a number of sine curves superposed. The process of finding a set of sine curves to represent a given variation is called HARMONIC ANALYSIS, p. 145 and p. 311 (*q.v.*).

Sirocco.—A name used on the Northern shores of the Mediterranean indiscriminately for any warm Southerly wind, whether dry or moist. Such winds blow in front of depressions advancing Eastward. The typical Sirocco however is hot and very dry, and is probably in many places a FÖHN wind.

Sleet.—Precipitation of rain and snow together. See p. 341.

Snow.—Precipitation in the form of feathery ice crystals. See p. 342.

Snow Crystals.—Thin flat ice-crystals of a hexagonal form. There are many patterns, and when snowflakes of various size are observed on any one occasion they differ only by containing a larger or smaller number of these crystals.

Solar " Constant."—The amount of radiant energy which would be received in one second from every square centimetre of cross-section of a beam of solar radiation if it had undergone no absorption in the atmosphere. Recent investigations indicate that the solar "constant" is not invariable. The mean value is about 135 milliwatts per square centimetre.

Solar Day.—See EQUATION OF TIME.

Solarisation.—Exposure to direct sunlight; the same as INSOLATION (*q.v.*). See also RADIATION, p. 330.

Solar Radiation Thermometer.—A thermometer whose bulb is blackened with lamp black, placed in a vacuum, and exposed to the direct rays of the sun. It is used for obtaining some indication of the intensity of the sun's RADIATION.

Solstice.—The time of maximum or minimum declination of the sun, when the altitude of the sun at noon shows no appreciable change from day to day. The summer solstice for the northern hemisphere, when the sun is farthest north of the equator, is about June 21st, and the winter solstice, when it is farthest south, is about December 21st. After the summer solstice the days get shorter until the winter solstice and *vice versa*.

Sounding.—Generally means a trial of the depth of the sea, but in meteorology it is used for a trial of heights in the atmosphere with measures of pressure, temperature, humidity or wind-velocity. " Soundings of the ocean of air " can be carried out by means of kites, PILOT BALLOONS or BALLONS-SONDES.

Spells of Weather.—Long spells of the same type of weather are often experienced. Anticyclonic weather may maintain itself for weeks. Depressions often follow one another on nearly the same track for weeks or even months; if they pass North of us we get a warm Southerly, alternating with a Westerly, type, and accordingly rains, gales and fine intervals succeeding one another with some regularity, as in the Autumn and Winter of 1915 to 1916. If the depressions pass to the

South we get Easterly and North-Easterly winds, with cold weather and rain, or snow in Winter, as in the cold spell in February and March, 1916.

. **Spring.**—Meteorologically in the northern hemisphere, the three months March, April and May. Astronomically, spring is defined as the period from the vernal EQUINOX, March 21st, to the summer solstice, June 21st. See SEASONS.

Squall.—A strong wind that rises suddenly, lasts for some minutes, and dies suddenly away. It is frequently associated with a temporary shift of the wind, and heavy showers of rain or snow. The thundersquall is a cool outrushing wind, probably katabatic, that often precedes a thunderstorm.

Stability.—A state of steadiness not readily upset by small events. For stability of the atmosphere, see ENTROPY.

Standard Time.—Time referred to the mean time of a specified meridian. The meridian of Greenwich is the standard for Western Europe. The standard meridian of other countries is chosen by international agreement, so that it differs from Greenwich by an exact number of hours or half hours.

State of the Sky.—The fraction of the sky obscured by cloud. It is usually measured on a scale, of 0 (quite clear) to 10 (overcast). A rougher classification suitable for synoptic charts divides the cloudiness into four classes represented by the symbols : b, bc, c, and o, which correspond to cloudiness of 0–3, 4–6, 7–8, and 9–10 respectively.

Statics.—A branch of mechanics, dealing with the forces which keep a body at rest.

Station.—A place where regular meteorological observations are made. The classification of British stations is :—

(1.) *First order stations of the International Classification. Normal Meteorological Observatories :* at which continuous records, or hourly readings, of pressure, temperature, wind, sunshine, and rain, with eye observations at fixed hours of the amount, form, and motion of clouds and notes on the weather, are taken.

(2.) *Second order stations of the International Classification. Normal Climatological Stations :* at which are recorded daily, at two fixed hours at least, observations of pressure, temperature (dry and wet bulb), wind, cloud and weather, with the daily maxima and minima of temperature, the daily rainfall and remarks on the weather. At some stations the duration of bright sunshine is also registered.

(3) *Third order stations of the International Classification. Auxiliary Climatological Stations :* at which the observations are of the same kind as at the Normal Climatological Stations, but (*a*) less full, or (*b*) taken once a day only, or (*c*) taken at other than the recognised hours.

Statoscope.—A very sensitive form of aneroid barometer, used to show whether a balloon is rising or sinking. The range of its index is very small and it has to be set from time to time by opening a tap leading to the interior of the box.

Storm.—Is commonly used for any violent atmospheric commotion, a violent GALE or a THUNDERSTORM, a rainstorm, duststorm or snowstorm. A gale of wind is classed as a storm when the wind reaches force 10.

Storm Cone.—See GALE WARNING.

Strato-cumulus.—The most common form of cloud of moderate altitude, sometimes covering the whole sky. It consists of 'flattish masses, often arranged in waves or rolls. See CLOUDS.

Stratosphere.—The external layer of the atmosphere in which there is no convection. The temperature of the air generally diminishes with increasing height until a point is reached where the fall ceases abruptly. Above this point lies the stratosphere, which is a region where the temperature changes slowly in a horizontal direction, and is practically uniform in the vertical (see BALLON-SONDE). The height at which the stratosphere commences is often about ten kilometres, but varies. It is higher in regions nearer the equator.

Stratus.—A sheet of low cloud without definite form ; virtually fog above the level of the ground. See CLOUDS.

Summer.—Meteorologically in the northern hemisphere the months of June, July, and August. Astronomically, the period from the summer solstice, June 21st, to the autumnal equinox, September 22nd See SEASONS.

Sun.—The central body of the solar system, round which the various planets revolve. Almost all meteorological processes depend directly or indirectly upon the radiation received from the sun.

Sun-dogs.—Another word for MOCK SUNS or PARHELIA ; *i.e.*, images of the sun occurring most often on the halo of 22° radius. Sometimes also used for portions of a rainbow.

Sun Pillar.—A column of light extending for about twenty degrees above the sun, most often observed at sunrise or sunset. The colour is usually white, but sometimes red. It is due to the reflection of light from snow crystals.

Sunset Colours.—See . BLUE OF THE SKY and TWILIGHT, p. 344.

Sunshine.—An important climatological factor that is determined by a sunshine recorder, an instrument in which the rays of the sun are focussed by means of a glass sphere upon a card graduated into hours. To obtain comparable results the instrument must satisfy a precise specification. The sun will also record its appearance on photographic paper and in many other ways, but in dealing with climatological records it is of the first importance that they should be made on a comparable basis.

For the British Isles a set of Monthly Maps of normals for the duration of sunshine, together with those for temperature and rainfall, is given in an *Appendix to the Weekly Weather Report* for 1913. The only point to which attention will be called here is that when one takes the values for the whole year, so that the possible amount is the same for all stations, there is a gradual falling off in the percentage of possible duration shown on the records, as one goes northward, from nearly 45 per cent. in the Channel Isles to 25 per cent. in the Shetland Isles. This difference raises the question whether there are any parts of the globe where the average percentage of the possible duration of sunshine is zero, where in fact the screen of cloud is perpetual.

If there is a region of that character, judging from the meteorological conditions that are known to us, we should expect to find it somewhere near the Arctic Circle in the North Atlantic and the North Pacific, and anywhere along the Antarctic Circle in the Southern Ocean. And, on the other hand, we know that, except in those regions where the belts are interrupted by the trade winds and monsoons, there is hardly any interference with the sun's rays by cloud in the high pressure belts along the Tropics of Cancer and Capricorn. We are not able at present to give the figures which represent these conclusions, but they lead on to speculation as to the causes which account for the distribution of cloud and sunshine and as to why cloud and rain are not confined to special localities or regions.

PERCENTAGES OF POSSIBLE DURATION OF SUNSHINE FOR THE WHOLE YEAR FOR DISTRICTS IN THE BRITISH ISLES (AVERAGES FROM RECORDS EXTENDING OVER THE 30 YEARS, 1881—1910).

Western Side.	Per cent.	Middle Districts.	Per cent.	Eastern Side.	Per cent.
Scotland, W.	30	Scotland, N. ...	26	Scotland, E. ...	30
Ireland, N. ...	29	England, N.W. ...	32	England, N.E.	31
Ireland, S. ...	32	Midland Counties	31	England, E. ...	36
		England, S.W. ...	38	England, S.E.	38
		English Channel	43		

Sunshine Recorder: See *Observer's Handbook.*

Sunspot-Numbers: the numbers which are used to represent the variation in the sun's surface from year to year as regards spots. The occurrences of dark spots, sometimes large, sometimes small, which are to be seen from time to time on the sun's face between its equator and forty degrees of latitude north or south, have long been the subject of observation. An irregular periodicity in their number was discovered by Schwabe of Dessau in 1851, using 25 years of observation. Professor R. Wolf of Zurich, by means of records in a variety of places, made out a continuous history of the sun's surface from 1610 to his own time, which is now continued by his successor, Professor Wolfer. The sunspot-number N is obtained by the formula $N = k\,(10g + f)$, in which g is the number of groups of spots and single spots, f is the total number of spots which can be counted in these groups and single spots combined, k is a multiplier representing " personal equation " which depends on the conditions of observation and the telescope employed. For himself when observing with a three-inch telescope and a power of 64 Wolf took k as unity.

The method of obtaining the number seems very arbitrary, but from the examination of photographic records by Balfour Stewart and others it is proved that the numbers correspond approximately with the " spotted area " of the sun. One hundred as a sunspot-number corresponds with about 1/500 of the sun's visible disc covered by spots including both umbras and penumbras. (See " The Sun," by C. G. Abbot, 1912.)

Spots are now regarded as vortical disturbances of the sun's atmosphere. They have a definite relation to the amplitude of the regular diurnal changes in terrestrial magnetism : their exact relation to magnetic storms is still unknown. Very many attempts have also been made to connect the phenomena of weather with the sunspot-numbers, Indian famines dependent on Indian rainfall, cyclones in the South Indian Ocean, Scottish rainfall, commercial catastrophes have all been the subject of investigation. The mean period of frequency of spots is 11·1 years and anything with a period approximating to 11 years or a multiple or sub-multiple thereof, may suggest a connexion with sunspots. The most recent and the most effective relation that has come to the knowledge of the Meteorological Office is the direct relation between the sunspot-number and the variation of level of the water in Lake Victoria at Port Florence. The CORRELATION in this case is + ·8.

The following is the list of sunspot-numbers since 1750 :—

TABLE OF SUNSPOT-NUMBERS, 1750–1916.

—	0	1	2	3	4	5	6	7	8	9
1750 ...	83	48	48	31	12	10	10	32	48	54
1760 ...	63	86	61	45	36	21	11	38	70	106
1770 ...	101	82	66	35	31	7	20	92	154	126
1780 ...	85	68	38	23	10	24	83	132	131	118
1790 ...	90	67	60	47	41	21	16	6	4	7
1800 ...	14	34	45	43	48	42	28	10	8	2
1810 ...	0	1	5	12	14	35	46	41	30	24
1820 ...	16	7	4	2	8	17	39	50	62	67
1830 ...	71	48	28	8	13	57	122	138	103	86
1840 ...	63	37	24	11	15	40	62	98	124	96
1850 ...	66	65	54	39	21	7	4	23	55	94
1860 ...	96	77	59	44	47	30	16	7	37	74
1870 ...	139	111	102	66	45	17	11	12	3	6
1880 ...	32	54	60	64	64	52	25	13	7	6
1890 ...	7	36	73	85	78	64	42	26	27	12
1900 ...	10	3	5	24	42	64	54	62	49	44
1910 ...	19	6	4	1	10	46	55	—	—	—

Surge.—First used by Abercromby to denote the general alteration of pressure that seems superposed upon the changes related to a low pressure centre.

Synoptic.—Giving a general or "bird's eye" view. Synoptic charts show the weather at one point of time, or its mean values for the same interval, over a large area upon a single map.

Tangent.—A straight line that touches a curve and does not cut it even when produced. Trigonometrically, the ratio perpendicular : base. See SINE.

Temperature.—The condition which determines the flow of heat from one substance to another. Difference of temperature plays the same part in the transfer of heat as does difference of pressure in the transfer of water. Temperature must be clearly distinguished from HEAT, heat being a form of ENERGY, temperature a factor which affects the availability of the energy. Temperature is measured by a THERMOMETER.

Temperature-Gradient.—A change of temperature with distance (see GRADIENT); but the usual meaning of the term is the lapse rate or rate of decrease of temperature that is found as greater altitudes are reached.

In most parts of the earth near the surface a fall of temperature of 1°F. for every 300 feet occurs, so that a tableland on the summit of a mountain 3,000 feet high will have a mean temperature 10°F. lower than stations near sea level in the same neighbourhood.

In the free atmosphere the temperature gradient is usually measured in degrees centigrade per kilometre of height. The decrease is a little slower than that found by mountain observations. It amounts to about 6°C. per kilometre in England in the lower strata, but increases to from 7° to 8° in the strata that lie between 5 and 9 kilometre height. Above 11 or 12 k. the fall ceases altogether. In the tropics the temperature gradient of 7° or 8° per kilometre is continued up to 15 k. height or more. See Tables under BALLON-SONDE and DENSITY.

Tension of Vapour.—See VAPOUR.

Terrestrial.—Having reference to the earth. The term Terrestrial Radiation refers to the heat radiated from the earth. ·

Thaw.—The term used to denote the cessation or break-up of a frost ; usually the result of the substitution of a South-Westerly type for a North-Easterly type in this country, or of the sudden incursion of a CYCLONE from the west. In more northern latitudes the " spring thaw " is a periodic event, denoting the seasonal progression, the unlocking of ice-bound seas and the melting of the snow. In these latitudes, in Western Europe, though not in Canada or Asia, the sun is generally at sufficient ALTITUDE about noon, except near mid-winter, to effect a partial thaw by day, even in the midst of a protracted frost, if the sky is clear.

Thermodynamics.—That part of the science of heat which deals with the transformation of heat into other forms of energy. See ENERGY and ENTROPY.

Thermogram.—The continuous record of temperature yielded by a thermograph.

Thermograph. — A self - recording thermometer generally consisting of a " Bourdon " tube or a bimetallic spiral with a suitable index. A large spirit thermometer with a float is also used. A mercury thermometer can also be arranged to give a photographic record, as at the observatories of the Kew type.

Thermometer.—An instrument for recording temperature, usually by means of the changes in volume of mercury or spirit contained in a glass tube with a bulb at one end, but not infrequently by the change of an electrical resistance. Generally the temperature of the air is required, and this is not easily obtained, particularly in sunny weather. Readings of thermometers exposed in a Stevenson screen, however, are sufficiently accurate for practical purposes.

Thunder.—The noise that follows a flash of lightning, attributed to the vibrations set up by the sudden heating and expansion of the air along the path of the lightning. The distance of a lightning flash may be roughly estimated by the interval that elapses between seeing the flash and hearing the thunder, counting a mile for every five seconds.

It is somewhat astonishing in common experience at what little distance thunder ceases to be audible: the interval between flash and sound seldom reaches a full minute,* which would set a limit of twelve miles to the distance of audibility. Considering the violence of the commotion in the immediate neighbourhood of a flash it might be expected that the sound would be perceptible at far greater distances. Two considerations affect the question—first, it is a common experience with balloonists that sounds from the balloon are less easily audible on the ground than sounds from the ground to the balloon and this observation is confirmed by the experience on mountains that sounds from below are more easily audible upwards than sounds from above downwards ; the second consideration is that in thunder-weather there are great discontinuities in the structure of the atmosphere, so that the distortion of the rays of sound, which partly accounts

---

* Capt. Cave cites an occasion on which not less than two minutes elapsed.

for the smaller audibility of sounds from below, is much exaggerated on the occasion of a thunderstorm.

Thunderstorm.*—In the British Isles, except at the stations on the Atlantic Coasts, well developed thunder-storms occur most frequently in the summer, and especially during the afternoon. The barometric disturbances with which they are associated are generally too limited in area to be called cyclones, but like cyclones they frequently move towards the East. They are nearly always accompanied by heavy rain, which is sometimes preceded by a squall that blows outward from the advancing storm, while the barometer rises suddenly and then remains comparatively steady. The squall brings with it cool air. See LINE SQUALL.

Lightning is seen, and thunder heard, before the arrival of the storm itself, but the flashes are generally most brilliant during the heavy rain. The thunder then follows the flashes after a very short interval, showing that the discharge has taken place at no great distance.

The thunder-cloud seems to be an extreme development of the cumulus cloud, in which the ascending currents have reached to a considerable height and spread outwards at the top. In consequence they often have the shape of an anvil. The thunder type of cumulus has a rounded summit, with a clearly defined border. Observations of the time and place of occurrence of thunder-storms show that they are generally long and comparatively narrow, and move broadside across the country. The precise conditions that lead to their formation are not understood. In some parts of the tropics thunderstorms are frequent and very violent.

---

* See photographs under CLOUDS and MAMMATO-CUMULUS.

IMMUNITY FROM THUNDERSTORMS IN VARIOUS PARTS
EXTENDING MAINLY OVER THE 25 YEARS

Table of " odds against one ", expressing the random chance

	STATION.	Spring.	Summer.	Autumn.	Winter.
SCOTLAND. North.	Sumburgh Hd. (Island)	767	164	569	450
	Deerness (Island) ...	135	30	57	68
	Stornoway (Island) ...	192	77	134	102
	Wick (E. Coast) ...	110	30	103	225
	Fort Augustus (Inland)	108	56	606	225
East.	Nairn (N.E. Coast) ...	192	32	284	1,120
	Aberdeen (E. Coast) ...	135	20	142	1,120
	Braemar (Inland) ...	74	25	162	281
	Dundee (E. Coast) ...	55	15	84	750
	Leith (E. Coast) ...	115	23	228	375
West.	Laudale (W. Coast) ...	34	24	39	33
	Rothesay (Island) ...	44	33	71	80
	Glasgow (W. Coast) ...	68	26	162	204
	Pinmore	92	45	97	118
	Douglas (Isle of Man)	53	24	49	250
IRELAND. N.	Malin Hd. (N. Coast)...	92	36	120	134
	Blacksod Pt. (W. Coast)	109	58	152	73
	Markree Castle (Inland)	72	32	175	78
	Armagh (Inland) ...	97	25	505	391
	Donaghadee (E. Coast)	115	46	175	1,120
S.	Dublin (E. Coast) ...	61	18	99	250
	Valencia (S.W. Coast)...	92	60	78	750
	Roche's Pt. (S. Coast)...	82	43	108	150
SCILLY & CHANNEL ISLANDS.	Scilly (St. Mary's) ...	82	42	65	68
	Jersey (St. Aubin's)	36	16	28	58

OF THE UNITED KINGDOM AS SHOWN BY OBSERVATIONS
1881–1905 (COMPILED BY F. J. BRODIE).

of a thunderstorm on any day in the several seasons of the year.

	STATION.	Spring.	Summer.	Autumn.	Winter.
ENGLAND. N.E.	N. Shields (E. Coast) ...	74	20	95	375
	Durham (Inland) ...	27	10	79	562
	York (Inland)	27	13	81	2,250
	Spurn Hd. (E. Coast) ...	32	11	62	375
ENGLAND. E.	Hillingdon (Inland) ...	21	8	37	205
	Yarmouth (E. Coast) ...	45	13	87	562
	Norwich (Inland) ...	19	9	40	209
	Cambridge (Inland) ...	27	10	47	750
MIDLAND COUNTIES.	Worksop	27	10	61	225
	Cheadle	17	8	25	125
	Churchstoke	36	15	76	220
	Loughborough	31	11	65	1,000 ?
	Cheltenham	29	14	87	161
	Oxford	40	14	63	750
S.E.	London (Brixton) ...	25	11	53	225
	Margate (E. Coast) ...	55	20	103	1,120
	Dungeness (S. Coast) ...	53	17	51	562
	Southampton (Inland)	45	17	58	225
	Hurst Castle (S. Coast)	74	29	76	322
ENGLAND. N.W.	Aysgarth (Inland) ...	27	13	39	237
	Stonyhurst (Inland) ...	23	10	27	94
	Liverpool (W. Coast) ...	74	27	114	321
	Llandudno (W. Coast) ...	68	29	60	141
	Holyhead (W. Coast) ...	72	30	69	374
S.W.	Pembroke (W. Coast) ...	209	92	95	562
	Falmouth (S.W. Coast)	177	56	73	150
	Cullompton (Inland) ...	72	30	108	150

Time.*—For all common purposes Greenwich mean civil time is now used in all places in Great Britain, except at Canterbury, and clocks are set by telegraphic signal from Greenwich. Previously, each town or village clock kept its own local mean time and had to be set by the local time keeper, usually the parson, with the aid of a sundial or some other means of ascertaining the time from the sun. In Ireland clocks are set according to Dublin time, which is 25 minutes after Greenwich time. In meteorology the hours of the civil day are numbered from 1 to 24, the counting beginning from midnight. Thus the hours of observation for telegraphic reporting are, 1h., 7h., 13h., 18h., with a subsidiary observation at 21h. Meteorologists are closely interested in good time-keeping, because punctuality is of importance, both with climatological observations and with those that are made for the maps used in forecasting. For the former local time, and for the latter Greenwich time is taken as the standard. The records of self-recording instruments, when the sheet is changed once a week, are for many purposes useless unless marks are made on the trace at definite times, so as to allow for irregularities in the running from day to day. See STANDARD TIME.

Tornado.—A short lived, but very violent wind. In West Africa the tornado is the squall which accompanies a thunderstorm; it blows outward from the front of the storm at about the time the rain commences, and in all parts of the world similar squalls occur, associated with thunder. It is also the name applied to small but very

---

* In 1916 "Summer Time," one hour in advance of Greenwich Time, was used in the United Kingdom from May 21st to September 30th; in 1917 from April 8th to September 17th; between the limiting dates (September 30th, 1916, and April 8th, 1917), G.M.T. was used in Ireland.

violent whirlwinds of one or two hundred yards diameter. These whirlwinds often do immense damage in the United States, where they are known as cyclones, completely destroying every tree and building in their track. They are not unknown in England, but are less frequent and less violent than in North America.

Torricelli, Evangelista.—The inventor of the barometer, born at Piancaldoli in 1608. At the age of 20 he went to Rome to study mathematics. In 1641 he met Galileo, and remained with him as his amanuensis till the death of Galileo three months later. Torricelli then became professor to the Florentine Academy; he lived in Florence till his death in 1647. Torricelli explained the fact, already known, that water will only rise about 32 feet in the pipe of a suction pump; he argued that if this was due to the pressure of the atmosphere the column of mercury that would be supported would be a little under $2\frac{1}{2}$ feet, since mercury is $13\frac{1}{2}$ times as heavy as water. He performed the experiment that confirmed his theory. He also enunciated various fundamental principles in hydro-dynamics.

Trade Winds.—The word " trade " in this expression is said to mean " track " and trade winds are winds which keep to a fixed track. We naturally turn to tropical or subtropical regions for track winds. The easterly wind on the margin of the ice in the Antarctic is very persistent but not very steady. The best known examples of track winds are the North East Trade and the South East Trade of the Atlantic Ocean. In a publication of the Meteorological Office, M.O. 203, on the Trade winds of the Atlantic Ocean the areas selected for the observations are for the North East Trade from 10° N. to 30° N. between 30° W. long. and the West Coast of Africa, and for the

South East Trade the two pairs of ten-degree squares
0° to 20° S., .0° to 10° W. and 10° to 30° S., 0° to 10° E.
The Canary Islands and Cape Verde Islands come in the
region selected for the North East Trade, and St. Helena
in that selected for the South East Trade. At St. Helena
there is a self-recording anemometer at a point 1,960 feet
above sea level, which is maintained for the Meteorological
Office.

The coast of Africa disturbs the regularity of the North
East Trade in the Eastern part of the area selected, but
the monthly results for the whole area give a wind with
a mean direction for the whole year of N. 30° E., varying
between N. 18° E. in May and N. 48° E. in January, and
a mean velocity for the whole year of 10·6 miles per hour
(4·7 m/s), varying from 7·4 miles per hour (3·3 m/s) in
October to 13·5 miles per hour (6 m/s) in April. The
South East Trade shows a mean direction for the year of
S. 38° E., varying from S. 35° E. in February and October
to S. 41° E. in August and November, and a mean velocity
of 14·2 miles per hour (6·4 m/s) varying from 13·1 miles
per hour (5·9 m/s) in January to 15 miles per hour
(6·7 m/s) in April, June and August. Thus, the North
East Trade shows more variation in direction than the
South East, and its velocity exhibits a marked seasonal
variation, with a maximum in April and a minimum in
October, which has no counterpart in the South East.
These are taken from observations made by ships at sea,
the velocities being determined by a scale of equivalents
of " Beaufort estimates." See BEAUFORT SCALE. When
the measures of the direction and velocity at St. Helena
are taken they show the monthly values oscillating about
S. 40° E., from S. 35° E. in October to S. 42° E. in April,
and a very marked seasonal change of velocity from

13 miles per hour (5·8 m/s) in May to 20 miles per hour (8·9 m/s) in September. This is very nearly the counterpart of the seasonal variation of the North East Trade. The mean of the velocities of the two "trades" works out at about 11·6 miles per hour (5·2 m/s) throughout the year. The flow which is represented by these winds comprises two streams about 1,000 miles wide, the courses of which are kept steadily from N.E. or from S.E. for about 2,000 miles. These steady currents carry an enormous amount of air. Taking the run at 300 miles per day over a thousand mile front the flow for a thickness of 1 mile would be 300,000 cubic miles a day; it would take rather less than 10 years for the whole of the atmosphere to pass through; if it be two miles thick the circulation would be complete in five years. And on the same assumption, the two trades acting together—yet they use only one-twentieth part of the belt of the earth's surface available for approaching the equator from North and South—would deliver the equivalent of the whole of the atmosphere in the course of about two and a half years.

So far, we have considered only the trade winds of the Atlantic Ocean between the African and American coasts. Similar winds under similar conditions exist to the Westward of the American coast where, it may be remarked, the coast line bends away, for a 1,000 miles or more, to the Westward after crossing the equator from the Southward, very much in the same way as the African coast line does, so that the North-East Trade wind of the Eastern Pacific lies to the West of, and not opposite to, its South-East partner, just as in the Atlantic. These are the only regions where the recognised characteristics of the Trade winds are well marked. In the Indian Ocean they are replaced by the Monsoon winds, which are continued across the equator from the North East in the winter and from the South East in the summer, when the air current from the south is carried forward as a South-West monsoon over India. A suggestion of "Trade" conditions appears in the Western Pacific to the North East of Australia, but it is less well marked than in the Atlantic and Eastern Pacific.

It should be noted that in the West Indian region in June the wind varies from North East to South East, and the same is true off the coast of tropical South America in December. Locally it is still known as the Trade wind, although it may be blowing from the South East, away from the equator.

The explanation of the origin of the Trade winds which is given in all books on Physical Geography is due originally to Edmund Halley, a personal friend of Newton's, secretary of the Royal Society, and subsequently Astronomer Royal at the beginning of the eighteenth century. It attributes the flow of air southward and northward on either side of the line to the replacement of air which has been heated by the warmth of the equatorial belt, and has, in consequence, ascended to the upper air and passed away. ~~John~~ Hadley, also a personal friend of Newton's, associated with him in the invention of the sextant, explained the easterly component by bringing the rotation of the earth into account. Whatever real ground there may be for a flow of air towards a belt of high temperature along the equator on the ground of local heating, it appears clear from the maps that the great arterial currents which we have described, and which are commonly understood as Trade winds, are really parts of the general circulation of the

George Hadley, who was a brother of John Hadley

Atmosphere, governed by the distribution of pressure. A map of the distribution of pressure and winds over the globe, such as that for January in the Barometer Manual for the Use of Seamen (M.O. publication No. 61) shows that there are two belts of high pressure on either side of the equator, about latitude 30° N. and 30° S. respectively. These belts are not continuous but form a succes-ion of anticyclonic areas, each with its appropriate circulation.

The southern hemisphere pr sents the simpler arrangement, because the land areas which cause disturbance of the order are less extensive. Along the parallel of 30° S. latitude we have anticyclonic areas with centres, (1) at 100° W., 30° west of South America, (2) at 10° W., nearly midway between South Africa and South America, (3) a system with double centre between the Cape and Australia, which extends along the Southern shore of Australia and develops a secondary centre there. The regularity of the distribution is thus much distorted by the Australian continent. The channels of low pressure between the anticyclonic areas are breaches in the belt of high pressure through which the great arterial currents of the trade winds flow over the Eastern Atlantic and Eastern Pacific. And these great currents are in reality features of a circulation round the isolated regions of high pressure. There seems little possibility of any alternative for the distribution thus described. Halley's explanation of the trade winds supposes a low pressure area over the equatorial belt, continually maintained by the convection of the rising air, and continually fed by a flow of air from a belt of higher pressure north or south. So that the flow of air is thought of as from high pressure to low pressure. Whatever may be the actual state of things close to the equatorial belt, the arterial currents of the trade winds are clearly shown by the map to be great streams of air with 2,000 miles of run, and with high pressure on the one side and low pressure on the other, such as we may find in all cases of well established air currents over the earth's surface, whether they last only for a few hours, a few days, as in the intermediate and polar regions, or the whole year, as in the regions of the trade winds.

If we cross the great currents from west to east we are travelling towards lower pressure; from east to west towards higher pressure. Obviously, we cannot continue this process all round the globe, and going westward we see that the pressure soon gets to a maximum and then falls off again, and the falling off is associated with a change in the direction of the current from south-east to east or north-east, or from north-east to east and south-east. The WIND-ROSES show that the western boundary of the high pressure is a fluctuating boundary, not a fixed one. Going Eastward we are brought up by the great land areas of Africa, where our knowledge of the distribution of pressure is little more than guessing from a few isolated stations which are affected by the uncertainties of REDUCTION TO SEA-LEVEL. But further investigation must lead to a distribution which corresponds with a low pressure at sea-level. That these great currents are really part of a great circulation which is governed by the distribution of pressure may be illustrated by comparing with the steadiness of the winds at St. Helena* (lat. 16° S., long. 5°·42 W.), the following table of the winds at Suva, Fiji, which is in latitude 18° S., long. 178°26 E. :—

---

* See *Trade Winds of the Atlantic Ocean*, M.O. publication No. 203.

TABLE OF WIND DIRECTION AT 9 A.M. AT SUVA, FIJI, IN 1911.

—	N.	N.E.	E.	S.E.	S.	S.W.	W.	N.W.	Calm.
uary ...	6	3	1	5	—	4	—	—	12
ruary ...	4	5	1	5	2	2	—	—	9
ch ...	4	6	1	2	—	2	—	3	13
il ...	7	12	1	1	—	—	1	4	4
...	2	15	6	2	—	2	—	3	1
e ...	3	6	3	1	1	1	—	5	10
...	1	5	3	4	1	1	1	4	11
ust ...	4	6	4	5	—	1	—	4	7
ember ...	2	10	8	3	—	3	2	2	—
ber ...	1	10	7	4	3	2	—	1	3
mber ...	—	16	6	3	1	—	—	—	4
mber ...	9	10	9	2	—	1	—	—	—
Year ...	43	104	50	37	8	19	4	26	74

rom this it appears that the wind conditions at the places are quite different, though their relations to equatorial belt of high temperature are altogether lar.

'e must, therefore, regard the trade winds as the main ims of air in the general circulation by which the rtropical region is supplied. The greater part of the ply turns eastward and gets away from the equatorial on again by passing round the western boundaries of anti-cyclonic regions. Some part of it may go to feed rain storms of the doldrums, but what fraction of the le supply is so used is not known.

he extension of Halley's theory of the trade winds

provides that the air after ascending in the equatorial region should flow back again away from the equator,and on account of the rotation of the earth the northward flow should be diverted towards the east, and thus become a south-west wind. Accordingly, south-west and north-west winds are to be expected above the north-east and south-east trades. Two thousand miles is a long way for the air to travel with no more diversion than $45°$ from the path of its desire when the rotation is taking place at the rate of $15 \sin \lambda$ degrees per hour unless the distribution of pressure interferes, but the theory seems to be confirmed by an observation made in 1856, by Piazzi-Smyth (then Astronomer Royal for Scotland) of a south-west wind at the top of the peak of Tenerife, 12,500 feet high, over the north-east trade flowing below. The transition is at about 10,000 feet, and the existence of a south-westerly current over the north-east trade over the ocean was verified by balloon observations by Teisserenc de Bort, although the question was the subject of some discussion at the time.

If, however, we regard the surface winds of the trades as part of the general circulation of the atmosphere controlled by pressure, we cannot do otherwise in the case of the upper currents, consequently we ought to find our explanation of the south-westerly current over the north-east trade as evidence of low pressure over the central region of the Atlantic north and south of the equator, and high pressure over the African land adjoining, giving rise to a gradient for equatorial winds up above, or for polar winds below. We should then have to conclude that the high pressure belts of the tropics are reversed in the upper regions, a conclusion that carries with it some consequences which at first sight are not easily disposed of.

The trade winds have an interest for meteorologists quite independent of their geographical interest and of their place in the general circulation. They are a sort of laboratory in which one can study the properties of a great current of air of known temperature and humidity flowing steadily over the surface of the sea and affected by the turbulent motion caused by the surface.

Professor Piazzi-Smyth, spent part of July, August and part of September, 1856, in the main stream of the north-east trade at Tenerife at a height of 8,900 feet or more. He found the air remarkably dry, while below him at a height of about 5,000 feet he could see the long strings of cumulus clouds that are characteristic of the trade wind forming a level horizontal layer upon which it seemed that one might walk to the neighbouring Canary Islands if it were not for a gap between the cloud sheet and the cloud actually in contact with the mountain, which was some 1,000 feet below the trade wind cloud. The wind at 8,900 feet was generally light. Cirrocumulus clouds, moving from south-west, were sometimes visible in the sky above at a height estimated at 15,000 feet. Occasionally the north-easterly wind got nearly to gale force at the high level, and on other occasions the wind blew strongly from the south-west there. The intermediate region between the north-east trade and the south-west counter trade was found to be generally a region of light winds, while the trade wind clouds were formed at the middle height of the trade.

It would appear, therefore, that we have in the body of the trade wind, an analogy, but on a smaller scale, of the separation of the troposphere from the stratosphere which is universal. The boundary between the two is the limit of convection 'from the surface. In the trade winds the boundary of convection is marked by the layer of clouds, above that level the moist air does not penetrate. The uniformity of level suggests that the limit is dependent upon the turbulent motion due to the eddies caused by the friction at the surface, the effect of which extends upwards to a height which depends upon the length of the "fetch." The convection is therefore in this case partly dynamical, and it is curious that the clouds formed are often spoken of as rollers.

Piazzi-Smyth speaks of summer and winter conditions as though he were dealing with a climate of temperate latitudes instead of a region to the south of the line of tropical high pressure.

The observations of St. Helena, which are made at about 2,000 feet above sea level in the south-east trade, show persistent south-easterly winds, with a mean humidity for the year of 89 per cent., ranging from 88 in January to 91 in March, and the normal amount of cloud works out at 8·5 (on the scale 0–10, or 85 per cent) for the year. The mean temperature reaches a maximum of 291·9a, 66·1°F., in March, and a minimum of 287·1a, 57·3°F., in September, and the rainfall has a normal maximum of 131 mm. in March and a minimum of 40 mm. in November. Hence, there is a definite seasonal variation, but it lags behind the corresponding changes in higher latitudes of the same hemisphere.

Trajectory.—The path traced out by a definite particle of air in a travelling storm, or the horizontal projection of the course followed by a pilot balloon : the trajectory, as worked out from theodolite readings, may be plotted on squared paper, and the direction and velocity of the wind at any given height deduced therefrom.

Tramontana.—An Italian word for the northerly winds of Italy which blow from the mountains.

. **Transparency.**—The capacity for allowing rays of light or some other form of radiation to pass. Thus glass is transparent for the visible radiation of light. Rock-salt is specially transparent for the rays of radiant heat. See VISIBILITY.

Tropic.—One or other of the circles of $23\frac{1}{2}°$ of latitude north and south of the equator, which represent the furthest position reached by the sun in summer and winter in consequence of the tilting of the earth's axis with reference to the plane of the ecliptic. The term applies also to the zone of the earth lying between them. The northern circle is called the tropic of Cancer, the southern the tropic of Capricorn.

Tropical.—Belonging to the regions of the tropics, or similar to what is experienced there. The word tropical is often used for the region between the tropics, which is more strictly called intertropical.

Tropopause.—The lower limit of the STRATOSPHERE.

Troposphere.—A term suggested by Teisserenc de Bort for the lower layers of the atmosphere. The temperature falls with increasing altitude up to a certain height (see TEMPERATURE GRADIENT), and the part of the atmosphere in which this fall occurs is called the troposphere. In these latitudes (50°) it extends from the surface for a thickness of some 7 miles, or 11 kilometres; in the tropics the thickness may reach 10 miles, or 16 kilometres.

Trough.—The period of lowest barometer during the passage of a depression. Taking the fluctuations of the barometer to be analogous to the fluctuations of level caused by waves, which is, however, not a very good analogy, the trough of the wave suggests as its counterpart the lowest reading of the barometer. With the barometer the passage of the trough is generally marked by phenomena of the type of a LINE SQUALL, a sudden rise of pressure, veer of wind, drop of temperature, and one or more squalls ; nothing of that kind takes place in the trough of a wave.

Twilight.—See p. 344.

Twilight Arch.—On a clear evening after sunset a dark arch with a pink edge may be seen to rise from the eastern horizon ; the distinction between the darkness below the arch and the brighter sky above it becomes rapidly less as the arch rises in the sky. The dark space is really the shadow of the earth. In mountainous countries shadows cast by mountains between the sun and the observer may be seen to rise from the twilight arch. The pink edge of the arch is due to reflection from particles in the atmosphere which are illuminated by rays of the sun that have lost nearly all their blue light from lateral scattering (see BLUE OF THE SKY).

Type.—Different distributions of atmospheric pressure are characterised by more or less definite kinds of weather, and accordingly when a certain form of distribution is seen on a chart the weather is described as belonging to such and such a type. The types are defined as cyclonic, anti-cyclonic and indefinite, and by terms denoting the direction of the isobars. Thus, a "southerly type" denotes a weather chart on which the isobars are shown as more or less parallel lines running north and south. A northerly type will also have isobars running north and south ; the distinction will be that in the southerly type barometric pressure will be high in the east, whereas in the northerly type the higher pressure will be in the west. In each season each type has more or less definite kinds of weather. Thus, the anti-cyclonic type will have dry weather, the cyclonic wet ; the southerly type will in general be warm, the northerly cold.

Typhoon.—A word of Chinese origin applied to the tropical cyclones occurring in the western Pacific near Japan and the Philippine Islands. They are extremely violent circular storms of 50 to 100 miles diameter, and travel slowly. Exactly similar storms are known as hurricanes in the West Indies, and as cyclones in the Bay of Bengal. The hurricanes of Mauritius are also similar to typhoons. See HURRICANE.

Upbank thaw.—A state of affairs in which the usual fall of temperature with height is reversed, a thaw, or an increase of temperature occurring on mountains sometimes many hours before a similar change is manifested in the valleys.

It is due to the superimposition of a warm wind blowing from a direction differing from that of the surface wind, and occurs most usually at the break-up of a frost, on the approach of a cyclonic system, but sometimes during the prevalence of anti-cyclonic conditions, when a down-current of air is dynamically heated in its descent from a great height. Under these conditions, at 9 a.m. on February 19th, 1895, at the end of a great frost, the temperature at the summit of Ben Nevis was 9·8a., 17°·6 F. higher than at Fort William, 4,400 feet below.

It is probable that this INVERSION of the normal temperature gradient is the cause of the phenomenon known as GLAZED FROST (*q.v.*).

V-shaped depression.—Used to describe isobars having the shape of the letter V, which enclose an area of low pressure. The point of the V is always towards the south or east.

Vapour-pressure.—The pressure exerted by a vapour when it is in a confined space. In meteorology vapour-pressure refers exclusively to the pressure of water-vapour. When several gases or vapours are mixed together in the same space each one exerts the same pressure as it would if the others were not present, and the vapour-pressure is that part of the whole atmospheric pressure which is due to water-vapour. See AQUEOUS VAPOUR, RELATIVE HUMIDITY.

Vapour-tension.—A now obsolete term for vapour-pressure. There seems now to be no reason why this should be called tension.

Vector.—A straight line drawn from a definite point in a definite direction. Thus a radius vector of the earth in its orbit is the line drawn from the sun to the earth. A vector quantity is a quantity which has a direction, as well as magnitude, and of which the full details are not known unless the direction is known. In meteorology the wind and the motion of the clouds are examples of vector quantities ; the directions, as well as the magnitudes, are required, whereas in the case of the barometer or the temperature the figures expressing magnitude tell us everything. They are called scalar quantities. All vectors obey the parallelogram law. That is to say, that any vector A may be exactly replaced by any two vectors B and C, provided that B and C are adjacent sides of any parallelogram, and A the diagonal through the point where B and C meet. Also the converse holds.

The position of an airship a given time after starting is

an example. The two vector quantities that bring about the final result are the velocity and the direction of the airship through the air, and the velocity and direction of the air, *i.e.*, the wind. Suppose an airship pointing S.W. and with speed of 40 miles an hour. After two hours its position on a calm day is 80 miles S.W. of the starting point. Now suppose the airship has to move in a S. wind of 30 miles an hour; after two hours this wind alone would place the airship 60 miles N. of the starting point. The real position will be given by drawing two lines representing these velocities and finding the opposite corner of the parallelogram of which they form adjacent sides. See COMPONENT.

Veering.—The changing of the wind in the direction of the motion of the hands of a watch. The opposite to BACKING.

Velocity.—Velocity is the ratio of the space passed over by the moving body to the time that is taken. It is expressed by the number of units of length passed over in unit time, but in no other sense is it equal to this space. It can be expressed in a variety of units. For winds metres per second, kilometres per hour and miles per hour are most common. When a velocity is variable a very short time is chosen in which to measure it. Thus the statement " at 11 a.m. the wind was blowing at the rate of 60 miles per hour " means that for one second or so at just 11 a.m. the wind had such a rate, that had that rate continued for an hour the air would have travelled 60 miles in that hour.

From the time of its establishment in 1854 until the final evaluation of the Beaufort Scale in 1905 it was the custom of the Meteorological Office to measure wind velocity by the cup anemograph which gave the " run " of an hour in miles. Miles per hour were accordingly the accepted unit of velocity, but when it became certain that for anemometers of the standard size (9-in. cups and 2-ft. arms) the "factor" was not 3 but 2·2, so that the miles were not really miles after all, some change of nomenclature was necessary to mark so great a change of habit. The pressure-tube anemograph gave the opportunity of measuring the velocity at any instant instead of the run during an hour : a gust that lasts only part of a minute is more appropriately measured by the distance which the wind travels in a second than by the distance which it might travel in an hour if it remained unchanged throughout the hour. Moreover in all questions of dynamical calculation the second is the unit of time. Gunners use the foot per second as their unit. The metre per second is more suitable for units on the C.G.S. system, and is now used in all the publications of the Meteorological Office.

Vernier.—A contrivance for estimating fractions of a scale division when the reading to the nearest whole division is not sufficiently accurate. The vernier is a uniformly divided scale which is arranged to slide alongside the main scale of an instrument. Information as to the graduation of a vernier and the method of reading is given in *The Observer's Handbook.*

Vertical.—The direction of the force of gravity or of the plumb line, so called because it refers to the vertex, *i.e.*, to the zenith. A vertical line is perpendicular to the surface of still water, which is horizontal. When produced it passes through the zenith and close to the centre of the earth. Two vertical lines can therefore never be parallel, although if they are near together they are very nearly so. A vertical plane at any point likewise passes through the zenith and very close to the centre of the earth. A vertical circle is a GREAT CIRCLE passing through the zenith and the nadir ; and the vertical circle also passing through the east and west points is called the prime vertical.

Viscosity.—The property of a liquid or gas whereby it resists the tangential motion of its parts. See DIFFUSION.

Visibility.—A term used in describing the effect of the atmosphere, and the amount of light in the sky, on the maximum distance at which an object can be seen, and the clearness with which its details can be made out. The visibility of the atmosphere depends chiefly on the amount of solid or liquid particles held in suspension by the air. On a cloudy day it is usually equally good in all directions, but on a sunny day the visibility is usually better, *i.e.*, objects can be seen more clearly, when looking away from the sun than when looking towards it.

In England the visibility of the atmosphere is usually bad towards the end of a spell of fine, calm weather ; but in these cases the occurrence of a shower of rain frequently clears the air and gives rise to good visibility. On the other hand during rainy weather the visibility is frequently bad, even when it is not actually raining.

The visibility of objects on the ground, when looked at from an aeroplane, is sometimes bad even when the visibility between two points on the ground is good and the sky is cloudless. This condition usually arises in calm, anti-cyclonic weather and is due to a layer of haze at a definite height above the ground.

The occurrence of haze during fine dry weather can frequently be connected with the proximity of a large town. A light north-easterly wind sometimes carries haze to a distance of 70 miles south-west of London, On one such occasion, it was found that at Farnborough, 35 miles from London, the haze extended to a height of 7,000 feet. Above that height the atmosphere was perfectly clear.

It frequently occurs that an aeroplane can be seen from the ground at a time when the ground cannot be seen from the aeroplane. This condition arises when there is a low haze or mist which prevents a large part of the sun's rays from reaching the ground. The aeroplane itself is brightly lighted by the direct rays of the sun, while the light reflected upwards from the top of the haze towards the aeroplane overpowers the feeble rays from the less brightly lighted ground. The effect is similar to that of a lace curtain over a window, which enables the occupants of a room to see out, while the interior cannot be seen from the outside.

Occasionally it happens that an aeroplane can see the ground while remaining invisible itself. The condition arises only on sunny days, but its cause is not understood.

The limit of visibility depends chiefly on the number of dust particles per cubic centimetre of the atmosphere. An apparatus for counting this number has been designed (see DUST-COUNTER), and used by Mr. John Aitken, F.R.S., who has found as few as 16 and as many as 7,000 dust-particles per cubic centimetre in the open country. The distance of the furthest visible object was found to depend on the number of particles in the atmosphere, and on its humidity. For a given depression of the wet-bulb thermometer, the limit of visibility multiplied by the number of particles per c.c. of air was found to be roughly constant. This constant, however, increases as the air becomes drier.

For a given depression of the wet bulb, therefore, the number of particles in a column 1 sq. cm. in cross section and stretching from the observer to the limit of visibility is constant. Mr. Aitken's estimates of its values for different degrees of humidity are shown in the accompanying table.

Depression of wet-bulb. F.	Number of particles of dust to produce complete haze.
2° to 4°	12×10^9
4° to 7°	17×10^9
7° to 10°	22×10^9

Vortex.—See p. 347.

Water.—The name used for a large variety of substances such as sea-water, rain-water, spring-water, fresh water of which water, in the chemical sense, is the chief ingredient. Chemically pure water is a combination of Hydrogen and Oxygen in the proportion by weight of one part to eight, or by volume, at the same pressure and temperature, of two to one, but the capacity of water for dissolving or absorbing varying quantities of other substances, solid, liquid or gaseous, is so potent that the properties of chemically pure water are known more by inference than by practical experience. They are in many important respects different from those of the water of practical life.

The most characteristic property of ordinary water is that we find it in all three of the molecular states ; we know it in the solid state as ice, as a liquid, (over a considerable range of temperature so well recognised as to be used for graduating thermometers), and as a gas. Thus, freezing and boiling are the common experience of many specimens of the water of ordinary life, and yet it is difficult to say in what circumstances, if any, perfectly pure water can be made to freeze or to boil.

Ordinary water is a palatable beverage, and is a medium in which a variety of forms of vegetable and animal life can thrive, but pure water freed from dissolved gases is perfectly sterile and quite unpalatable.

Ordinary water has a mass of 1 gramme per cubic centimetre ($62 \cdot 3$ lbs. per cubic foot) at 277a. Sea-water contains dissolved salts to the extent of as much as 35 parts per 1000 parts of water, and its density varies from $1 \cdot 01$ to $1 \cdot 05$ g/cc

Rain-water is the purest form of ordinary water, it contains only slight amounts of impurity in the form of ammonium salts derived from the atmosphere. Spring-water contains varying amounts of salts dissolved from the strata of soil or rock through which it has percolated. The most common of these salts is carbonate of calcium, which is specially soluble in water that is already aerated with carbonic acid gas ; sulphates of calcium and other earthy metals are also found, and sometimes a considerable quantity of magnesia. These dissolved salts give the waters of certain springs a medicinal character. In some districts underground water is impregnated with common salt and its allied compounds to such an extent that it is no longer called water, but brine.

When impure water evaporates, the gas that passes away consists of water alone, the salts, which are not volatile, are left behind ; similarly when water freezes in ordinary circumstances the ice is formed of pure water, the salts remain behind in the solution ; so that, except for the slight amount of impurity due to mechanical processes, pure water can be got from sea-water or any impure water, either by distilling it, or by freezing it.

Besides the solid constituents which give it a certain degree of what is called " hardness," ordinary water contains also small quantities of gases in solution, presumably oxygen and carbonic acid. When the water freezes the ice consists of pure water, and the dissolved gases collect in crowds of small bubbles.

The thermal properties of water, in the state of purity represented by rain-water, are very remarkable. Starting from ordinary temperatures, such as 290a. (62·6°F.) and going upwards in the scale, the water increases in bulk, and part evaporates from the surface, until the boiling point is reached, a temperature which depends upon the pressure, as indicated on p. 300. Then the water gradually boils away without any increase of temperature, but with the absorption of a great amount of heat. Going downwards, the bulk of the water contracts slightly until the temperature of 277a. is reached (4°C., 39·1°F.) : that is known as the temperature of maximum density of water. From that point to the freezing point of water, there is a slight expansion of one eight-thousandth part, and in the act of freezing there is a large expansion amounting to one-eleventh of the volume of water. It is in consequence of this change of density in freezing that ice floats in water with a one-eleventh of its volume projecting, if the ice is clean, solid ice, and the water of the density of fresh water. Salt water would cause a still larger fraction to project, but floating ice carries with it a considerable amount of air cavities and sometimes a load of earth so that the relation of the whole volume of an iceberg to the projecting fraction is not at all definite.

Water-atmosphere.—A general term used to indicate distribution of water-vapour above the earth's surface. The limitation which is imposed upon the quantity of water-vapour in the atmosphere by the dependence of the pressure of saturation upon temperature, places the distribution of water-vapour on a different footing from that of the other gases. The atmosphere is enriched with water-vapour by EVAPORATION at the surface and it is distributed by the process of CONVECTION, but that process does not extend beyond the TROPOSPHERE, and the water-vapour beyond that limit must be attributed to the action of diffusion. Above the surface saturation is produced only by the reduction of temperature on rarefaction caused by convection, so that we cannot expect CLOUDS to' be formed beyond the range of convection. Hence for all the ordinary purposes of meteorology which are concerned with the formation of clouds and other forms of precipitation, the water-atmosphere is limited by the boundary of the troposphere.

Waterspout.—The term used for the funnel-shaped tornado cloud when it occurs at sea.

Waterspouts are seen more frequently in the tropics than in higher latitudes. Their formation appears to follow a certain course. From the lower side of heavy Nimbus clouds a point like an inverted cone appears to descend slowly. Beneath this point the surface of the sea appears agitated, and a cloud of vapour or spray forms. The point of cloud descends until it dips into the centre of the cloud of spray; at the same time the spout assumes the appearance of a column of water. It may attain a thickness (judged by eye) of 20 or 30 feet, and may be 200 to 350 feet in height. It lasts from 10 minutes to half an hour, and its upper part is often observed to be travelling at a different velocity from its base until it assumes an oblique or bent form. Its dissolution begins with attenuation, and it finally parts at about a third of its height from the base and quickly disappears. The wind in its neighbourhood follows a circular path round the vortex and, although very local, is often of considerable violence, causing a rough and confused, but not high, sea.

Water-Vapour.—See AQUEOUS VAPOUR.

Waves.—Any regular periodic oscillations, the most noticeable case being that of waves on the sea. The three magnitudes that should be known about a wave are the amplitude, the wave length, and the period. The amplitude is half the distance between the extremes of the oscillations, in a sea wave it is half the vertical distance between the trough and crest, the wave length is the distance between two successive crests, and the period is the time-interval between two crests passing the same point. In meteorological matters the wave is generally an oscillation with regard to time, like the seasonal variation of temperature, and in such cases the wave length and the period become identical.

If a quantity varies so as to form a regular series of waves it is usual to express it by a simple mathematical formula of the form $y = a \sin(nt + a)$. Full explanation cannot be given here, it must suffice to say that the method of expressing periodic oscillations by one or more terms of the form $a \sin(nt + a)$ is known as "putting into a sine curve," "putting into a Fourier series," or as "HARMONIC ANALYSIS." See p. 311.

Any periodic oscillations either of the air, water, temperature, or any other variable, recurring more or less regularly, may be referred to as waves. During the passage of sound waves the pressure of the air at any point alternately rises above and falls below its mean value at the time. A pure note is the result of waves of this sort that are all similar, that is to say, that have the same amplitude and wave length. The amplitude is defined in this simple case as the extent of the variation from the mean, while the wave length is the distance between successive maximum values. The period is defined as the time taken for the pressure to pass through the whole cycle of its variations and return to its initial value. Another good example of wave form is provided by the variations in the temperature of the air experienced in these latitudes on passing from winter to summer. This is not a simple wave form because of the irregular fluctuations of temperature from day to day, and the amplitude of the annual wave cannot be determined until these have been smoothed out by a mathematical process. Fourier has shown that any irregular wave of this sort is equivalent to the sum of a number of regular waves of the same and shorter wave length. In America "heat waves" and "cold waves" are spoken of. These are spells of hot and cold weather without any definite duration, and do not recur regularly.

Waves of Explosions are among the causes which may produce a rapid variation of pressure which begins with an increase, and is followed by a considerable decrease. The transmission is in the same mode as that of a wave of sound. The damage done by a wave of explosion is often attributed to the low pressure which follows the initial rise. In the same way the destructive effect of wind is sometimes due to the reduction of pressure behind a structure resulting in the bulging outwards of the structure itself in its weaker parts.

Weather.—The technical classification of different kinds of weather as given by the letters of the Beaufort notation, set out in detail in the *Introduction*, p. 10.

Weather Maxim.—A popular saying or proverb in connexion with the weather, sometimes expressed in rhymes. The best are the sailors' maxims which, at the

Meteorological Office, whether rightly or wrongly, are associated with Admiral FitzRoy. The relation with modern meteorology is often easily apparent.

> First rise after low
> Foretells a stronger blow

is quite characteristic of the passage of the TROUGH of a depression.

> If the wind backs against the sun,
> Trust it not for back it will run

is appropriate for the anticipation of a cyclonic depression in the Northern Hemisphere.

> Long foretold, long last,
> Short notice, soon past

is also good meteorology in relation to travelling depressions.

A useful essay might be written on the sailor's maxim quoted by Sir G. Nares—

> When the rain's before the wind
> Your topsail halyards you must mind,
> But when the wind's before the rain
> You may hoist your topsails up again.

Some of the land maxims also represent fair conclusions from experience.

> If hoar frost come on mornings twain
> The third day surely will have rain

provides a fair indication of the gradual transition from Easterly to Southerly weather.

A yellow sunset is regarded as a sign of stormy weather. Admiral FitzRoy's version of the maxim is "A bright yellow sunset presages wind ; a pale yellow wet."

A voluminous collection of maxims and legends has been compiled by Mr. Richard Inwards, a former President of the Royal Meteorological Society, under the title of „Weather Lore." Admiral FitzRoy was perhaps the last to attempt to draw up a scheme of weather prognostics according to the precepts of experience, as he was the first to introduce forecasts based on weather maps. Professor W. J. Humphreys of the United States Weather Bureau has given a physical explanation of many of the best known weather signs in the atmosphere.

An examination of Mr. Inwards' collection makes it apparent that the weather wisdom of ancient saws does not lend itself to systematic presentation. Variants of the same maxim sometimes contradict one another. A large number have to do with the saints' days of the calendar, and so with seasonal variations. The St. Swithin's legend has obvious reference to the transition from spring drought to autumn rainfall (see SEASON), and the fact that the hour of heaviest rainfall in the year [in London] is the third hour of the afternoon in July.

Many maxims are based upon the prevalent notion that every unusual occurrence is a *sign* of something to come. In modern days we prefer to regard the state of the crops and the behaviour of birds as the natural consequence of the *past* and *present*, not as the controlling cause of the future. No doubt, if the course of events in the physical universe is unique, that is to say, if the present is the only possible sequel to the past, then the relation of the future to the present is of the same order as the relation of the present to the past, and while we are looking for the one we may find the other. But what are offered as signs are obviously insufficient as causes. When we read

> Hark ! I hear the asses bray,
> We shall have some rain to-day,

we are supposed to regard the braying, not as a *cause* of rain, but as an evidence of superior intelligence in the quadruped, stimulated by sensations which are too delicate for our senses; but as a matter of practice it is doubtful if any serious action was ever based on that intelligent expression of the emotions.

Wedge.—Short for wedge of high pressure: an extension of a high pressure region, more or less in the shape of a wedge, that separates two neighbouring areas of lower pressure. See Plate XVI.

Weight.—The force with which the earth attracts bodies near its surface. In dynamics we distinguish between the amount of material substance which a body contains, and the force with which gravity attracts it, but experiments made by Galileo long ago led ultimately to the conclusion that apart from the resistance of the air, all bodies, large or small, are similarly affected by GRAVITY, so that every part of a composite mass is now recognised as separately affected by gravity, the result for the whole being simply proportional to the amount of material substance, irrespective of its particular nature Bodies immersed in a fluid, as a balloon in air, may rise, that is, apparently have less than no weight, because they displace fluid, air in this case, which weighs more than the bodies themselves. It should be noted that it is the weight of the heavier surrounding air that furnishes the driving force for the ascent of the balloon.

Wet Bulb.—An ordinary thermometer having the bulb coated with muslin that is kept moist. The evaporation cools the bulb, and makes the reading lower than that of a similar plain thermometer. See PSYCHROMETER.

Whirlwind.—A quite small revolving storm of wind in which the air whirls round a core of low pressure. Whirlwinds sometimes extend upwards to a height of many hundred feet, and cause dust storms when formed over a desert.

Wind.—The motion of the air. It appears certain that the general winds of the earth are maintained by the unequal warming of different parts of the earth by the sun, but the exact manner in which they arise, and the reason of their distribution, is not clearly understood. Some local winds may be explained, as, for instance, the wind accompanying the descent of an avalanche, or the land and sea breezes, but the problem of the general circulation is very much more difficult. In the open sea, away from the disturbing influence of the great continents, the general trend of the winds is as follows :—Round the equator are light variable winds, and on either side to 20°–30° north or south are to be found the TRADE WINDS, moderate in force from the N.E. in the northern and from the S.E. in the southern hemisphere. Further towards the poles in about latitude 40° and 50° there are winds blowing chiefly from westerly points, but by no means steady. They often reach the force of a gale. Concerning the polar regions comparatively little is known. The calm equatorial belt and the trade winds on either side follow the movements of the sun, being furthest north in our summer, and furthest south in winter. There is at present no exhaustive analysis of the facts which have been collected concerning the force and direction of the winds of the British Isles. The diagrams on pp. 281–285 represent the *monthly* frequency of winds of different forces at Deerness (for the northern Area), at Holyhead (for the Irish Sea), at Scilly (for the mouth of the English Channel), and at Yarmouth (for the East Coast). A diagram is also given for the frequency of the wind in January at ten stations. The monthly average duration of winds of gale force at these stations is given under GALE. The real fact which these diagrams illustrate is that no

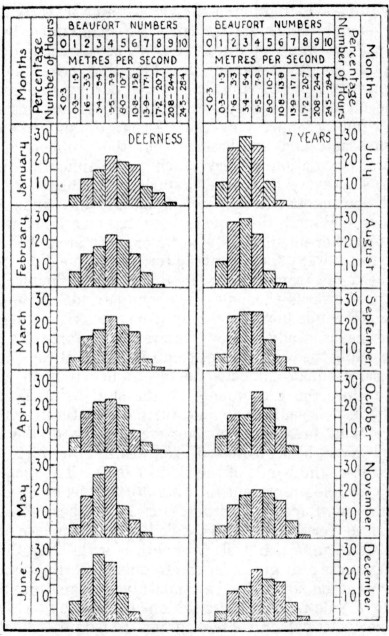

Monthly Average Wind Frequency at Deerness.

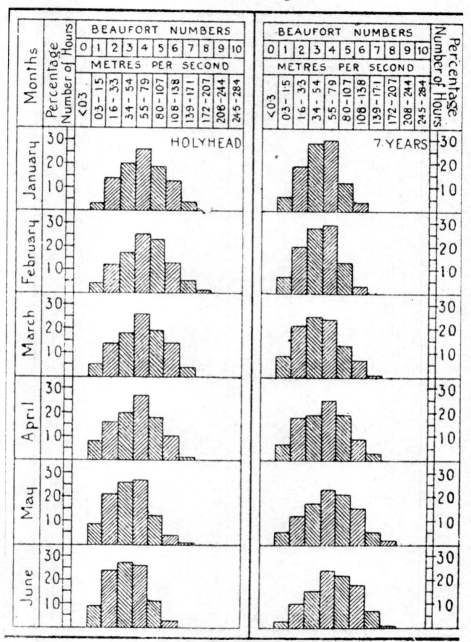

Monthly Average Wind Frequency at Holyhead.

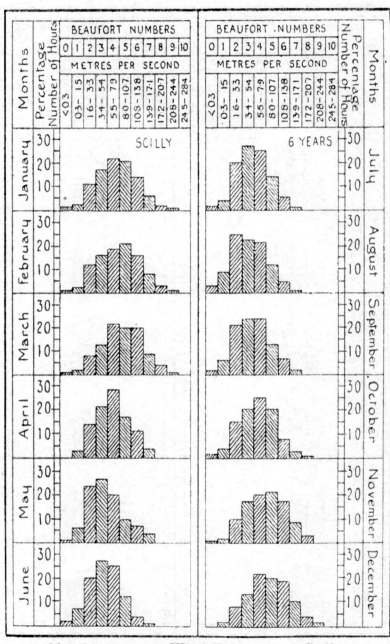

Monthly Average Wind Frequency at Scilly.

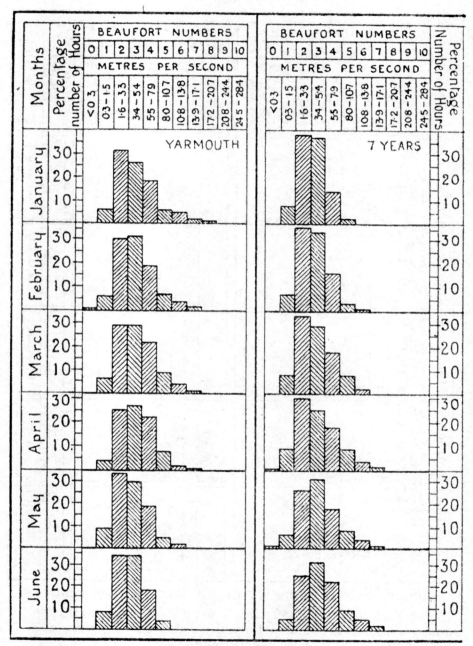

Monthly Average Wind Frequency at Yarmouth.

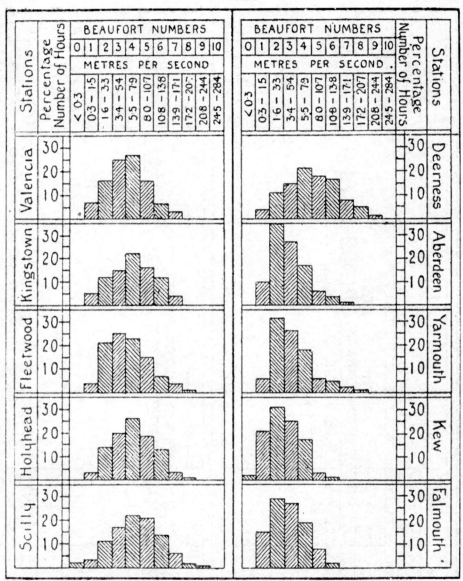

Average Wind Frequency in January for Ten Stations.

Note: From an investigation lately completed it appears that on the average the observed wind of force 6 is related to the theoretical or geostrophic wind at various stations as follows:—

Valencia, 62 per cent.   Aberdeen, 58 per cent.   Scilly, 63 per cent.
Yarmouth, 63 per cent.   Spurn Head, 71 per cent.

exact scientific meaning can be attached to the comparison
of measurements of wind when the observations are made
close to the surface of the earth. It is certain that near
the ground or near buildings the velocity of the air is
changing rapidly with height. It has for example
recently been determined by special observations of wind
quite near the surface that the velocity at 4 ft. is from
83 to 90 per cent. of the velocity at 6 ft. above ground
according to the nature of the ground. The velocity
doubles itself, more or less, within 500 metres ; the actual
figure depends upon the time of day among other things.
So a measure of wind is as much dependent upon the
exposure of the particular point at which the observation
was taken as of the unrestricted flow of air in an unobstructed position. In recent years at the Meteorological
Office we have found the wind computed from the isobars,
the geostrophic wind, a much more satisfactory standard
of reference than the anemometer readings.* Further
information about wind is given under the following
headings : BEAUFORT SCALE, EDDY, FRICTION, GALE,
GRADIENT WIND, GUST, ISOBARS, LINE SQUALL, SQUALL.
See also references in the index to Tables on p. 357.

Wind at the earth's surface is subject to considerable
diurnal variation, being greatest in the early afternoon
and least before dawn (see DIURNAL) : at the tops of
mountains and presumably at higher levels generally
the reverse is the case, as the following tabular summary
of the observations at the top of the Eiffel Tower (300
metres high) clearly shows :—

---

* Strictly speaking, in dealing with winds at a considerable height,
we should employ the system of isobars appropriate to that particular
level.

Jh.	Jan.	Feb.	Mar.	Apr.	May.	June.	July.	Aug.	Sept.	Oct.	Nov.	Dec.	Year.
1	10·69	10·52	10·25	9·70	9·27	8·79	8·79	9·16	9·34	10·11	9·79	10·30	9·73
2	10·57	10·39	10·13	9·65	9·13	8·62	8·69	9·08	9·16	10·07	9·75	10·19	9·62
3	10·54	10·34	10·03	9·47	9·09	8·42	8·36	8·96	9·00	9·98	9·80	10·08	9·50
4	10·45	10·40	9·98	9·38	9·07	8·33	8·14	8·76	8·83	9·85	9·74	10·00	9·41
5	10·57	10·38	9·90	9·28	8·93	8·22	8·01	8·67	8·76	9·76	9·64	9·96	9·34
6	10·65	10·24	9·86	9·15	8·69	7·60	7·56	8·60	8·64	9·78	9·64	10·07	9·21
7	10·62	10·25	9·69	8·66	7·63	6·61	6·42	7·86	8·36	9·71	9·66	10·10	8·55
8	10·57	10·40	9·38	7·67	6·70	5·78	5·52	6·76	7·57	9·35	9·55	10·00	8·27
9	10·34	9·88	8·58	7·05	6·53	5·76	5·39	6·14	6·51	8·82	9·27	10·08	7·86
10	9·94	9·15	8·15	7·03	6·83	6·09	5·67	6·29	7·14	8·00	8·62	9·83	7·73
11	9·44	8·69	7·96	7·27	7·22	6·35	6·08	6·59	6·41	7·60	7·99	9·36	7·58
12	8·98	8·46	8·11	7·60	7·28	6·61	6·36	6·72	6·60	7·56	7·57	8·93	7·57
13	8·76	8·30	8·27	7·75	7·30	6·67	6·55	6·96	6·71	7·68	7·51	8·76	7·60
14	8·75	8·41	8·47	8·70	7·56	6·97	6·79	7·13	6·79	7·73	7·55	8·75	8·05
15	8·98	8·51	8·71	7·95	7·81	7·11	6·89	7·25	7·00	7·97	7·71	8·88	7·90
16	9·45	8·70	8·79	7·97	7·87	7·22	7·01	7·42	7·21	8·32	8·18	9·31	8·12
17	9·89	9·20	8·86	8·11	8·02	7·33	7·19	7·52	7·41	8·98	8·96	9·83	8·44
18	10·34	9·78	9·12	8·18	8·21	7·41	7·29	7·74	8·03	9·84	9·43	10·29	8·81
19	10·65	10·36	9·76	8·81	8·36	7·66	7·56	8·21	8·96	10·32	9·71	10·48	9·24
20	10·81	10·61	10·03	9·48	8·78	8·15	8·06	8·96	9·46	10·53	9·91	10·64	9·62
21	10·86	10·76	10·19	9·80	9·22	9·75	8·77	9·42	9·81	10·73	9·98	10·59	9·99
22	10·81	10·85	10·33	9·93	9·51	9·06	8·87	9·47	9·95	10·56	10·02	10·58	9·99
23	10·77	10·71	10·40	10·04	9·51	9·14	8·95	9·32	9·91	10·39	9·98	10·48	9·97
24	10·70	10·48	10·41	9·82	9·45	8·96	8·99	9·30	9·65	10·31	9·81	10·47	9·86
Year	10·17	9·82	9·39	8·65	8·25	7·57	7·41	8·01	8·17	9·33	9·16	9·92	8·83

Winter.—In meteorology the months of December, January, and February. Astronomically, winter commences on December 21st, and ends on March 21st. See SEASONS.

Wireless Telegraphy has two types of application in meteorology, according as we deal with electromagnetic waves produced artificially or naturally. The former is exemplified by the wireless weather-reports from vessels at sea, enabling synoptic charts to be extended to ocean regions without the long delays otherwise involved, and by the distribution of meteorological information from high power stations. The other application is in the detection of distant thunderstorms. Very early in the history of Wireless Telegraphy it was found that lightning flashes emitted electromagnetic waves capable of affecting the detecting device then in use—the coherer. A coherer may be made to actuate an electromagnet the armature of which carries a pen for recording on a revolving drum, so that every lightning flash within 200 miles or more may thus automatically record itself. In the modern wireless receiver the electromagnetic waves set up by lightning cause clicks in the telephone. It seems probable that a large proportion if not all of the irregular and troublesome noises called atmospherics, strays, or X's, which are formidable obstacles in long distance wireless telegraphy may be referred to distant lightning.

Zenith.—The point of the sky immediately "overhead," or in the vertical produced upwards; the opposite of *nadir*, which is the point in the sky below one's feet, or in the vertical produced downward beyond the earth's centre and out the other side.

Zodiac.—The series of constellations in which the sun is apparently placed in succession, on account of the revolution of the earth round the sun, are called the Signs of the Zodiac, and in older writings give their names and symbols to the months, thus :—

March is associated with Aries, the Ram.
April   „   „   Taurus, the Bull.
May   „   „   Gemini, the Heavenly Twins.
June   „   „   Cancer, the Crab.
July ·   „   „   Leo, the Lion.
August   „   „   Virgo, the Virgin.
September   „   „   Libra, the Scales.
October   „   „   Scorpio, the Scorpion.
November   „   „   Sagittarius, the Archer.
December   „   „   Capricornus, the Goat.
January   „   „   Aquarius, the Watercarrier.
February   „   „   Pisces, the Fishes.

Owing to precession, the position of the sun relative to the above constellations has altered a good deal since classical times. The sun now enters Aries in April.

Zodiacal Light.—A cone of faint light in the sky, which is seen stretching along the Zodiac from the Western horizon after the twilight of sunset has faded, and from the 'Eastern horizon before the twilight of sunrise has begun. In our latitudes it is best seen from January to March after sunset, and in the Autumn before sunrise. In the TROPICS it is seen at all seasons in the absence of moonlight. It is supposed to be due to the reflection of sunlight from countless minute particles of matter revolving round the sun inside the Earth's orbit. Its light is usually fainter than that of the Milky Way.

SUPPLEMENTARY ARTICLES.

Absolute Humidity.—Aqueous vapour has a very large annual variation but a small diurnal variation, whether one considers the amount of vapour present, or the contribution which it makes to the atmospheric pressure. This is readily seen in consulting the two accompanying tables, which give respectively the quantity and the pressure of aqueous vapour at Richmond (Kew Observatory).

According to the first table the quantity of aqueous vapour in the atmosphere in the hottest months, July and August, is nearly double that in the coldest months, January and February. The quantity is slightly greater in the afternoon than in the morning hours, but the excess of the afternoon maximum over the morning minimum represents only 6 or 7 per cent. of the mean value.

As the second table shows, the mean vapour-pressure in July and August is fully double that in January and February. The diurnal variation is also a little more marked than it was for the quantity of vapour. The maximum pressure in the afternoon occurs decidedly later in the day at midsummer than at midwinter. The morning minimum, on the other hand, occurs a little earlier in summer than in winter.

vapour in grammes per cubic metre for each of the 24 hours in the several months.

Hour.	1	2	3	4	5	6	7	8	9	10	11	12	13	14	15	16	17	18	19·20	21	22	23	24	Mean.
Jan.	5·2	5·2	5·2	5·2	5·2	5·2	5·2	5·2	5·2	5·3	5·4	5·4	5·5	5·5	5·5	5·5	5·4	5·4	5·4	5·3	5·3	5·3	5·3	5·3
Feb.	5·2	5·2	5·1	5·1	5·1	5·1	5·1	5·1	5·2	5·3	5·4	5·4	5·5	5·5	5·5	5·5	5·5	5·5	5·4	5·3	5·3	5·3	5·2	5·3
March	5·4	5·4	5·4	5·3	5·3	5·3	5·3	5·4	5·5	5·7	5·7	5·7	5·8	5·8	5·8	5·8	5·8	5·7	5·7	5·6	5·6	5·6	5·5	5·6
April	6·1	6·1	6·0	6·0	5·9	6·0	6·1	6·2	6·3	6·3	6·4	6·3	6·4	6·3	6·4	6·3	6·3	6·3	6·3	6·3	6·2	6·2	6·2	6·2
May	7·2	7·2	7·1	7·1	7·1	7·2	7·4	7·5	7·5	7·5	7·5	7·5	7·5	7·5	7·6	7·6	7·6	7·5	7·6	7·5	7·5	7·4	7·4	7·4
June	8·9	8·8	8·8	8·7	8·8	8·8	9·1	9·1	9·2	9·2	9·3	9·3	9·3	9·2	9·2	9·2	9·3	9·3	9·4	9·2	9·2	9·2	9·0	9·1
July	10·1	9·9	10·0	9·9	10·0	10·1	10·3	10·3	10·2	10·3	10·3	10·3	10·3	10·3	10·4	10·4	10·5	10·5	10·6	10·5	10·5	10·4	10·3	10·3
Aug.	10·1	10·0	10·0	10·0	10·0	10·0	10·2	10·4	10·4	10·3	10·3	10·3	10·3	10·3	10·3	10·4	10·4	10·5	10·6	10·6	10·5	10·4	10·3	10·3
Sept.	9·2	9·2	9·0	9·0	8·8	8·9	9·1	9·2	9·4	9·4	9·5	9·4	9·5	9·4	9·4	9·4	9·5	9·6	9·6	9·5	9·4	9·3	9·2	9·2
Oct.	7·6	7·6	7·5	7·5	7·4	7·4	7·4	7·5	7·8	7·9	8·0	7·8	8·0	7·9	8·0	8·0	8·0	8·0	7·9	7·8	7·8	7·7	7·6	7·8
Nov.	6·4	6·4	6·3	6·3	6·3	6·3	6·2	6·3	6·4	6·5	6·6	6·7	6·7	6·7	6·7	6·7	6·7	6·5	6·5	6·4	6·4	6·4	6·4	6·5
Dec.	5·5	5·5	5·4	5·4	5·5	5·4	5·4	5·4	5·5	5·6	5·7	5·7	5·8	5·8	5·8	5·8	5·7	5·7	5·6	5·6	5·6	5·5	5·5	5·6
Mean	7·2	7·2	7·2	7·1	7·1	7·1	7·2	7·3	7·4	7·4	7·5	7·5	7·5	7·5	7·5	7·5	7·6	7·5	7·6	7·5	7·4	7·4	7·3	7·4

RICHMOND (KEW OBSERVATORY) Pressure of aqueous vapour in millibars at each hour of the day in the several months of the year.

Hour.	1	2	3	4	5	6	7	8	9	10	11	12	13	14	15	16	17	18	19	20	21	22	23	24	Day.
Jan.	6·7	6·7	6·6	6·6	6·6	6·6	6·6	6·6	6·7	6·8	6·9	7·0	7·1	7·1	7·1	7·1	6·9	6·9	6·9	6·9	6·8	6·8	6·7	6·7	6·8
Feb.	6·6	6·6	6·6	6·6	6·5	6·5	6·5	6·5	6·7	6·8	6·9	7·0	7·0	7·0	7·0	7·0	7·0	7·0	6·9	6·8	6·8	6·8	6·7	6·7	6·8
March	7·0	6·9	6·9	6·8	6·7	6·7	6·7	6·9	6·9	7·3	7·3	7·4	7·4	7·4	7·4	7·4	7·5	7·4	7·3	7·3	7·2	7·2	7·1	7·1	7·1
April	7·9	7·9	7·7	7·7	7·7	7·7	7·9	8·1	8·1	8·2	8·3	8·3	8·4	8·3	8·4	8·3	8·3	8·3	8·2	8·2	8·1	8·1	8·0	8·0	8·1
May	9·4	9·3	9·3	9·2	9·2	9·3	9·7	9·7	9·8	9·9	10·0	10·0	10·0	10·0	10·0	10·1	10·1	10·1	10·0	9·9	9·9	9·8	9·6	9·6	9·7
June	11·7	11·6	11·6	11·4	11·5	11·7	12·0	12·1	12·2	12·2	12·4	12·3	12·4	12·4	12·4	12·4	12·5	12·5	12·6	12·5	12·3	12·2	12·1	11·5	12·1
July	13·5	13·1	13·2	13·1	13·2	13·4	13·7	13·7	13·7	13·6	13·6	13·6	13·7	13·7	13·6	13·9	14·0	14·0	14·2	14·0	14·1	14·0	13·8	13·7	13·7
Aug.	13·5	13·3	13·2	13·1	13·0	13·2	13·6	13·8	13·9	13·8	13·7	13·7	13·8	13·7	13·8	13·8	13·9	14·0	14·2	14·1	14·0	14·0	13·8	13·7	13·7
Sept.	12·1	12·0	11·8	11·7	11·6	11·6	11·8	12·1	12·4	12·5	12·7	12·6	12·6	12·6	12·6	12·6	12·8	12·8	12·7	12·6	12·5	12·4	12·2	12·1	12·3
Oct.	9·8	9·8	9·7	9·7	9·6	9·6	9·6	9·8	10·1	10·4	10·5	10·5	10·5	10·4	10·5	10·5	10·5	10·5	10·4	10·3	10·2	10·1	10·0	9·5	10·1
Nov.	8·2	8·2	8·1	8·1	8·0	8·0	8·0	8·1	8·2	8·4	8·6	8·7	8·7	8·7	8·7	8·7	8·6	8·5	8·4	8·4	8·3	8·2	8·2	8·2	8·3
Dec.	7·0	7·0	6·9	6·9	7·0	6·9	6·9	6·9	7·0	7·2	7·3	7·3	7·5	7·4	7·4	7·4	7·3	7·3	7·2	7·2	7·1	7·1	7·1	7·1	7·1
Mean	9·5	9·4	9·3	9·2	9·2	9·3	9·4	9·5	9·7	9·8	9·9	9·9	9·9	9·9	9·9	9·9	9·9	9·9	9·9	9·5	9·8	9·7	9·6	9·6	9·7

Accumulated Temperature.—A term used to describe the excess or defect of temperature in relation to a selected base-level, prevailing over a more or less extended period of time, *e.g.*, a week, a month, or even a year. Accumulated temperature is employed mainly in connection with agricultural statistics, and the base-level adopted in this and in most Continental countries is a temperature of 279a, equivalent to 42°F., or 10° above the freezing point. This temperature was suggested many years ago by Prof. A. Candolle, an eminent Swiss physicist, as the level above which the growth of vegetation commences and is maintained. Temperatures *above* 42°F. may therefore be regarded as *effective*, inasmuch as they tend to the promotion of active plant-growth. Temperatures *below* 42°F. may be regarded as *non-effective* at the best, and at certain seasons of the year, when the defect is large, as positively injurious. In the Weekly Weather Report the amount of effective and non-effective heat is expressed in what are described as "day-degrees." A "day-degree" Fahrenheit signifies 1° above or below 42°F. continued over a period of 24 hours, or, in inverse proportion, 2° continued over 12 hours, 3° over 8 hours, and so on. At the Meteorological Office the amount of Accumulated Temperature above and below 42°F, is computed from the daily readings of the maximum and minimum thermometers, in accordance with formulæ proposed more than 30 years ago by Sir Richard Strachey, at that time Chairman of the Meteorological Council. The actual method of computation is described in the preface to the Weekly Weather Report for 1884 and subsequent years. As examples of the results attained, the following statistics may be of interest. In the table the amount of Accumulated Temperature above and below 42°F. is given respectively for the exceptionally warm summer of 1911, in contrast with the cool summer of 1907; and for the cold winter of 1916–17 in contrast with the mild winter of 1912–13.

The period embraced is, in each case, the 13 weeks comprised as nearly as may be within the three months June to August and December to February. The winter of 1916–17 was, it need scarcely be said, prolonged far beyond the ordinary winter boundary. The averages with which the actual results are compared are those for the 35 years 1881–1915.

	ACCUMULATED TEMPERATURE.			
	Above 42°F.		Below 42°F.	
	Day degrees.	Difference from average.	Day degrees.	Difference from average.
Summer of 1911 ...	1,940	+297	0	0
„ „ 1907 ...	1,423	−220	0	0
Winter of 1916–17	54	−126	598	+237
„ „ 1912–13	278	+98	185	−176

Atmospheric Electricity treats of the various electrical phenomena observed at or near the earth's surface. If we regard the earth as a sphere of radius R, carrying an electrical charge of uniform surface density σ, the electrical force on unit charge at any radial distance r not less than R is the same as if the whole charge $4\pi\sigma R^2$ were collected at the centre, and is thus $C \times 4\pi\sigma R^2/r^2$, where C is a numerical constant depending on the units adopted. On the electrostatic system C is unity. Charges of like sign repel one another, and it is usual when talking of electrical force to regard it as the force experienced by a positive unit. Thus the above force is upwards or downwards according as σ is positive or negative. In fine weather σ is normally negative and so the force is downwards. The force at any surface-point is really determined by the charge in its immediate vicinity, and thus whether σ be uniform or not the force is given correctly by $-4\pi\sigma C$, where σ is the surface density at the point. If we take a point at a height h small compared with R and suppose ρ to be the mean electrical charge per unit volume throughout the height h, we find in a similar way that the electrical force at the point is $-4\pi C (\sigma + \rho h)$.

If F denote the attraction towards the earth on a unit charge at height h, in order to raise it to a slightly greater height h' an amount $F(h'-h)$ of work must be done, which is transformed into a rise of potential (*i.e.*, capacity to do work). If the potential rises during the operation from V to V', then $F(h'-h) = V' - V$. Thus the force downwards is $F = (V' - V)/(h' - h)$.

It is usual to consider the change of potential per metre of height, which is known as the potential gradient. If we write P for $(V' - V)/(h' - h)$, we finally get

$$P_o = -A\sigma \quad , \quad P_h = -A(\sigma + \rho h),$$

where P_o and P_h are the values of the potential gradient at ground level and at height h respectively. A is here a numerical constant, equal to 4π in the electrostatic system of units.

P_o is positive, *i.e.* the potential increases as we leave the ground, if the force on a positive charge is directed downwards, *i.e.* if σ is negative. This is almost always the case in fine weather. As we go up, P will increase if ρ is negative like σ, but diminish if ρ is positive. In fine weather P diminishes as we go up, or ρ is positive. At Kew Observatory the potential gradient in fine weather averages about 300 volts per metre. At most other stations somewhat lower values have been observed. The potential gradient has a large annual variation, being lowest in summer. There is also a large diurnal variation, with usually two maxima and two minima in the 24 hours. At Kew the lowest value occurs in the early afternoon in summer, but in the early morning in winter.

As we go up from the earth, the potential gradient normally diminishes, *i.e.* each successive metre adds less to the potential, but all contributions being in the same direction the potential goes on mounting, and at the levels attained by aircraft may reach hundreds of thousands of volts. Any body remaining at one level gradually assumes the potential of the surrounding air, the process being accelerated if the body is provided with sharp edges or points, or with an engine emitting fumes, or if it is discharging ballast. But if a body makes a large rapid change of level, it may depart widely in potential from the surrounding air, and in an extreme case this may lead to discharge by sparking and consequent danger to an airship.

Besides its regular changes, potential gradient near the ground shows numerous if not perpetual irregular changes. Clouds sometimes carry large electrical charges, and heavy passing clouds usually cause large fluctuations of potential. During rain the potential gradient at ground-level is often negative.

The charge in the air evidenced by the change in

potential gradient with height may be carried by drops of water, but it is also carried by ions. There are always at least two kinds of these present in the atmosphere, usually known as light (or mobile) ions and heavy (or Langevin) ions. The latter seem the more numerous, especially near smoky towns, but they move very slowly, and as carriers of electricity are relatively unimportant. Also the numbers of heavy ions carrying positive and negative charges seem approximately equal, thus they·neutralise one another so far as influence on the potential gradient is concerned. On the other hand there is usually a marked excess of light positive ions, as suggested by the falling off of the gradient as height increases. The number of light positive and negative ions combined near ground level is usually of the order of 1,000 per c.c.

Air is often regarded as a non-conductor of electricity, and it is a very poor conductor compared with copper ; it conducts, however, to a certain extent. The negative charge on the earth and the positive ions in the atmosphere attract one another, a process equivalent to the passing of a current from the air to the earth. This current is extremely small if reckoned in amperes per cm.²—only in fact about 2×10^{-16} on the average—but for the earth as a whole this means fully 1,000 amperes, if we can accept the few stations where observations have been made as fairly representative.

The process by which this current is maintained is at present a mystery. The difficulty is analogous to that which puzzled philosophers who saw rivers flowing into the sea without the sea becoming fuller. Two explanations which seemed promising, though neither suggested a sufficiently regular source of supply, appear to have broken down. It was suggested that rain might restore the balance by bringing down negative electricity. But the observations hitherto made—too limited as yet perhaps to be wholly conclusive—indicate that while rain not infrequently brings down negative electricity, it brings down on the whole more positive. Another suggestion was that the balance might be restored by lightning. Mr. C. T. R. Wilson has, however, recently devised a method of determining the sign and the quantity of the electricity brought to the earth by a lightning flash, and his results suggest that on the whole the charge brought down is at least as often positive as negative.

Observations made from balloons indicate that at heights above 1 or 2k a rapid increase takes place in the ionisation of the atmosphere. At heights of 90 to 150k AURORA is a frequent phenomenon in high latitudes, and it is natural to suppose that at such heights the electrical conductivity is much greater than near the ground.

Aurora takes a great many forms. In addition to arcs, bands, rays and isolated patches, there are sometimes displays resembling curtains or draperies, also so-called " coronae," representing a concentration of rays directed towards a limited space of the heavens.

Of the accompanying figures, one shows an arc, the other a curtain. The arc is the most symmetrical and stable form of aurora, sometimes persisting with little visible variation for several minutes. Auroral curtains, when seen in the zenith in high latitudes, seem very thin in the direction perpendicular to their length, and are usually in rapid motion. The lower edge, both of arcs and curtains, is usually much the best defined.

Aurora is very rare in the south of Europe, and is but

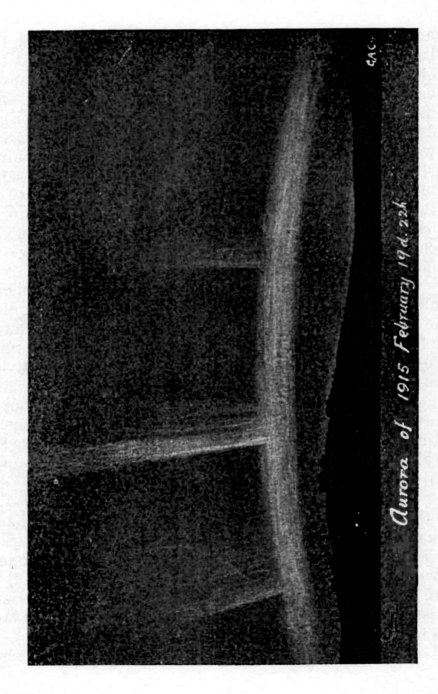

AURORA OF 1915, FEBRUARY 19d. 22h.

Aurora of 1915 February 19.d. 22h

13204

AURORA OF JANUARY 4, 1917. SKETCHED AT ABERDEEN BY G. A. CLARKE.

Phase I. 20h. 20m.

seldom seen in the south of England. But the frequency increases rapidly as we go north, and in Orkney and Shetland Aurora is a comparatively common phenomenon. A zone of maximum frequency passes from the North of Norway to the South of Iceland and Greenland. Aurora is also common in high southern latitudes, but its distribution there is still imperfectly known. The visibility of weak aurora is much affected by moonlight, and even the strongest aurora seems to be invisible if the sun is above the horizon. Thus there is some difficulty in assigning definite laws for its frequency of occurrence. In the British Isles and similar northern latitudes it is most common in the late evenings and near the equinoxes; but in the north of Norway and Greenland it appears to be most frequent near mid-winter. Of late years Professor Störmer has devised a method of photographing aurora, including reference stars in the photograph, and by means of photographs taken simultaneously at the two ends of a measured base he has obtained numerous results for the altitude. Heights exceeding 200 k. are not unusual, but a great majority of the heights lie between 90 k. and 130 k.

Aurora is undoubtedly an electrical discharge, and we thus infer that at heights of 100 k.—at least in high latitudes—the atmosphere must often, if not always, be a vastly better conductor of electricity than it is near the ground. Some distinguished travellers have claimed to see aurora come down between them and distant mountains. If this be the case, aurora must occasionally come down to much lower levels than any measured by Störmer, and there may be truth in the belief held by some meteorologists that cirrus cloud is sometimes the seat of aurora.

When visible in England, aurora is nearly always accompanied by a magnetic storm, but this is not the case when it is confined to high latitudes. The spectrum of aurora consists of a number of lines, one of which in the green is particularly characteristic, but it has not yet been identified with certainty with that of any known gas. It is not at all improbable that eventually we may learn much from the spectrum of aurora as to the constitution of the atmosphere at heights far greater than those accessible to balloons.

Boiling-points.—It is customary to say that a thermometer is graduated so that the freezing-point and boiling-point of water come at specified figures, *e.g.*, 32° and 212° on the Fahrenheit, or 273 and 373 on the absolute scale, and the importance of defining the pressure under which the water is boiling is frequently overlooked. In the process of boiling, bubbles of vapour are formed in the interior of the liquid. If the pressure of the air above the liquid is low the bubbles are formed and grow more readily, *i.e.*, at a lower temperature than when the pressure is high, so that the boiling-point is lowered by decrease of pressure, raised by increase of pressure.

Except on rare occasions pressure at sea level in England is between 1,040 mb. and 960 mb. Under the pressure 1,040 mb., water would boil at 373·73 a, under 960 mb. at 371·49 a. Under 1,000 mb. the boiling-point is 372·63 a. The standard pressure used in the definition of the temperature 373 a (or 212°F.) is that due to 760 mm. of mercury at the freezing point of water at sea level in latitude 45°, *i.e.*, 1,013·2 mb.

When we leave sea-level and ascend to places where the pressure is much lower, the temperature at which water boils is reduced. For example, at Pretoria, 5,200 ft. above sea-level, the average pressure is 871 mb., corresponding with a boiling-point 369a.

This change in the boiling-point in the course of an ascent is made use of in the measurement of heights by the HYPSOMETER, a method which is convenient, as the apparatus required is more portable than a mercury-barometer, and more reliable than an aneroid. At 21,600 ft., the greatest height reached by the Duke of the Abruzzi on the Himalayas, the pressure would be about 420 mb. and the boiling-point 350a. At great altitudes there is much difficulty in cooking, owing to the comparatively low temperature of the boiling water.

It should be mentioned that the figures which have been given above refer to the boiling of pure water. The addition of salts in solution raises the boiling-point. Sea water of average density boils at about 0·5a. above pure water under the same pressure. By adding 40 grammes of salt to 100 grammes of water the boiling-point can be raised by 9a.

Calorie or gramme-calorie—*i.e.*, the heat required to raise the temperature of 1 g. of water by 1a. at 288a.—is often used in connection with measurements of solar radiation. The amount of solar radiation is accordingly often given as so many gramme-calories per square centimetre per minute. At the Meteorological Office we use instead the milliwatt (per square centimetre), because that is the accepted unit of "rate of working" in Thermodynamics. Even in the total absence of cloud the amount of solar radiation which reaches a given area on the earth's surface at a given time is very variable. It depends on the altitude of the sun and the transparency of the earth's atmosphere. Thus it is by no means a simple thing to estimate the " Solar Constant," *i.e.*, the radiation which would be received in one minute by a square centimetre outside the earth's atmosphere, at the mean distance of the earth from the sun, the incidence of the radiation being normal. From a long series of investigations, Dr. Abbot, of the Smithsonian Institution, Washington, U.S.A., has arrived at 1·93 calories per square centimetre per minute or 135 milliwatts per square centimetre, as the mean value of the solar constant. Dr. Abbot concludes, however, that solar radiation, outside the earth's atmosphere, is not really constant, the fluctuations being presumably due to changes in the solar atmosphere.

Contingency.—In expressing the relationship between two variables, the correlation co-efficient " r " can only be used when both variables are given quantitatively. The correlation ratio η can be used when one or both variables are expressed quantitatively.

If, however, both variables are given qualitatively, it is not possible to use either the correlation co-efficient or the correlation ratio. In such cases it is usual to calculate the co-efficient of mean square contingency, C_1. This co-efficient C_1 is of the same nature· as the correlation co-efficient r.

The method of calculating C_1 can be obtained from any text-book on the Theory of Statistics*. An excellent astronomical example is given on page 167, " The Combination of Observations," Brunt (Camb. Univ. Press), in which it is shown that there is a close relationship between spectral type and the colour of stars. See Correlation.

Correlation Ratio.—A measure of the relationship

* An Introduction to the Theory of Statistics—by G. Udny Yule.

between two variables. In calculating a correlation co-efficient it is assumed that the regression is linear, *i e.*, that the observations themselves, or the means of grouped observations, when plotted, lie approximately along a straight line. In the calculation of the correlation ratio η, linear regression is not assumed. The correlation ratio may be defined as a generalised coefficient which measures the approach towards a curved linear line of regression of any form.

If η, r be respectively the correlation ratio, and correlation coefficient, found from a set of observations, $\eta^2 - r^2$ is a measure of the deviation from linearity of the curve of regression. See Computer's Handbook, pp. V 29-52.

Duration of Rainfall.—A climatic feature of some importance. Many forms of self-recording raingauge have been designed to determine the distribution of rain in time, but it is only in recent years that adequate attention has been paid to the matter, and the pattern of gauge has not yet been standardised in this country. During the 34 years, 1881–1914, at the headquarters of the British Rainfall Organization, in North-west London, the average annual duration of rain (snow and other forms of precipitation included) was 433 hours, about seventeen days, or 5 per cent. of the year, the extreme annual values ranging from 299 hours to 689 hours ($12\frac{1}{2}$ days to 29 days, $3\frac{1}{2}$ per cent. to 8 per cent.). In the wet regions of Cumberland, Wales and Western Scotland, the annual duration exceeds 1,000 hours (11·5 per cent. of the year) and in the wettest parts in the wettest years sometimes approaches 2,000 hours, or between a quarter and a fifth of the year.

The duration values for the year 1915 (a wet year) are given for the Observatories of the Meteorological Office, together with the total amount of rainfall and the mean rate of fall per hour :—

—	Rainfall.	Duration.	Rate per hour.
	mm.	hrs.	mm.
Kew	805	461	1·75
Falmouth ...	1,322	744	1·78
Eskdale ...	1,224	790	1·55
Aberdeen ...	805	589	1·37
Valencia ...	1,516	761	1·98
Armagh ...	741	530	1·40

The highest duration value for the year 1915, according to tables set out in the annual publication *British Rainfall* was 1,303 hours, or 15 per cent., near Kinlochleven, Argyll, a few miles S.E. of Ben Nevis, and the lowest value 442 hours at Nottingham.

In the London district the mean rate of fall increases with the mean temperature, reaching its maximum in July and minimum in January. The actual duration, on the average, is least in July and September, when it is little more than 25 hours, and greatest in November, when that figure is nearly doubled.

The CORRELATION COEFFICIENT between annual amount and annual duration of rainfall for 35 years in N.W. London is + ·81.

Dust.—The atmosphere is permeated by dust up to great heights ; the dust may be derived from deserts, or from any dry surface. from evaporated sea-spray, from plants in the shape of pollen grains, from the debris of meteorites, from volcanoes. Dust is important meteorologically in that water vapour condenses on dust particles. Dust-free air may be cooled considerably below the dew-point without condensation occurring.

Dust Counter.—Aitken has devised three types of instrument for estimating the number of dust-particles in a sample of air ; a large model with artificial illumination, suitable as a permanent part of the equipment of a first-class observatory ; a portable model suitable for testing locally polluted air, *e.g.*, in sanitary work ; and a pocket instrument for use in country districts where the variations in the dustiness are small. This last instrument will be described briefly, as it embodies the same principle as the others, but with fewer working parts.

Into a receiving chamber, lined with moist blotting paper, a measured quantity of the air to be tested is introduced. This chamber contains a horizontal glass stage, having fine cross lines 1 mm. apart etched upon it so as to divide the surface into a network of squares. A sudden reduction of the pressure of the saturated air in this receiver, which is effected by means of a pump, causes the aqueous vapour to condense upon the dust-particles, and the small raindrops so formed fall upon the glass stage. The average number that fall upon one of the small squares is then counted, with the aid of a lens let into the roof of the receiver, and so an estimate of the number of dust-particles in 1 cc. of the air can be made. The method of measuring the volume of the sample of air is ingeniously simple. When the piston is drawn down in making a stroke of the pump, the air in the receiver expands by a fraction which is read off upon a scale engraved upon the barrel of the pump for this purpose. If now the receiver is put into communication with the outer air, a sample of air having this volume enters and restores the pressure inside to that of the outside air. The complete instrument can be packed in a box $4\frac{3}{8} \times 2\frac{1}{2} \times 1\frac{1}{4}$ inches and weighs barely half-a-pound.

The following table shows the number of dust-particles found by Aitken in 1 cc. of air at various localities :—

Cannes (April)	1,500—150,000
Simplon Pass (May)	500— 14,000
Summit of Rigi (May)	200— 2,350
Eiffel Tower (May)	226—104,000
Paris (Garden of M.O.) (May) ...	134,000—210,000
London (Victoria Street) (June) ...	48,000—150,000
Dumfries (Oct.-Nov.)	395— 11,500
Ben Nevis (August)...	335— 473

False Cirrus.[*]—False cirrus may be defined as a type of cloud resembling cirrus but occurring at lower altitudes. It consists of snow, may occur at any height, and may be divided into two main classes :—

(1) Consisting of isolated tufts of large masses of considerable height.

(2) Spread out in extensive sheets.

Type (1) is commonly seen on the tops of showers. The rounded top of a cumulus, consisting of minute particles causing diffraction rings, often turns to false cirrus ; this may afterwards be carried for considerable distances both vertically and horizontally. As the shower dissolves away, the false cirrus may remain for some time

---

[*] Contributed by Lieut. C. K. M. Douglas, R.F.C.

afterwards, and may consist of white tufts or dull grey masses, with edges resembling cirrus. It occasionally forms direct, and not from other clouds. For instance, on April 1st, 1917, near Edinburgh large tufts of false cirrus formed at a height of about 6,000 feet, apparently caused by convection currents. Snow showers resulted but only a few flakes reached the ground.

Type (2) is distinguished by its more regular formation and covers large areas. It sometimes has a dull uniform grey appearance, being then usually classed as "alto-stratus"; it has then often very great thickness. Sometimes it assumes the well-known cirrus form, resembling cirro-stratus sheets, but never causing a halo. No very definite dividing line can be drawn between "false cirrus" and cirro-stratus. False cirrus sheets may change to thin wavy clouds resembling cirro-cumulus, causing diffraction rings; this most often happens in the evening, and the clouds may afterwards dissolve away entirely. Dense masses of false cirrus from the south with surface winds from the north-east often precede heavy thunder-storms.

Glacier.—A river of ice flowing slowly but irresistibly down the valleys of those regions which have a perpetual supply of snow to feed the head of the glacier. The explanation of the gradual flow of ice down valleys under the action of gravity, forms a special section of physics and is another illustration of the peculiarities of the material of which water is composed. Glaciers are not only of climatic importance but in dynamical meteorology, with rivers, they deserve consideration as showing the line along which air flows when the excess of density due to cooling is the primary reason for the movement.

From the analogy we may conclude that a gully is no protection against *katabatic* winds but rather the reverse.

Gravity relates to the attraction between material bodies. The law of universal gravitation is that every mass attracts every other mass with a force which varies directly as the product of the attracting masses and inversely as the square of the distance between them. It is convenient to regard the attracted body as of unit mass. The law then implies that the force exerted is independent of the temperature or velocity of the attracting body. Both these conclusions have been attacked of late years, but it is not questioned that they are sufficiently exact for meteorological purposes.

It is easily shown mathematically that a sphere whose density varies only with the distance from the centre attracts an external body exactly as if the whole mass were collected at the centre, and that a similarly constituted spherical shell—*i.e.*, a mass bounded by two concentric spherical surfaces—while attracting an external body as if its mass were collected at the centre, exerts no attraction at any internal point. Let us apply this to a point in the atmosphere at height h above the ground, regarding the earth as a perfect sphere of radius R, and assuming the density, whether of the earth or the atmosphere, to vary only with the radial distance. The atmosphere outside the spherical surface of radius $R+h$ exerts no attraction, while the earth's mass M' within the surface of radius $R+h$ attract as if collected at the centre. Thus the attractive force is $G(M+M')/(R+h)^2$, where G is a constant. This becomes $g_0(1+M'/M)(1+h/R)^{-2}$, where $g_0 = GM/R^2$ is the corresponding force at the earth's surface, *i.e.*, wholly within the atmosphere. Counted in kilogrammes M' is large, but even if we went to the confines of the atmosphere M'/M would be less than 1/1 million. Thus the attraction of the atmosphere may be neglected, at least for meteorological purposes. The variation with height in the earth's own attraction is much more important. At all heights attained by balloons we may neglect h^2/R^2, and so replace $(1+h/R)^{-2}$ by $1-2h/R$. But at a height of say 10 miles this represents a reduction of one part in 200 in gravity.

In reality the earth is not a sphere, but approaches to a spheroid whose equatorial radius is 10·7 k. longer than its polar radius. Also it rotates, and the " centrifugal force " due to the rotation reduces gravity, especially near the equator. The earth's surface is also irregular in outline, and the density variable, at least near the surface. Thus the formulæ actually advanced to show the variation of gravity at different parts of the earth's surface are complicated.

The following formula, due to Helmert, is perhaps the best known. In it g denotes the acceleration of gravity in C.G.S. units, *i.e.*, in cm/s^2 :

$$g = 978\cdot000\ (1+0\cdot00531\ \sin^2\ \phi) \times$$

$$\left(1 - \frac{2h}{R} + \frac{3h}{2R}\frac{\delta}{\Delta} - \frac{h'\ (\delta-\theta)}{2R\Delta} + y\ \right)$$

Here ϕ is the latitude, R the earth's mean radius, h the height above sea level, h' the thickness of surface strata of low density, Δ the earth's mean density (approximately 5·6 times that of water), δ mean density of surface strata (usually taken as 2·8), θ the actual density of surface strata for the region, and y

a so-called orographical correction arising from neighbouring mountains and so on. At sea level, supposing
$\delta=\theta$, and y negligible, this becomes

$$g=978\cdot600\,(1+0\cdot00531\,\sin^2\,\phi),$$

or more conveniently $g=980\cdot5966-2\cdot5966\,\cos\,2\phi$.

Thus g has its mean value where $\cos\,2\phi$ vanishes, *i.e.*,
where $2\phi=90°$, or $\phi=45°$. This explains why it is usual
to reduce gravity to latitude 45°. This means reducing
some measure actually made—e.g. of the height of the
barometer—to what it would have been if gravity had
possessed its mean value. The formula does not, of
course, imply that gravity has the same value at every
spot in latitude 45°, irrespective of its height above sea
level or other local peculiarities.

The determination of g absolutely at any spot with the
precision which the formulæ suggest is extremely difficult,
but relative values of g, or, differences between its values
at different places, can be determined with very high precision by means of pendulum observations.

If t and t' be the times of oscillation of a certain pendulum at two stations, the corresponding values g and g'
of gravity are connected by the relation $g'/g=(t/t')^2$.

This enables gravity at any station to be determined in
terms of gravity at a base station. For accurate work
corrections have to be applied to the observed times of
swing to allow for departures of temperature and pressure
from their standard values, also for chronometer-rate and
flexure of the pendulum-stand. When all the known
corrections are carefully made a very high degree of
accuracy is obtainable. For instance, taking 981·200 as
the value of g at Kew Observatory, this being the value
accepted for the purposes of the Trigonometrical Survey

of India, the last two comparisons instituted between Greenwich and Kew, the one made by the United States Coast and Geodetic Survey, the other by the Trigonometrical Survey of India—using two different sets of half-second pendulums, gave for *g* at Greenwich the respective values 981·188 and 981·186. ·

Pendulum and other geodetic observations have led to a theory of *isostasy* which has received strong support of late years, especially in the United States. According to this theory if we start at about 100 k. below sea level we find between there and the free surface an approximately uniform quantity of matter irrespective of whether the free surface is mountainous or not. A lesser density under lofty mountains and a higher density under deep seas act as compensations.

While the mass of a body is independent of its position, its weight, *i.e.*, the gravitational attraction exerted on it varies with *g* and so increases as we pass from the equator towards either pole. Denoting by g_ϕ the value of *g* in latitude ϕ we obtain from the formula

$$g_{90} = 983\cdot19, \quad g_0 = 978\cdot00.$$

In other words, gravity at the poles exceeds gravity at the equator by 1 part in 189.

Harmonic Analysis.

—There are many meteorological phenomena which recur with some approach to regularity day by day. If the changes of such a variable as temperature are represented by a curve, then the portions corresponding to successive days bear a strong likeness to one another. If for the actual record for each day the record for the average day were substituted, the variation for a long period would be represented by a

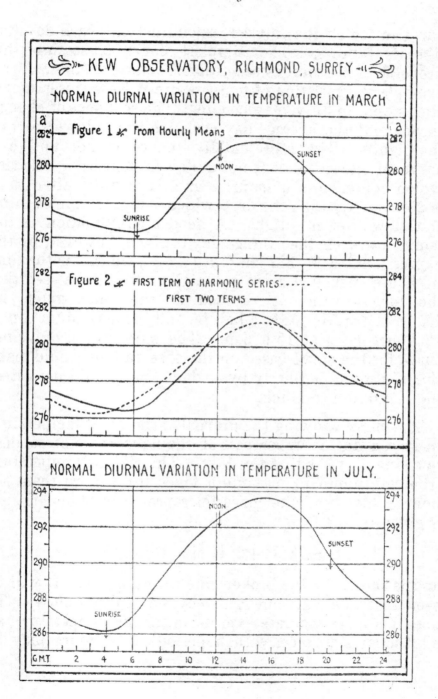

KEW OBSERVATORY, RICHMOND, SURREY

NORMAL DIURNAL VARIATION IN TEMPERATURE IN MARCH

Figure 1 — From Hourly Means

SUNRISE NOON SUNSET

Figure 2 — FIRST TERM OF HARMONIC SERIES - - - -
FIRST TWO TERMS ———

NORMAL DIURNAL VARIATION IN TEMPERATURE IN JULY.

NOON SUNSET

SUNRISE

GMT 2 4 6 8 10 12 14 16 18 20 22 24

curve in which the part corresponding with each day was like its fellows. The simplest curve possessing this property of continuous repetition is a curve of sines. As an example the variation of temperature at Kew Observatory, Richmond, in July, may be cited. The sequence of change throughout the average day is shown in the lower part of the figure. The representative curve is not unlike a curve of sines, but it is not quite symmetrical. The rise which commences at sunrise and lasts until after 15 h. is more steady than the drop which is rapid in the evening and slow after midnight. A good approximation to the temperature on the average day is given, however, by the expression $289 \cdot 9 + 3 \cdot 7 \sin (15t + 224\frac{1}{2}°)$ where t is the time in hours reckoned from midnight. It will be seen that the lowest value is reached at the time given by $15t + 224\frac{1}{2}° = 270°$ *i.e.* at 3 h. 6 m. and the maximum comes 12 hours later at 15 h. 6 m. The substitution of a sine-curve for the curve based on the observations would make the minimum too early by an hour, but would not affect the maximum so much.

The curve showing the diurnal variation of temperature in March (in the upper part of the figure) is not so near to a sine-curve as that for July. The rise in temperature from minimum to maximum takes little more than six hours. The best sine-curve for representing the variation is given by the formula

$$\theta = 278 \cdot 74 + 2 \cdot 47 \sin (15t + 222°)$$

and is shown by the broken line in the figure. It will be seen that the agreement is by no means close. To obtain a more accurate expression for the temperature, an additional sine term with a period of 12 hours may be introduced. The best formula containing such a term is

$$\theta = 278 \cdot 74 + 2 \cdot 47 \sin (15t + 222°) + 0 \cdot 63 \sin (30t + 39°)$$

The new term $0 \cdot 63 \sin (30t + 39°)$ is positive in the early morning and in the early afternoon, so that it delays the drop to the minimum and makes the maximum earlier. In Figure 2, the continuous curve which corresponds with the proposed formula crosses the simple sine-curve at intervals of six hours. The resemblance to the curve based on the observations is greatly improved. A closer resemblance would be obtained if additional terms

$$0 \cdot 08 \sin (45t + 330°) + 0 \cdot 12 \sin (60t + 190°)$$

were included in the formula.

The harmonic representation of a diurnal inequality may be expressed in either of the alternative forms—

$$a_1 \cos (15° \times t) + a_2 \cos (30° \times t) + a_3 \cos (45° \times t)$$
$$+ a_4 \cos (60° \times t) + \ldots$$
$$+ b_1 \sin (15° \times t) + b_2 \sin (30° \times t) + b_3 \sin (45° \times t)$$
$$+ b_4 \sin (60° \times t) + \ldots ,$$

$$P_1 \sin (15° \times t + A_1) + P_2 \sin (30° \times t + A_2) +$$
$$P_3 \sin (45° \times t + A_3) + P_4 \sin (60° \times t + A_4) + \ldots ,$$

where t denotes the time in hours counting from some fixed hour, usually midnight. The latter is the form which has been adopted in the previous part of this note, as it best exhibits the physical significance of the results, but the first form is that employed for the actual numerical calculation of the harmonic coefficients. We first calculate the a, b coefficients and then derive the P, A coefficients from the relations

$$\tan A_n = a_n / b_n ; \quad P_n = a_n / \sin A_n = b_n / \cos A_n ;$$

where n may be 1, 2, 3, 4, &c.

For brevity, let 0, 1, 2 . . . . . 23 represent the algebraical departures from the mean value for the day of an element such as temperature or pressure at the successive hours midnight (or 0), 1, 2 . . . . Then using the following closely approximate values 0·966 for cos 15° or sin 75°, 0·866 for cos 30° or sin 60°, 0·707 for cos 45° or sin 45°, 0·259 for cos 75° or sin 15°, and noticing that 0·5 is the exact value of cos 60° or sin 30°, we have the following mathematical expressions for the a, b coefficients of the first 4 orders :—

$$12a_1 = (0-12) + 0·966\{(1+23)-(11+13)\} + 0·866\{(2+22) \\ -(10+14)\} + 0·707\{(3+21)-(9+15)\} \\ + 0·5\{(4+20)-(8+16)\} + 0·259\{(5+19)-(7+17)\},$$

$$12a_2 = (0+12)-(6+18)+0·866\{(1+23)-(5+19)-(7+17) \\ + (11+13)\} + 0·5\{(2+22)-(4+20)-(8+16) \\ + (10+14)\},$$

$$12a_3 = (0-12)-(4+20)+(8+16)+0·707\{(1+23)-(3+21) \\ -(5+19)+(7+17)+(9+15)-(11+13)\},$$

$$12a_4 = (0+12)-(3+21)+(6+18)-(9+15) \\ + 0·5\{(1+23)-(2+22)-(4+20)+(5+19)+(7+17) \\ -(8+16)-(10+14)+(11+13)\},$$

$$12b_1 = (6-18) + 0·966\{(5-19)+(7-17)\} + 0·866\{(4-20) \\ + (8-16)\} + 0·707\{(3-21)+(9-15)\} \\ + 0·5\{(2-22)+(10-14)\} + 0·259\{(1-23)+(11-13)\},$$

$$12b_2 = (3-21)-(9-15)+0·866\{(2-22)+(4-20)-(8-16) \\ -(10-14)\} + 0·5\{(1-23)+(5-19)-(7-17) \\ -(11-13)\},$$

$$12b_3 = (2-22)-(6-18)+(10-14)+0·707\{(1-23)+(3-21) \\ -(5-19)-(7-17)+(9-15)+(11-13)\},$$

$$12b_4 = 0·866\{(1-23)+(2-22)-(4-20)-(5-19)+(7-17) \\ + (8-16)-(10-14)-(11-13)\}.$$

The terms are arranged in pairs for facility of calculation, as will be better understood on consulting the numerical example given presently. It will be noticed that in the case of the b coefficients we have to do invariably with differences, and that the sum of the two numerals (representing the observational hours) which form the pair is invariably 24. Similarly in the case of the a coefficients, with two apparent exceptions, we have the sum of observational values at hours which together amount to 24. The exceptions (0 ± 12) are only apparent; they really represent $\frac{1}{2} \{(0 + 24) \pm (12 + 12)\}$. The hours 0 and 24 alike represent midnight.

Take for illustration the case already given of the diurnal variation of temperature at Kew Observatory during March. The 24 hourly differences from the mean of the day on the average of the 45 years 1871 to 1915 were as follows :—

0,12	1,23	2,22	3,21	4,20	5,19
−1·35	−1·51	−1·75	−1·91	−2·10	−2·19
+2·03	−1·04	−0·72	−0·29	+0·11	+0·70

6,18	7,17	8,16	9,15	10,14	11,13
−2·31	−2·14	−1·62	−0·49	+0·43	+1·41
+1·42	+2·26	+2·69	+2·93	+2·77	+2·58

The headings denote the hours to which the observational data immediately below refer. For instance, the departures from the mean value of the day at 0 h. and 12 h. were respectively −1°·35 and +2°·03.

Referring to the formulæ it will be seen that we want the algebraical sum and difference of the two entries which appear in the same column. These are respectively :—

sums ... $+0.68$ -2.55 -2.47 -2.20 -1.99 -1.49
-0.89 $+0.12$ $+1.07$ $+2.44$ $+3.20$ $+3.99$
differences -3.38 -0.47 -1.03 -1.62 -2.21 -2.89
-3.73 -4.40 -4.31 -3.42 -2.34 -1.17

For calculating the b coefficients we require only the differences; for the a coefficients in addition to the sums we require only the first difference.

We thus have
$$12a_1 = -3.38 + 0.966\,(-2.55-3.99) + 0.866\,(-2.47-3.20)$$
$$+ 0.707\,(-2.20-2.44) + 0.5\,(-1.99-1.07)$$
$$+ 0.259\,(-1.49-0.12).$$

Employing Crelle's Tables, or logarithms, or straight-forward multiplication, we get $12a_1 = -3.38 \; -6.32 \; -4.91 \; -3.28 \; -1.53 \; -0.42 = -19.84$, and so $a_1 = -1.653$.

Similarly we find $12a_2 = +4.83$, and so $a_2 = +0.403$;
$$12a_3 = -0.53 \quad , \quad a_3 = -0.044;$$
$$12a_4 = -0.32 \quad , \quad a_4 = -0.027.$$

Coming next to the b's, we have
$$12b_1 = -3.73 + 0.966\,(-2.89-4.40) + 0.866\,(-2.21-4.31)$$
$$+0.707\,(-1.62-3.42) + 0.5\,(-1.03-2.34)$$
$$+0.259\,(-0.47-1.17),$$

$$= -3.73 - 7.04 - 5.65 - 3.56 - 1.69 - 0.42 = -22.09,$$
and so $b_1 = -1.841$.

Similarly we find

$$12b_2 = +5\cdot86, \text{ and so } b_2 = +0\cdot488\,;$$
$$12b_3 = +0\cdot79 \quad ,, \qquad b_3 = +0\cdot066\,;$$
$$12b_4 = -1\cdot39 \quad ,, \qquad b_4 = -0\cdot116.$$

The deduction of the P, A, constants is simple. Take, for example, the case of P_1, A_1, *i.e.* the 24-hour term. We have $\tan A_1 = \dfrac{a_1}{b_1} = \dfrac{-1\cdot653}{-1\cdot841} = +0\cdot8978.$

The angle whose tangent is $+0\cdot8978$ may be $41°55'$ or $41°55' + 180°$, *i.e.* $221°55'$.

To determine which, we notice that a_1 and b_1 are both minus, so that $\sin A_1$ and $\cos A_1$ are both minus. Thus A_1 lies in the third quadrant, between $180°$ and $270°$, and consequently is $221°55'$, or to the nearest degree $222°$.

The formula $P_1 = a_1/\sin A_1$ gives us $P_1 = \dfrac{1\cdot653}{0\cdot668} = 2\cdot47.$

We need not trouble about the sign, as the P's are all positive. The values of A_2, P_2, A_3, P_3, A_4 and P_4 are derivable exactly in the same way.

The process of finding the trigonometric series to give the best representation of a periodic function is known as harmonic analysis. The reverse process, determining the value of the function at any time when the components are known, is harmonic synthesis. Both processes can be carried out by suitable machines, and also by arithmetical computation from given data. The latter process is the more usual except in the case of the prediction of tides.

In any term $P \sin (nt + A)$ the coefficient P which determines the range is called the amplitude, $nt + A$ is called the phase-angle, A being the phase-angle for midnight. It may be mentioned that the alternative form

$P \cos n(t-t_0)$ where t_0 is the time of the maximum, has certain advantages; it was adopted by General Strachey for the discussion of harmonic analysis of temperature in the British Isles.

By comparison of the amplitudes and phase-angles for different places and different seasons, climates may be classified. For èxample, the amplitude of the whole-day term for temperature in July at Falmouth is 2·1a, and the phase-angle for local apparent midnight is 250°. In comparison ˙with Kew, the amplitude is small and the maximum occurs early. This difference in phase is typical of the difference in conditions on the coast and inland. It may be stated, however, that as regards temperature, harmonic analysis has not yielded information which can not be obtained more readily from the curves showing the daily variation. With pressure more important results have been discovered.

For temperature the first or all-day term in the expansion in trigonometric series is by far the most important. With pressure the second term is comparable in size with the first, and at most stations there are two maxima and two minima in the course of 24 hours. The first term is found to depend on the situation of the station, whether near the coast or inland, in a valley or on a mountain-side, whereas the second or twelve-hour term depends principally on the latitude. The daily changes represented by the first term are clearly understood, they are the effects of local heating of the air. No adequate explanation of the surge of pressure which is represented by the second and higher terms has been put forward.

The daily variation of pressure at Cairo in July is represented graphically by the second Figure.

Daily variation of the Barometer at Cairo [*Abbassia Observatory*] *in July.*

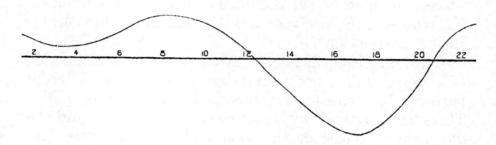

The departure of the pressure from the mean for the day is given in millibars by the expression

$$\cdot92 \sin (15t + 17°) + \cdot66 \sin (30t + 140°)$$
$$+ \cdot12 \sin (45t + 348°) + \cdot05 \sin (60t + 250°).$$

The first term represents an oscillation with the maximum and minimum at about 5h. and 17h. respectively. It indicates that as the air is warmed in the daytime it expands and overflows from the Nile valley over the surrounding high ground and over the neighbouring seas.

The second term represents an oscillation with maxima at 10h. 20m. and 22h. 20m. These hours are almost the same all over the globe. The amplitude depends on the latitude and to a certain extent on the time of year. The mean value for the year at Cairo is 0·8 mb. It is about 1·3 mb. at the equator, 0·5 in latitude 45°, 0·35 in London and 0·1 mb. in latitude 60°.

The third term is interesting as it changes its phase by 180° at the equinoxes. The first maximum occurs at 2h. in summer, the first minimum at the same hour in winter.

It has been mentioned that the all-day term depends largely on local conditions. An interesting contrast is offered by the British observatories. At Richmond, Surrey, the amplitude of this term in July is about 0·3mb., and it has about the same value at Cahirciveen, but the phases are opposite : at Richmond the maximum occurs at 5h., whereas at Cahirciveen it is the minimum which occurs in the morning (at 7h).

Harmonic Analysis may be extended to the investigation of changes which are caused by forces having different periods. The classical instance is that of the tides. The. Tides being caused by the attraction of the sun and the moon show as periods the solar and also the lunar day. The process by which the heights and the times of tides are foretold in practice depends on harmonic analysis and synthesis.

Ice.—Owing to the large amount of heat absorbed in melting (80 CALORIES for one gramme melted) a mass of ice represents a powerful reservoir of cold. Masses of ice or snow can attain to such dimensions in Nature that the heat absorbed during melting is of climatological importance. An excellent example is furnished by the icebergs observed by Antarctic explorers. The largest of these appear to be portions of the great Ross Ice-barrier that have broken away during the summer months. They are generally several hundred feet thick and may exceed 20 miles in length. The amount of heat required to melt one 20 miles long, 5 miles broad and 600 feet thick would be sufficient to raise the temperature of the air over the whole British Isles from the ground up to a height of 1 kilometre (3,281 feet) by over 40°C.

When ice forms upon a pond during frosty weather the cooled water at the surface is continually replaced by warmer water from below until the whole mass has fallen to 277a (39°F), which is the temperature at which water has its greatest density. The surface can then cool undisturbed until the freezing point is reached and ice begins to form, but when ice first begins to form in a flowing river is a complicated question about which Professor H. T. Barnes, F.R.S., has written.

When the sea freezes the crystals formed contain no salt but cannot easily be separated from the brine which is mixed up with them, consequently the water obtained by melting genuine sea-ice is salt. When, however, this ice forms hummocks under the action of pressure the brine drains out and leaves pure ice. Newly-formed sea-ice has a surprising degree of flexibility due to the fact that the crystals are separated by layers of brine or salt, and even when it is several inches thick the surface can be moved up and down unbroken by a swell. As the thickness increases this can no longer happen, and the sheet is broken up into pieces, which grind together and soon form the beautiful " pancake-ice " familiar to polar explorers.

Ionisation in the atmosphere arises from the presence of free + and − ions. Charged ions move along the lines of force in an electric field, carrying their charges with them. This is equivalent to an electric current. The current increases with the number of free ions present, and with their *mobility* (*i.e.*, the velocity which an ion possesses in a field of unit strength). An increase of current for a given strength of field is equivalent to an increase of conductivity in the medium.

There are at least two distinct kinds of ions in the atmosphere, usually known as light or mobile ions, and as heavy or Langevin ions, so-called after their discoverer,

Prof. Langevin. The heavy ions are the more numerous, at least, in the polluted air ordinarily met with near large towns, but their mobility is so small that they are of minor importance so far as the conductivity of the atmosphere is concerned. The light ion has a velocity of the order of 1 cm. per second in a field of 1 volt per cm.

Ionic charges in the atmosphere are usually measured with the Ebert apparatus. This consists of a hollow cylindrical tube—vertical in the more recent forms—containing a co-axial cylindrical rod, which is insulated and connected to the fibres of a " string electrometer." The rod is charged to a potential of from 100 to 20) volts, the cylindrical tube being earthed. Air is pulled through the tube by a turbine, the amount passing being recorded on an anemometer. Supposing the rod charged negatively, the positive ions in the admitted air are attracted to the rod, and as the air passes give up their charge to it. The length of the rod and the potential to which it is charged are such as to ensure that no mobile ion will escape capture. The readings of the electrometer taken before and after the admission of the air, the capacity of the electrical system being known, inform us how much the charge on the rod has been diminished. A small part of the loss—determined by a separate experiment—is due to imperfect insulation ; the balance represents the free electrical charge opposite in sign to that on the rod existing in a measured volume of air. Two experiments are made, the rod being charged negatively in the one case, positively in the other. We thus get the free charges present per c.c. in the atmosphere. These charges are highly variable, but are usually of the order of 1000×10^{-20} in electromagnetic units. The number of ions per c.c. is often published and may be deduced by dividing the charge, whether +. or −, by the charge on an ion, for which the value accepted at present is 159×10^{-22} in electromagnetic units.

In all, or nearly all the earlier work done on the subject, the ionic charge was given a value 29 per cent. less than that now accepted, leading to an overestimate of the number of ions. It is also the case that part of the charge is derived from the heavy ions, though the percentage of these caught by the Ebert apparatus is undoubtedly small. The mobility of the ions may also be measured with the Ebert apparatus, but the process is somewhat complicated, and the accuracy of individual determinations is not high.

Observations at the earth's surface have usually given a decided excess in the number of + ions. The + and − ions naturally tend to combine, and their presence thus points to the existence of some agency producing ions. Several possible agencies are recognised, including radio-active substances, and solar radiation, especially ultra-violet light. Near the ground the radio-active substances ordinarily present in the ground may be the chief source. Balloon observations have shown that the ionisation diminishes somewhat at first as we leave the ground, but at heights of 1 k to 2 k it begins to increase again, and at heights of 9 k or 10 k it seems to be very much larger than near the ground. The ionising agent there is presumably RADIATION of some kind from the sun.

Lightning, Protection from.—The region between the earth and a thundercloud is one of great electrical stress. It may appear paradoxical that a lightning-conductor, intended to protect a structure within that region from damage, acts primarily by increasing this stress. The lightning-conductor consists of a metallic point or set of points connected by a metal rod to a conductor of considerable area buried in moist earth. This conducting point, projecting some short distance above the highest point to be protected, increases the intensity of the stress between itself and the cloud, till one of two things happens. A silent "brush" discharge may take place, in which the induced electrification of the earth streams comparatively gently from the point (selected because of its well-known property of facilitating brush-discharge), and thus finally reduce the stress to a limit insufficient to produce a violent lightning discharge. If, on the contrary, a lightning discharge does occur in the region, it will pass to the point because of the increased stress, and the rod will carry the current harmlessly to earth.

The old idea of an "area of protection" is no longer tenable, and pointed conductors should therefore be provided on every vertical projection of the structure to be protected, and at intervals along the ridge of a long roof. These should be connected by metal rods or cables and the rods connected at several places to earth. The connecting rods should run as straight as possible since electrical inertia will make the discharge jump across an air-gap in preference to rounding a sharp bend or loop in the rods. Iron rods are preferable to copper both electrically and economically, and may be painted for preservation. The rods should be held at a distance of some inches from walls, but should be fixed, not by insulators, but by metal holdfasts fastened in or on the walls. Metal roofs, gutters, pipes and other masses of metal should be electrically continuous and connected to earth.

Inside the building, pipes, bell-systems and all large metallic masses should also be earth-connected, since violent oscillations may be induced in them by a discharge through the external conductor, and they may cause fire by sparking to earth if they are not so connected.

The only complete protection is attained by enclosing the structure in a "birdcage" arrangement of conductors, well connected to earth at several points. A metal building, whose parts are electrically connected amongst themselves and to earth, is probably the most perfect protection possible, but here also internal metal-work should be earth-connected.

The personal danger from lightning in the open country is at least twice as great as in towns, owing to the number of buildings in the latter protected intentionally (as by lightning conductors), or unintentionally (as by overhead wiring for light, power, telephones, etc.). It seems to be a definitely established fact that certain trees, particularly the Oak, are more frequently struck than others. The relative danger of lightning stroke, taking the Beech as 1, is Oak 50–60, Scotch Pine 30–40, Spruce 10, but is of course much affected by environment. Isolated and prominent trees are more frequently struck than average forest trees.

The safest course in the open—though perhaps not the most comfortable—is to lie in a ditch or furrow, failing these to lie on the ground. To shelter under isolated trees or on the edges of a wood is dangerous : well inside the wood the danger is probably not great. Immediately under a line of over-head wires is also a relatively safe area.

The protection of aircraft against lightning is a difficult problem, complicated by such appendages as wire cables in the case of balloons and radio-telegraphic aerials on aeroplanes. The trail of hot gases from the engine exhaust acts as a comparatively good conductor, which may work for good or harm according to the position of the craft relative to the thundercloud, but on the whole, by acting as a lightning-conductor and thus facilitating discharge along a path passing through the machine, probably adds a good deal more to the danger than it takes from it..

Magnetism.—The branch of knowledge relating to magnetic phenomena. Terrestrial magnetism is concerned with the earth's magnetism. The earth has been happily described as a great magnet: the distribution of magnetic force at its surface may as a first approximation be regarded as that due to a uniformly magnetised sphere, whose magnetic axis, however, is inclined at some 10° or 12° to the earth's axis of rotation (polar axis). The magnetic poles are the one to the north of Canada, the other in the Antarctic. At these poles the dip needle is vertical, and the horizontal component of magnetic force vanishes ; the compass needle has no guiding force and points anyhow. At what may be called the magnetic equator, which is nowhere very far from the geographical equator, the vertical force vanishes ; the dip needle is horizontal, and the horizontal force has its largest values. The horizontal force in London is only about half that where the magnetic equator crosses India. The compass needle points in the direction of the local horizontal component of magnetic force, and this direction is exactly north and south only along two lines or narrow belts, one of which at present crosses Asia Minor and European Russia, while the other crosses the United States and Canada. The position of these " Agonic " lines as they are called, and the direction of the magnetic needle, change gradually with time, having what is known as " secular change." The inclination of the magnetic needle to the geographical meridian is called the declination, or sometimes, rather unfortunately, the magnetic variation. As we travel westward from the Asiatic-European Agonic line, the declination becomes increasingly westerly, until we pass the western limits of Europe. Thus, at present, approximate values are at Cairo $1\frac{3}{4}°$ W., at Athens $3\frac{3}{4}°$ W., at Pola $7\frac{1}{2}°$ W., at Copenhagen $8\frac{1}{2}°$ W., at Brussels $12\frac{1}{4}°$ W., at London 15° W., and at Valencia Observatory (Co. Kerry) 20° W. In Europe westerly declination is at present diminishing at a rate of nearly 10′ a year. Besides the secular change, declination has a regular diurnal variation, and also frequent irregular changes, which when large are known as magnetic storms. In the Northern hemisphere the prominent part of the regular diurnal variation is a westerly movement from about 7h. to 13 h. (1 p.m.), followed by a slower easterly movement. Speaking generally the range of the regular diurnal variation is least near the magnetic equator, where it may average less than 3′, and the greatest near the magnetic poles, where it may exceed 1°. It varies with the season of the year. At Richmond, for instance, in the average year it varies from about $3\frac{1}{3}′$ in December to 11′ in August, the mean from all months of the year being about 8′. It also varies considerably from year to year, showing a remarkably similar progression to that of sunspot frequency. In a year of sunspot maximum the range may be 50 per cent. or more larger than a few years earlier or later at sunspot minimum. Few days are wholly free from irregular changes of declination, and these are sometimes much larger than the regular changes. Thus the actually observed daily range at Kew sometimes exceeds 1°, and in high latitudes ranges of 5°, or even 10° or more, are occasionally observed. In latitudes, however, below 60° in Europe departures of more than 30' from the mean value for the year are rare. On the occasions of very large magnetic changes AURORA is generally observed, even in the South of England, and there is usually some interference with ordinary telegraphy.

The direction of the compass-needle is practically independent of the height above the ground, except in localities where some large underground source of disturbance exists. In such a case, moreover, the higher one goes up the less is the effect of the local disturbance.

All objects of iron are liable to become magnets, especially when they are long and disposed with their length nearly in the magnetic meridian, and are thus apt to introduce errors in the readings of compasses in their vicinity. This warning applies particularly to large objects like ships, girders and large guns ; but even small articles of iron, such as some buttons or spectacle frames, when close to a compass, may cause quite a serious error. Some forms of rock, especially dark-coloured basalt, are strongly magnetic, and large disturbing effects are caused by the strong electric currents used in connection with electric tramways and railways when the system is a direct-current one.

Precipitation.—A term borrowed from chemistry to denote any one of the results of the conversion of the invisible water-vapour to visible water or ice, thus comprising not only rain, hail, snow, sleet, dew, hoar-frost and rime, but cloud, mist and fog. In practice, however, the use of the word is limited to appreciable deposit in either the solid or the liquid form at the earth's surface, the definition of " Day of precipitation " being identical with that of RAIN-DAY (*q.v.*). At low levels it is rare for appreciable deposit of water in the rain-gauge to result from precipitation of cloud, mist or fog, but in mountainous districts wet-fog and SCOTCH-MIST (*q.v.*) are responsible for a considerable quantity of " rainfall." See RAIN, HAIL, SNOW, etc.

Radiation, Solar and Terrestrial.—Radiation is the process by which heat is transferred from one body to another without altering the temperature of the intervening medium. All life upon the earth and all meteorological phenomena are dependent upon the radiant heat and light received from the sun. See INSOLATION.

The earth itself is always radiating into space, and according to Stefan's law the rate of radiation is given by σT^4, where T is the absolute temperature and σ a constant. During the day normally the earth receives directly from the sun and indirectly from the atmosphere, including the clouds, more radiation than it gives out. At night the reverse is the case. The rate of loss of heat from a plate freely exposed at the earth's surface at night tells us the balance of loss, *i.e.*, the excess of the earth's radiation outwards over what it receives from the atmosphere. With the aid of Stefan's law we can form an estimation of radiation received from the atmosphere. According to Professor Millikan, who has recently reviewed the literature of the subject, the most probable value of σ in Stefan's formula in watts per sq. cm. is $5 \cdot 72 \times 10^{-12}$, or in gramme‑calories per sq. cm. per minute 77×10^{-12}. For the radiation at 288a this gives $77(288)^4 \times 10^{-12}$ or $0 \cdot 53$ gramme-calories per sq. cm. per minute, and similarly for any other temperature.

Combining this with observations of the balance of loss experienced at different heights at different temperatures, we have the following results, the heat-data being in gramme-calories per sq. cm. per minute :—

Height (metres)	440	950	3100	3100
Temperature absolute ...	288	267	261	271
Balance of loss	0·13	0·15	0·20	0·20
Radiation by Stefan's law...	0·53	0·39	0·36	0·42
Radiation received from atmosphere	0·40	0·24	0·16	0·22

Recent experiments by Anders Ångström show that aqueous vapour exercises a potent influence in reducing the balance of loss of heat by nocturnal radiation.

In a paper read before the Royal Meteorological Society in February, 1917, and published in the Quarterly Journal for April, Mr. W. H. Dines, F.R.S., gives the following values for the amount of solar radiant energy absorbed and reflected by the earth and its atmosphere, and of radiation of the earth's heat and its absorption and transference.

The values are expressed in gramme-calories per sq centimetre per day.

Radiant energy received by the earth per day 720
(An amount capable of warming the atmosphere 3a per day.)
Radiant energy absorbed by the earth per day ;
for the whole earth 300
(The Callendar instrument at the Meteorological Office gives about 200 ; Hann gives 166 for Kiev (50°N.) ; and 46 for Taurenberg Bay (79°N.) ; 300 is the value for London at the beginning of May or August.)
Radiant energy absorbed by the air 60
(The value seems low, but there is no observational evidence against it.)

Outward radiation from the earth 500
    (Obtained by using the most probable
   value of σ in Stefan's law [*vide supra*].)
Heat radiated by earth reflected back by
   atmosphere ... .·. 60
Heat radiated by earth absorbed by atmosphere 360
Heat radiated by earth transmitted beyond the
   outer limit of atmosphere 80
Transference of heat from earth to air 200
Radiation from air downwards 340
Radiation from air upwards 280

Effect of the whole daily solar radiation when applied to raise the temperature of the air in the first 1, 2 and 3 kms. of the atmosphere.

According to Angot (quoted from Hann) the following are the proportionate values of the solar radiation per cm^2. in each latitude.

0°	10°	20°	30°	40°	50°	60°	70°	80°	90°
350	345	331	308	277	240	199	166	150	145

If the value of the solar constant be taken as 2 gramme-calories the daily receipt of heat per cm. strip on the equator is $2r \times 2 \times 60 \times 24$ where r is the earth's radius, and the receipt per cm^2. per day is $2r \times 2 \times 60 \times 24/2\pi r = 916$.

The amounts for each latitude are therefore—

0°	10°	20°	30°	40°	50°	60°	70°	80°	90°
916	904	869	807	725	629	521	435	393	380

Taking a mean pressure of 1014 mb. the water-equivalent of the atmosphere is a layer of water 250 cm. deep, hence dividing the above numbers by 250, the number of degrees that the whole radiation is capable of raising the whole atmosphere is given below for each latitude.

0°	10°	20°	30°	40°	50°	60°	70°	80°	90°
3·7	3·6	3·5	3·2	2·9	2·5	2·1	1·7	1·6	1·5

With a mean surface temperature of 288a and a lapse-rate of 6a per k. the percentage of the whole quantity of air found under 1 k. height is 11·3, under 2 k. 21·7 and under 3 k. 30·8. The amounts for each latitude are shown in the following table, the figures indicating the rise of temperature in degrees that would occur if the whole solar radiation were concentrated in the layer and no loss of heat occurred.

Latitude	0°	10°	20°	30°	40°	50°	60°	70°	80°	90°
Under 1 k. ...	32·5	32·0	30·8	28·6	25·7	22·3	18·4	15·4	13·9	13·4
Under 2 k. ...	16·9	16·6	16·0	14·9	13·4	11·6	9·6	8·0	7·2	7·0
Under 3 k. ...	11·9	11·7	11·3	10·5	9·4	8·2	6·7	5·7	5·1	4·9

The above figures represent mean conditions as to density. A fall of pressure will increase the values and so also will a rise of temperature, because with a rise of temperature a smaller proportion of the whole atmosphere will be found in the given layer. The mean conditions hold in about latitude 40°; in the equatorial regions some 4 per cent. must be added to the values, and in latitude 55° some 4 per cent. deducted.

The values given are interesting, but it must be remembered that the whole solar heat is not absorbed by the lower strata, probably only a small proportion of the whole, also as the loss per 24 hours is about the same as the gain in the 12 hours that the sun is on the average above the horizon, the rise of temperature, quite apart from convection, would be only half the values given in the table.

Size and Rate of Fall of Raindrops.

Raindrops.—The size of raindrops can be measured If, for example, a shallow tray containing dry plaster of Paris is exposed for a few seconds during rain, each drop which falls into the tray will make a plaster cast of itself which can easily be measured. A better method is to collect the drops upon thick blotting paper. If, while still wet, the paper is dusted over with a dye powder a permanent record will be obtained consisting of circular spots whose diameter is a measure of the size of the drops. By comparing the diameters of the discs produced by raindrops with those produced by drops of water of known size, the amount of water contained in the former can be found. The following table contains some results obtained by P. Lenard in this way at nine different times :—

Drops.			No. of drops per m.^{2} per second.								
Diameter.		Volume.	(1)	(2)	(3)	(4)	(5)	(6)	(7)	(8)	(9)
mm.	in.	mm.^{3}									
0·5	·019	0·066	1000	1600	129	60	0	100	514	679	7
1·0	·039	0·523	200	120	100	280	50	1300	423	524	233
1·5	·059	1·77	140	60	73	160	50	500	359	347	113
2·0	·079	4·19	140	200	100	20	150	200	138	295	46
2·5	·098	8·19	·0	0	29	20	0	0	156	205	7
3·0	·118	14·2	0	0	57	0	200	0	138	81	0
3·5	·138	22·5	0	0	0	0	0	0	0	28	32
4·0	·157	33·5	0	0	0	0	50	0	0	20	39
4·5	·177	47·8	0	0	0	0	0	200	101	0	0
5·0	·196	65·5	0	0	0	0	0	0	0	0	25
Total number ...			1480	1980	486	540	500	2300	1840	2190	500
Rate of rainfall (mm./min.)			0·09	0·06	0·11	0·05	0·32	0·72	0·57	0·34	0·26

(1) and (2) refer to a rain "looking very ordinary" which was general, over the north of Switzerland. The wind had freshened between (1) and (2).

(3) Rain with sunshine-breaks.

(4) Beginning of a short fall like a thundershower. Distant thunder.

(5) Sudden rain from a small cloud. Calm; sultry before.

(6) Violent rain like a cloudburst, with some hail.

(7), (8) and (9) are for the heaviest period, a less heavy period, and the period of stopping of a continuous fall which at times took the form of a cloudburst.

We see then that in a general rain, such as the normal type which accompanies the passage of a depression over Northern Europe, by far the greater number of drops have a diameter of 2 mm. or less. In short showers, especially those occurring during thunderstorms, the frequency of large drops is much greater. In such showers the diameter of the largest drops appears to be about 5 mm. We shall see later that there is a limit to the size of drops determined by the fact that it is impossible for a drop, whose diameter exceeds 5·5 mm. or rather less than a quarter of an inch, to fall intact.

The rate at which a raindrop, or any other object, can fall through still air depends upon its size. When let fall its speed will increase until the air-resistance is exactly equal to the weight, when it will continue to move at that steady speed (*see* EQUILIBRIUM). The manner in which this "terminal velocity," as it is called, varies with the size of the raindrops is shown in the following table, due to Lenard.

TERMINAL VELOCITIES OF WATER-DROPS FALLING IN AIR.

Diameter of drop.		Terminal Velocity.		Diameter of drop.		Terminal Velocity.	
mm.	in.	m/s.	mi/hr.	mm.	in.	m/s.	mi/h
0·01	0·0004	0·0032	0·007	3·0	0·118	6·9	15·
0·1	0·0039	0·32	0·71	3·5	0·138	7·4	16·
0·5	0·020	3·5	7·9	4·0	0·157	7·7	17·
1·0	0·039	4·4	9·8	4·5	0·177	8·0	17·
1·5	0·059	5·7	12·6	5·0	0·200	8·0	17·
2·0	0·079	5·9	13·2	5·5	0·216	8·0	17·
2·5	0·098	6·4	14·3				

We may look upon this table in another way. T]
frictional resistance offered by the air to the passage of
drop depends upon the relative motion of the two, and
is of no consequence whether the drop is moving and tl
air still, or the air moving and the drop still, or both a
and drop moving if they have different velocities. T]
velocities given in the tables are those with which the a
n a vertical current must rise in order just to keep tl
drops floating, without rising or falling. The abo
results were, in fact actually determined by Lenard i
his way, by means of experiments with vertical ai
currents on drops of known size. We see that beyond
certain point the terminal velocity does not increase wil
the size of the drops. This is due to the fact that tl
drops become deformed, spreading out horizontally, wit
the result that the air-resistance is increased. For dro]
greater than 5·5 mm. diameter, the deformation

sufficient to make the drops break up before the terminal volocity is reached.

An important consequence of Lenard's results is that no rain can fall through an ascending current of air whose vertical velocity is greater than 8 m/s. In such a current the drops will be carried upwards, either intact or after breaking up into droplets. There is good reason for believing that vertical currents exceeding this velocity frequently occur in nature.

On account of their inability to fall in an air current which is rising faster than their limiting velocity, rain-drops formed in these currents will have ample opportunity to increase in size, and the electrical conditions will usually be favourable for the formation of large drops. These large drops can reach earth in two ways ; either by being carried along in the outflow of air above the region of most active convection, or by the sudden cessation of or a lull in the vertical current. The violence of the precipitation under the latter conditions may be particularly disastrous. (See also *Cloudburst* and *Hail*.)

Electrification of Waterdrops by Splashing.

If drops of water are allowed to splash upon a metal plate, the water acquires a minute positive charge of electricity, and an equal negative charge is shared by the plate and the air contiguous to the splashing drop. It is possible to show this by means of delicate apparatus. The largest charges are found when distilled water is used, and even small amounts of dissolved substances in the water make a considerable difference to the results obtained. With sea-water, indeed, the effect is reversed, the water becoming negatively charged after splashing.

The presence of a solid obstacle to cause splashing is not really necessary to produce the separation of electricity. The breaking up of a jet of water into spray and the splitting of large drops of water in a current of air produce similar effects. The last-named case is of particular importance in meteorology because it forms the basis of the theory put forward by Dr. G. C. Simpson to account for the production of the enormous electrical stresses in the atmosphere which precede the discharge of lightning in thunderstorms.

The first necessity for a thunderstorm is the formation of a cumulus cloud, and this requires an ascending current of air. In ascending the air expands and gets rapidly cooler, with the result that before long the water-vapour in the air begins to condense and form visible droplets. The cloud is, in fact, the visible result of this condensation. Once formed, the drops rapidly increase in size and would ordinarily fall as rain. But if the ascending current is sufficiently violent the raindrops will not be able to fall through it, but will be carried up with the air. The vertical velocity required to hold up drops of all sizes is 8 m/s., and there is no reason to doubt that such currents can easily be produced. Now in such a current it is impossible for a drop to grow beyond 5·5 mm. in diameter (see *Size and Rate of Fall of Raindrops*). At that point it becomes unstable and divides into droplets. These in their turn go through the same process of growing and dividing. Each time a division occurs the droplets gain a positive charge, and the air which is carried up with the current gains an equal negative charge. In this way the waterdrops in the region of the ascending current rapidly become very highly charged, and as soon as the potential gradient anywhere amounts to 30.000 volts/cm. a lightning-flash will óccur. Although the charge produced by a single division is very small, we have only to suppose that the same quantity of water may take part in many hundreds of divisions—and there is nothing improbable in this—to be able to account for the production of sufficiently high potentials.

The negatively charged air will be carried right to the top of the column and there dispersed. Its presence should be shown by a negative charge on the rain which falls some distance from the storm-centre, while that falling near the centre should be positively charged. Such observations as exist tend to support this conclusion of the theory.

Regression Equation.—A regression equation shows the most probable form of the relationship between two varying quantities insofar as such relationship can be definitely determined from the set of statistical data on which it is based. It is formed from the correlation co-efficient and the matter is best explained by an example. See also under CORRELATION.

The strength of the wind and the steepness of the barometric gradient at the same time and place are closely related, and a regression equation may be formed between them. Let W denote the strength of the wind, W_m its mean value, and δW the departure from the mean, and let G, G_m and δG be the corresponding values for the steepness of the gradient. Then if the gradient is known the strength of the wind is given by a regression equation in the form

$$W = W_m + a\, \delta\, G + \varepsilon.$$

In this equation ε will in general have some value, positive or negative, differing on each occasion, and the a will be so chosen that the sum of the squares of the ϵ's will be as small as possible. The W, δG and ϵ are variable quantities, the a a constant. It is usual, for the sake of brevity, to write the equation $\delta W = a \delta G$, but it must be remembered that the ϵ has been omitted ; ϵ is called the residual error, and since ϵ is often fairly large, it is not permissible to write ~~$\delta R = \delta W / a$~~. $\delta G = \dfrac{\delta W}{a}$

There are two errors involved in a regression equation. The value of a can in general only be found at all correctly when the number of observations is large. The residual error ϵ may be as large as the term $a \delta G$ unless the correlation co-efficient is nearly 1 or $- 1$. When the correlation is $+ .1$ the term ϵ is nothing ; also, when the correlation is known to·be large (it cannot be proved to be large from a few observations) the value of a can be determined with greater certainty than when the correlation co-efficient is small.

The following are three examples all dependent on fairly high correlation co-efficients.

Thickness of TROPOSPHERE $= 10,600 + 112 \, \delta P_9$ metres,
> where P_9 denotes the pressure of the air at a height of nine kilometres expressed in millibars. (Europe.)

Hay crop per acre $= 28 + 4 \, \delta R$ cwts.,
> where R denotes the spring rainfall in inches. (East of England.)

Number of deaths in England during July, August and September $= 150,000 + 7,200 \, \delta T$,
> where T denotes the mean temperature in degrees F of June, July and August. (On the assumption that the present population is forty millions.)

Scotch-Mist.—In mountainous or hilly regions, rain-clouds (nimbus) are often adjacent to the ground, and precipitation takes place in the form of minute water-drops, the apparent effect being a combination of thick mist and heavy drizzle.

The upland character of the greater part of Scotland and the consequent frequency of occurrence of the phenomenon in that country have secured for it the appellation by which it is generally known-in the British Isles.

The base of a true nimbus or rain-cloud rarely exceeds about 7,000 ft. (2·1 k.) in elevation, and sometimes descends to within a few hundred feet of sea-level, so that Scotch-mist may be experienced in comparatively low-lying regions.

In the uplands of the Devon-Cornwall peninsula the same phenomenon, which is there of very frequent incidence, is known as " mizzle."

Sleet.—Precipitation of rain and snow together or of partially melted snow. In America the name " sleet " is used for small dry pellets of snow which might be classed as soft-hail. Sleet is, perhaps, snow that passes through a stratum of comparatively warm air (see INVERSION) and, undergoing partial liquefaction therein to an extent varying with the temperature and thickness of the layer, reaches the ground in a semi-liquid condition. If the stratum of warm air is not adjacent to the ground, and if the surface-temperature is below the freezing-point, a phenomenon similar to GLAZED FROST (*q.v.*) may result, the re-freezing of the half-melted snow occasioning the formation of a layer of ice on all objects exposed to the precipitation. Marked instances of this occurred in London during the winter of 1916–1917, and road traffic, and in some cases even rail-locomotion, was rendered difficult or impossible.

Snow.—Precipitation in the form of feathery ice-crystals; other forms of ice-precipitation are the powdery ice-crystals or needles which are commonly experienced in the snow-storms of intensely cold weather on mountain tops and in the arctic or antarctic regions—in the snow-storms, in fact, of which the "BLIZZARD" has become the descriptive name; soft hail or graupel. *i.e.*, snow in which the needles are agglomerated to form minute snow-balls, sometimes striated in texture, which break with a splash on reaching hard ground; and true hail, which began as rain frozen and sustained in rapidly-ascending currents of dynamically cooling air. Snow may perhaps be the result of the direct congelation of water-vapour, the omission of the intermediate liquid-state being the essential difference between the hail and snow processes. Snowflakes are formed of one or more ice-crystals arranged in symmetrical hexagonal patterns of which there is an almost infinite variety. Many are figured as photomicrographs in the *Monthly Weather Review* of the United States Weather Bureau, Washington, for 1902 (W. A. Bentley). When snow falls with comparatively high temperature, large, wet flakes often result; with lower temperature the flakes are smaller, and with the thermometer reading far below the zero of the Fahrenheit scale, we have the "snow-dust" or "ice-needles"; fine ice-crystals or needles also characterise the deposits which are formed in foggy, frosty weather, particularly on mountain-tops, where wreaths of such crystals sometimes grow out to windward. The hexagonal formation of a snowflake may be well observed under a low-power microscope; it will be noticed that each one of the constituent "spiculæ" is set at an angle of 60 degrees to its fellows. The ratio which an inch of rain bears to an inch of snow depends upon the density of the snow ; as a rough approximation for the most common kind of snow a ratio of 12 to 1 is usually taken in this country. In exceptional cases the divergences from this value are very wide indeed ; according to Colonel Ward, the range may be from about 5 to 1 to about 50 to 1—that is to say, a foot of snow on the ground may yield, when melted in the RAIN-GAUGE, the water-equivalent to 2·4 in. of rain at the one extreme, or to 0·24 in. at the other. One foot of snow to one inch of rain is, however, a convenient generalisation.

Soft-Hail.—The English term for the form of ice-precipitation known in German as Graupel. It consists in reality of pellets of closely agglomerated ice-needles, sometimes striated in texture, and thus falls under the category of snow. rather than under that of hail. On colliding with any hard substance, soft-hail breaks up with a splash, and may thus be distinguished from true hail, the form of which is not affected by the impact. The French equivalent for "soft-hail" or "graupel" is "grésil."

Sun-dial.—Little use is made of the sun-dial at the present time, except as an ornament for the garden. There are various forms, the commonest being a horizontal stone slab upon which a rod or style, called the gnomon, is set up in the astronomical meridian, inclined to the horizontal at an angle equal to the latitude of the place, or, in other words, parallel with the earth's axis. The line traced by the shadow of the style at each hour of the day is engraved upon the slab. When the vertical plane through the style lies correctly in the meridian, after applying a correction for the EQUATION OF TIME (*q.v.*), such a dial will give mean solar time whenever the sun is visible. To obtain Greenwich Mean Time a constant correction must be applied depending upon the longitude of the place.

By taking account of the length of the shadow as well as the line on the dial, the time of year can be indicated, and some dials are elaborately graduated as a perpetual calendar as well as time-keeper.

Twilight.—Twilight is caused by the intervention of the atmosphere between the sun and the earth's surface. With no atmosphere, darkness would set in sharply at the moment of sunset, and would give place suddenly to light at sunrise, as on the moon. But when the sun is some distance below the horizon the upper layers of air are already illuminated, and are reflecting light to us. The amount of reflected light diminishes as the sun's distance below the horizon increases, because higher, and so less strongly reflecting, layers alone are in direct sunlight.

So early as the 11th century the period of Astronomical Twilight, between sunset and the onset of " complete " darkness, was determined as ending when the sun is 18° below the horizon, and this value has not been modified by later observations. If we assume direct reflection as the sole cause of twilight, this value, 18°, would indicate that the atmosphere above a height of some 80 kilometres is incapable of reflecting an appreciable amount of light.

Long before the end of Astronomical Twilight, however, the light has become insufficient for ordinary employments, hence another period, Civil Twilight, is recognised, ending when the sun is about 6° below the horizon, and conditioned by the insufficiency of light for outdoor labour after that time.

The duration of twilight depends on the season and the

latitude. At midsummer the sun is $23\frac{1}{2}°$ North of the equator. Hence within the Arctic circle, latitude $90°-23\frac{1}{2}°=66\frac{1}{2}°$, the sun never sets, so that there is no twilight. Between the Arctic circle and latitude $90°-23\frac{1}{2}°-18°=48\frac{1}{2}°$ there is a belt with no true night, twilight extending from sunset to sunrise. At midwinter, in the Arctic circle, the sun does not rise, but up to latitude $90°-23\frac{1}{2}°+18°=84\frac{1}{2}°$, there is an alternation between twilight and night. North of $84\frac{1}{2}°$ there is continuous night. •

At London (latitude $51\frac{1}{2}°$) Astronomical Twilight has a minimum duration of about 1 hour 50 minutes on March 1st and October 1st, with a secondary maximum in midwinter of just over 2 hours, and lasts all night at midsummer.

At the Equator the minimum duration is 1 hour 9 minutes, the solstitial maxima 1 hour 15 minutes.

Civil twilight at the Equator varies between 21 and 22 minutes, at London it has minima of 33 minutes in March and October, maxima of 40 minutes in December, and 45 minutes in June.

The duration of either twilight at any latitude and season may be found by using the equation

$$\cos h = \frac{\sin a - \sin \phi \sin \delta}{\cos \phi \cos \delta}$$

where h = sun's hour angle from the meridian,

a = sun's altitude,

ϕ = latitude,

δ = sun's declination,

$a = -50'$ at beginning of twilight (allowing for sun's semi-diameter and refraction),

$-6°$ at end of civil, and $-18°$ at end of astronomical twilight;

thus to find duration of civil twilight, find cos h for the two cases, $\alpha = -50'$ and $\alpha = -6°$, convert the two values of h to time, and the difference is the required duration.

The intensity of twilight depends to some extent on cloud, dust, haze, or other obscurity in the atmosphere. Dust in the higher layers, as in the case of the sunsets of 1883–5 (after the eruption of Krakatoa), may much increase the intensity of illumination during twilight, by increasing the reflected light. In a cloudless sky the intensity falls off rapidly at first, then more slowly from about 35 foot-candles at sunset to 0·5 foot-candles at the end of civil twilight, and to ·0001 foot candle at the end of astronomical twilight. These intensities are to the light of the full moon in the zenith as 1750, 25, and ·005 respectively to 1.

The optical phenomena of twilight occur in the following sequence ; for explanations, reference should be made to the corresponding articles in the Glossary. As the sun sinks towards the horizon it is shining through an increasing thickness of haze and dust-laden air, and scattering (see BLUE OF THE SKY) causes less and less of the blue light to reach us, so that the sun appears increasingly red. A yellow band now appears on the Western horizon, extending for about 60° to either side of the sun. Gradually the yellow deepens to orange or red as the proportion of blue decreases. As the sun passes below the horizon the pink TWILIGHT ARCH (better called the Anti-Twilight Arch) rises from the Eastern horizon, the space under it being strikingly darker than the rest of the sky. While this arch is rising in the East the PURPLE LIGHT has appeared at an altitude of about 25° in the West, above the point of sunset. This light attains its maximum intensity when the sun is about 4°

below the horizon, and disappears on the Western horizon when the sun is about 6° below, at the end of Civil Twilight. Just before its disappearance the purple light has become a narrow arch over the yellow glow near the horizon and thus forms the " Western Twilight Arch."

The purple light is often seen to be intersected by dark blue stripes radiating from the position of the sun. These are the shadows of clouds on or below the horizon, and are frequently called Crepuscular Rays. On very clear nights a second dark segment in the East and a second Purple Light in the West may be observed.

Evening conditions have been assumed above, but obvious inversions make the discussions applicable to the mornings.

Vortex.—A special form of rotatory motion in fluids. Two forms of vortex have figured much in mathematical literature, the vortex-ring and the long straight vortex, and both are believed to be represented in nature. The mathematical vortex-ring in its simplest form is shaped like a perfect anchor-ring or hoop, whose circular aperture is very large compared with the diameter of the circular wire of which it is composed. The cross-section of the material of the ring—a liquid or gas—is everywhere a circle of radius e, and the centres of all these circles lie on a larger circle, the aperture, of radius a. There is complete symmetry round the axis, *i.e.*, the perpendicular to the plane of the aperture through its centre. Any plane through the axis cuts the ring at right angles in two circles of radius e, situated at opposite ends of a diameter of the aperture. If we take any one of these circular sections the liquid within it is everywhere circulating round and round within the circle. In the simplest case its rotational velocity increases as its distance from the centre, where it vanishes. But in addition to this the ring moves bodily. If it is alone in an infinite liquid, its centre travels in the direction of the axis, with a uniform velocity which is greater the greater a/e.

The straight vortex in its simplest form is a right circular cylinder, or pencil-shaped body, and if the vorticity is uniform over the cross section—the simplest case—the liquid spins round with a velocity proportional to the distance from the centre of the section, *i.e.*, the liquid forming the vortex turns round exactly as if it were a rigid body. A solitary straight vortex in an infinite liquid has no inherent tendency to translatory movement. The liquid forming the vortex simply goes on spinning round the axis of the cylinder; the liquid round it also rotates round this axis, but with a velocity which diminishes as the distance from the vortex increases.

The assumption ordinarily made that the liquid is infinite means that every part of the vortex is remote from a boundary. But some forms of vortex motion are possible in presence of a plane boundary, and a sphere whose radius is large compared with the largest dimension of a vortex may be treated as a plane. A vortex ring with its aperture parallel to a plane boundary behaves as if face to face in an infinite liquid with an equal " image " vortex, whose distance is double that of the real vortex from the plane. The two vortices repel one another. Again a theoretically possible case is that presented by the half of a complete vortex-ring—cut in two, as it were, by the boundary—the plane of the aperture being perpendicular to the boundary. The motion would be the same as if the ring were really complete and no boundary existed. Similarly there are two possible cases of a straight vortex in presence of a plane boundary. The vortex may be parallel to the boundary. The conditions are the same as if it were in an infinite liquid facing another equal vortex—in which the spin is in the opposite direction—the distance between the two being double the distance of the real vortex from the boundary. The vortex tends to move parallel to the boundary, in the direction perpendicular to its own length. In the second case the vortex is perpendicular to and abuts on the boundary; it then behaves as if it extended to infinity on both sides of the boundary, and so has no inherent tendency to translatory movement. Whether the vortex be straight or ring-formed, an essential feature of the mathematical theory is that the liquid, once incorporated in the vortex, remains in it. The beginning and ending of the existence of the vortex are events outside the compass of the mathematical theory.

Vortex rings are, easily created by human agency. A drop of one liquid falling into another suitable liquid forms a vortex-ring, and smoke-rings are familiar to most people. Whether they occur in nature is a more difficult question. Delicate optical measurements suggest that sunspots are whirls of electrified gases. It is noticed that sometimes sunspots move in pairs, and that the whirls in them deduced from the optical measurements are in opposite directions. It has been suggested that we have here really to do with the horse-shoe or semi-ring vortex. The two sunspots represent the portions of this which are nearly perpendicular to the sun's surface, and the connecting or crown portion extends into the more rarefied solar atmosphere and is not recognisable from the earth. This is merely a speculation, but the possibility of a similar phenomenon in the earth's atmosphere may be worth considering.

What seems to be at least an approach to the long straight vortex is exemplified by water spouts and by the dust-whirls sometimes seen on warm days. But the common belief that it is also exemplified by the ordinary cyclonic storm does not seem well founded. The belief is mainly based on the fact that the isobars during a cyclonic storm are often roughly circular. The direction of the wind, it is true, at some height above the ground, approaches that of the isobars. But the centre of the storm, *i.e.*, the centre of the system of isobars, is not stationary but moves with a velocity comparable with that of the wind itself. The actual path of the air is complicated. It is carried from without into the cyclone, but does not remain in it. The mathematical vortex, on the other hand, is composed of the same fluid from start to finish. The mathematical vortex, moreover, is a long thin body like a pencil. An ordinary cyclone, even supposing it extends some distance into the stratosphere, is a disk-like body, the height of which is small compared with its diameter. Again, in the straight mathematical vortex the velocity round the axis is the same at the same axial distance in all cross sections. Ordinarily the wind increases in velocity with the height above the ground. Supposing the core of a cyclonic vortex originally vertical, unless the motion of translation were the same at all heights, the core would depart more and more from the vertical, and, judging by what happens with water-spouts, dissolution would soon ensue.

The conditions compatible with real vortex motion in a cyclone are that the velocity should be independent of the height, that the horizontal diameter of the body of air possessing the motion should not be large, and that an unchanged body of air should have the translational velocity shown by the isobars. The necessary conditions are certainly not fulfilled near the centre of the ordinary large cyclonic storm. They seem much more likely to be encountered in the small "secondaries" that are sometimes met with on the outskirts of large depressions, or in the whirlwinds that occasionally leave a long narrow track of devastation. It is difficult to ascertain the exact meteorological conditions attending these special disturbances. A weather map, to show them satisfactorily, would have to be of exceptionally open scale and based on an unusually minute knowledge of local conditions. One or two cases of real vortical storms do seem, however, to have been observed in the British Isles, notably a storm on March 24, 1895, which caused much damage to trees in the Eastern Counties.

Wind Rose.—A diagram showing, for a definite locality or district, and usually for a more or less extended period, the proportion of winds blowing from each of the leading points of the compass. As a rule the " rose " indicates also the Strength of the wind from each quarter, and the number or proportion of cases in which the air was quite calm.

The simplest form of wind rose is represented by the accompanying figure, in which the number or proportion of winds blowing from each of the principal 8 points of the compass is represented by lines converging towards a small circle, the proportion of winds from each direction being indicated by the varying length of the lines. The figures in the circles give the number, or percentage, of cases in which the air was calm.

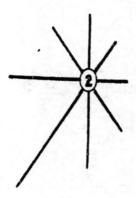

A "rose" may be, and occasionally is, devised in such a manner as to indicate the relation of other meteorological phenomena, such as cloud, rain, fog, &c., to the direction of the wind. As a result of an investigation recently undertaken in the Meteorological Office a series of roses has been constructed showing that on the western and southern coasts of the British Islands the bulk of the fogs experienced are sea fogs, *i.e.*, they occur with winds blowing (sometimes with considerable strength) from the surface of the ocean. On the north and east coasts summer fogs also come from the sea, but winter fogs more often from the land. The "roses" show further that over the inland parts of England the fogs are radiation fogs, and are accompanied by calm or very light winds blowing from various quarters.

The publications of the Meteorological Office have included from time to time wind roses of various designs. Specimens of these are reproduced on the two succeeding pages.

Showing Average Direction of Wind by shaded areas converging towards centre of diagram and Strength of Wind in numbers of Beaufort Scale by dots.

Prevalence of Calms indicated by diameter of central circle.

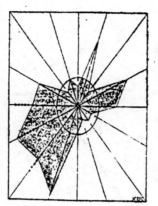

(Reproduced from " Wind Charts of North Atlantic," published in 1859.)

Relative prevalence of Wind for each point of the compass shown by length of arrows converging towards centre.

Force of Wind by curve intersecting wind arrows.

Calms by proportion of shaded to unshaded portions of large central area.

Additional information related to Ocean Currents and other matters of interest to Navigators.

(Reproduced from " Charts of Meteorological Data for Lat. 20°N. to 10°S., Long. 10°—40°W.," published in 1876.)

Irregularly shaped areas around outside circle indicate relative prevalence of Wind from various directions.

Radial lines converging towards central area indicate Wind Force.

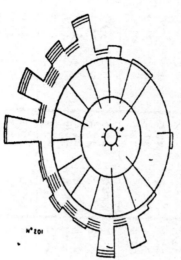

Shaded portions of outlying areas indicate prevalence of Gales.

Small central circle indicates by its diameter the proportion of Calms.

Star points around this circle indicate by their length the number of observations.

(Reproduced from " Charts of the Ocean District adjacent to the Cape of Good Hope," published in 1882.)

Arrows fly with the Wind towards centre of diagram.

Frequency of Wind from each direction is indicated by length of arrow.

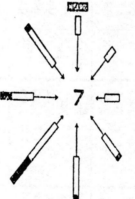

Force of Wind is indicated thus :—

Light,   Moderate,   Strong.

Figures in centre of diagram indicate percentage of Calms.

[Similar to Wind Roses published in current issues of Monthly Weather Report and in " Monthly Meteorological Charts of North Atlantic and Mediterranean."]

Ins.	Milli-bars.	Ins.	Milli-bars.	Ins.	Milli-bars.	Ins.	Milli-bars.	Ins.	Milli-bars.	Ins.	Milli-bars.
28.00	948.2	28.50	965.1	29.00	982.0	29.50	999.0	30.00	1015.9	30.50	1032.8
2	48.8	2	65.8	2	82.7	2	99.6	2	16.6	2	33.5
4	49.5	4	66.5	4	83.4	4	1000.3	4	17.3	4	34.2
6	50.2	6	67.1	6	84.1	6	01.0	6	17.9	6	34.9
8	50.9	8	67.8	8	84.7	8	01.7	8	18.6	8	35.5
28.10	51.6	28.60	68.5	29.10	85.4	29.60	02.4	30.10	19.3	30.60	36.2
2	52.2	2	69.2	2	86.1	2	03.0	2	20.0	2	36.9
4	52.9	4	69.8	4	86.8	4	03.7	4	20.6	4	37.6
6	53.6	6	70.5	6	87.5	6	04.4	6	21.3	6	38.2
8	54.3	8	71.2	8	88.1	8	05.1	8	22.0	8	38.9
28.20	54.9	28.70	71.9	29.20	88.8	29.70	05.7	30.20	22.7	30.70	39.6
2	55.6	2	72.6	2	89.5	2	06.4	2	23.3	2	40.3
4	56.3	4	73.2	4	90.2	4	07.1	4	24.0	4	41.0
6	57.0	6	73.9	6	90.8	6	07.8	6	24.7	6	41.6
8	57.7	8	74.6	8	91.5	8	08.4	8	25.4	8	42.3
28.30	58.3	28.80	75.3	29.30	92.2	29.80	09.1	30.30	26.1	30.80	43.0
2	59.0	2	75.9	2	92.9	2	09.8	2	26.7	2	43.7
4	59.7	4	76.6	4	93.5	4	10.5	4	27.4	4	44.3
6	60.3	6	77.3	6	94.2	6	11.2	6	28.1	6	45.0
8	61.0	8	78.0	8	94.9	8	11.8	8	28.8	8	45.7
28.40	61.7	28.90	78.6	29.40	95.6	29.90	12.5	30.40	29.4	30.90	46.4
2	62.4	2	79.3	2	96.3	2	13.2	2	30.1	2	47.1
4	63.1	4	80.0	4	96.9	4	13.9	4	30.8	4	47.7
6	63.7	6	80.7	6	97.6	6	14.5	6	31.5	6	48.4
8	64.4	8	81.4	8	98.3	8	15.2	8	32.2	8	49.1

CONVERSION OF DEGREES FAHRENHEIT INTO DEGREES CENTIGRADE AND DEGREES ABSOLUTE.

F.	°C.	a.	°F.	°C.	a.	°F.	°C.	a.	°F.	°C.	a.
20	−6·7	266·3	45	7·2	280·2	70	21·1	294·1	95	35·0	308·0
21	−6·1	266·9	46	7·8	280·8	71	21·7	294·7	96	35·6	308·6
22	−5·6	267·4	47	8·3	281·3	72	22·2	295·2	97	36·1	309·1
23	−5·0	268·0	48	8·9	281·9	73	22·8	295·8	98	36·7	309·7
24	−4·4	268·6	49	9·4	282·4	74	23·3	296·3	99	37·2	310·2
25	−3·9	269·1	50	10·0	283·0	75	23·9	296·9	100	37·8	310·8
26	−3·3	269·7	51	10·6	283·6	76	24·4	297·4	101	38·3	311·3
27	−2·8	270·2	52	11·1	284·1	77	25·0	298·0	102	38·9	311·9
28	−2·2	270·8	53	11·7	284·7	78	25·6	298·6	103	39·4	312·4
29	−1·7	271·3	54	12·2	285·2	79	26·1	299·1	104	40·0	313·0
30	−1·1	271·9	55	12·8	285·8	80	26·7	299·7	105	40·6	313·6
31	−0·6	272·4	56	13·3	286·3	81	27·2	300·2	106	41·1	314·1
32	0·0	273·0	57	13·9	286·9	82	27·8	300·8	107	41·7	314·7
33	+0·6	273·6	58	14·4	287·4	83	28·3	301·3	108	42·2	315·2
34	1·1	274·1	59	15·0	288·0	84	28·9	301·9	109	42·8	315·8
35	1·7	274·7	60	15·6	288·6	85	29·4	302·4	110	43·3	316·3
36	2·2	275·2	61	16·1	289·1	86	30·0	303·0	111	43·9	316·9
37	2·8	275·8	62	16·7	289·7	87	30·6	303·6	112	44·4	317·4
38	3·3	276·3	63	17·2	290·2	88	31·1	304·1	113	45·0	318·0
39	3·9	276·9	64	17·8	290·8	89	31·7	304·7	114	45·6	318·6
40	4·4	277·4	65	18·3	291·3	90	32·2	305·2	115	46·1	319·1
41	5·0	278·0	66	18·9	291·9	91	32·8	305·8	116	46·7	319·7
42	5·6	278·6	67	19·4	292·4	92	33·3	306·3	117	47·2	320·2
43	6·1	279·1	68	20·0	293·0	93	33·9	306·9	118	47·8	320·8
44	6·7	279·7	69	20·6	293·6	94	34·4	307·4	119	48·3	321·3

INDEX TO TABLES INCLUDED IN THE GLOSSARY.

	See under :—
Abbreviations. List of	p. 2.
Adiabatic expansion. Change in temperature of air on.	Adiabatic.
Aqueous Vapour—Mass of in saturated air. ...	Aqueous vapour.
Pressure of do. do. ...	Do.
Amount and Pressure of, at Kew.	Absolute Humidity.
Clouds. Types of	Clouds.
Correlation Coefficients. Selected examples ...	Correlation.
Density	Buoyancy.
Evaporation of Water	Evaporation.
Fog and Mist. Average No. of observations of Fog in British Isles.	Fog.
Frequency in English Channel of	Frequency.
Gales at some British anemometer stations ...	Gale.
Seasonal variation of	Gale.
Gradients. Steep pressure	Gradient.
Gusts. Range of fluctuation of	Gusts.
Strongest recorded	Gusts.
Hurricanes, cyclones and typhoons recorded in various parts of the World.	Hurricane.
Insolation. Calculated Insolation reaching Earth.	Insolation.
Pressure Units. Conversion table	p. 355.
Rain. Consecutive hours of rain in 1912 ...	Persistent rain.
Rainfall during the four seasons in S.E. England and N. Scotland.	Seasons.
Day rainfall and night rainfall ...	Seasons.
Relative Humidity. Frequency of occurrence of various values of	Relative humidity
Sunshine. Percentages of possible duration of	Sunshine.
Temperature. Boiling points of water at various pressures in the atmosphere up to 8,000 feet.	Hypsometer.
Conversion table	p. 356.
Normal weekly temperatures for S.E. England.	Seasons.
Some common temperatures ...	Absolute temperature.

	See under :—
Thunderstorms, Immunity from	Thunderstorms.
Upper atmosphere. Normal pressure at various heights.	Ballon-sonde.
Average temperature at different levels.	Ballon-sonde.
Average values of pressure, density and temperature of air over regions of high and low pressure.	Density.
Normal factors for the density of air at various heights.	Buoyancy.
Limit of height for the expenditure of ballast.	Buoyancy.
Depression produced on airships by rain or snow.	Buoyancy.
Wind. Monthly normals of wind velocity at some French and British stations.	Normal.
Normal hourly wind velocities at Kew	Normal.
Spells of N.E.-S.E. winds of specified duration over S.E. England and N. France.	Frequency.
Frequency of winds from different quarters over S.E. England and N. France.	Frequency.
Distance between isobars for various geostrophic winds.	Isobars.
Equivalents of wind force	Beaufort scale.
Wind direction at Suva, Fiji	Trade winds.
Hourly velocity at the top of the Eiffel Tower.	Wind.

Printed under the authority of His Majesty's Stationery Office
By DARLING and SON, Limited, Bacon Street, E.2.

CORRIGENDA.

In the Fourth Issue the plates representing various forms of pressure distribution which in the previous issue were placed with the separate articles: Anticyclone, Col, Depression, Secondary Depression, V-Shaped Depression, Wedge in alphabetical order are now put together in the article Isobars, and should have been re-numbered in order to correspond with the text. But the re-numbering, and in consequence the order, has failed. The following corrections should therefore be made in the numbering and order of the plates :—

Depression should be Plate XI. instead of XIII., and face page 174.

Secondary Depression should be Plate XII. instead of XIV., and face page 175.

Anticyclone should be Plate XIII. instead of XI., and face page 176.

Col should be Plate XIV. instead of XII., and face page 177.

The foot-note on page 177 should be omitted.

Page 75, line 1, "Sir Gilbert Walker" should read "Dr. Gilbert Walker."

Page 132, last line, "65 millibars" should read "5 millibars."

Page 256, line 24, "John Hadley," etc., should read "George Hadley, who was a brother of John Hadley," etc.

Page 262, line 18, "years" should read "year."

Page 271. In the column headed "Depression of Wet Bulb," the temperature scale F. should be indicated.

Page 295, line 1, R^1 should read R^2.

    „   „ line 12, $\rho\sigma$ should read σ.

    „   „ line 26, V^1 should read V'.

Page 308, line 27, "Earth's mass M'" should read "earth's mass plus that of atmosphere (M + M')."

Page 330, line 28, should read "$77\ (288)^4 \times 10^{-12}$."

Page 340, line 7, the equation should read $\delta G = \dfrac{\delta W}{a}$.

(23632—12.) Wt. 7924—185. 6000. 6/19. D & S. G. 3.

THIS BOOK IS DUE ON THE LAST DATE
STAMPED BELOW

AN INITIAL FINE OF 25 CENTS
WILL BE ASSESSED FOR FAILURE TO RETURN
THIS BOOK ON THE DATE DUE. THE PENALTY
WILL INCREASE TO 50 CENTS ON THE FOURTH
DAY AND TO $1.00 ON THE SEVENTH DAY
OVERDUE.

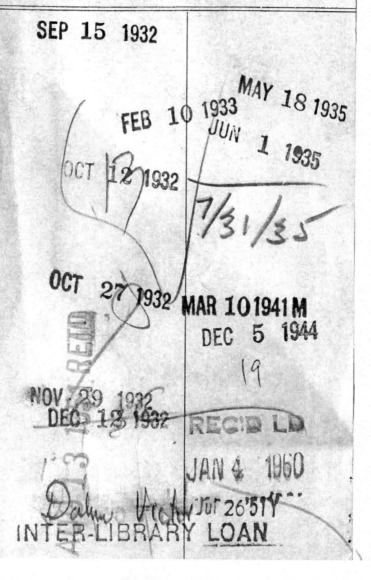

Lightning Source UK Ltd.
Milton Keynes UK
UKOW041330101012

200375UK00005B/21/P